THE THREE JEWELS

Also by Sangharakshita

A Survey of Buddhism
A Guide to the Buddhist Path
The Taste of Freedom
Peace is a Fire
Human Enlightenment
The Religion of Art
The Eternal Legacy
Travel Letters
Alternative Traditions
Who is the Buddha?
Ambedkar and Buddhism
Crossing The Stream
The History of My Going for Refuge
Flame in Darkness
The Ten Pillars of Buddhism
Vision and Transformation
New Currents in Western Buddhism
The Rainbow Road *(memoirs)*
Facing Mount Kanchenjunga *(memoirs)*
In the Sign of the Golden Wheel *(memoirs)*
The Inconceivable Emancipation
Ritual and Devotion in Buddhism
The Buddha's Victory
Tibetan Buddhism: An Introduction
The Priceless Jewel
The Drama of Cosmic Enlightenment
The FWBO and 'Protestant Buddhism'
Wisdom Beyond Words
Forty-Three Years Ago
The Meaning of Conversion in Buddhism
Complete Poems 1941–1994
Was the Buddha a Bhikkhu?
In the Realm of the Lotus
Transforming Self and World
Buddhism for Today – and Tomorrow
The Essence of Zen
What is the Dharma?
A Stream of Stars
Know Your Mind

Booklets

Going for Refuge
Buddhism and the West
Great Buddhists of the Twentieth Century
The Meaning of Orthodoxy in Buddhism
Extending the Hand of Fellowship
My Relation to the Order
Mind – Reactive and Creative

SANGHARAKSHITA

THE THREE JEWELS

The Central Ideals of Buddhism

WINDHORSE PUBLICATIONS

Published by Windhorse Publications
11 Park Road
Birmingham
B13 8AB

First published by Rider 1967
First Windhorse edition 1977
Fourth edition, revised and reset 1998

Printed by Biddles Ltd, Guildford, Surrey
Cover design Dhammarati

Cover details:
Buddha head, Gupta period
Flower / Photodisc
Wall painting from Ming-oi, 8th/9th century

British Library Cataloguing in Publication Data
A catalogue record for this book is available from the British Library

ISBN 1 899579 06 0
(Third edition ISBN 0 904766 49 7)

Thanks to Sagaramati, Nancy Nicolazzo, and Graham Patterson for their invaluable assistance in producing this new edition.

To help readers unfamiliar with Pali and Sanskrit, plurals have been indicated by an -s suffix rather than employ the technically correct orthography.

CONTENTS

I take my refuge in the Buddha, and pray that with all beings
I may understand the Great Way, whereby the Buddha-seed
may forever thrive.

I take my refuge in the Dharma, and pray that with all beings
I may enter deeply into the sutra-treasure, whereby our wisdom
may grow as vast as the ocean.

I take my refuge in the Sangha, and pray that with all beings
I may reign in great multitudes and have nothing to check
the unimpeded progress of Truth.

Avataṁsaka Sūtra

About the Author

Sangharakshita was born Dennis Lingwood in South London, in 1925. Largely self-educated, he developed an interest in the cultures and philosophies of the East early on, and realized that he was a Buddhist at the age of sixteen.

The Second World War took him, as a conscript, to India, where he stayed on to become the Buddhist monk Sangharakshita. After studying for some years under leading teachers from the major Buddhist traditions, he went on to teach and write extensively. He also played a key part in the revival of Buddhism in India, particularly through his work among the ex- Untouchables.

After twenty years in India, he returned to England to establish the Friends of the Western Buddhist Order (FWBO) in 1967, and the Western Buddhist Order in 1968. A translator between East and West, between the traditional world and the modern, between principles and practices, Sangharakshita's depth of experience and clear thinking have been appreciated throughout the world. He has always particularly emphasized the decisive significance of commitment in the spiritual life, the paramount value of spiritual friendship and community, the link between religion and art, and the need for a 'new society' supportive of spiritual aspirations and ideals.

The FWBO is now an international Buddhist movement with over sixty centres on five continents. In recent years Sangharakshita has been handing on most of his responsibilities to his senior disciples in the Order. From his base in Birmingham, he is now focusing on personal contact with people, and on his writing.

PREFACE

DURING THE LAST five decades interest in Buddhism has become widespread in the West. From being the closed preserve of professional orientalists, whose interest was largely linguistic and historical, and to whom Buddhism was little more than a particularly well-preserved mummy in the museum of Comparative Religion, the wise, compassionate, and vital teachings of the Buddha have started attracting the attention of an increasing number of sensitive and thoughtful people who, though having outgrown authoritarian creeds of every kind, are yet in search of a framework of psychological and spiritual reference ample enough to contain and elastic enough not to confine their aspirations. Whether choosing to describe themselves as Buddhists or not, those who feel 'at home' within the framework called Buddhism, and who settle down therein, in effect commit themselves to the realization of an ideal by following a certain way of life in the company of other people similarly committed. This is what is traditionally known as 'Going for Refuge' to the Three Jewels, an act which, though it may find ceremonial expression, is essentially a profound inner experience, a spiritual rebirth or 'conversion', as a result of which one's whole life is transformed and reoriented.

The Three Jewels are the Buddha, the Dharma, and the Sangha. By the Buddha or Enlightened One is meant not only the historical Śākyamuni, the founder of Buddhism, but the ideal of Enlightenment both in its universal aspect and its ultimate reality. The Dharma or Doctrine is not only the sum total of the Buddha's teachings but the whole body of moral and spiritual laws, discovered and revealed by him, of which the doctrinal teachings form the conceptual formulation and practical exemplification. Similarly the Sangha or Assembly is the spiritual community of those who, following the Dharma, have attained the same levels of spiritual experience, or observe a common rule of monastic discipline, or simply the whole body of the faithful going for refuge to the Three Jewels – enlightened and unenlightened, monastic and lay, real and nominal.

The Three Jewels are, therefore, of pivotal importance in Buddhism. Indeed, the Three Jewels are Buddhism.

Such being the case, it is astonishing that, although there have appeared in print numerous accounts of the life and teachings of the Buddha, both popular and scholarly, not a single work of importance has been dedicated to the Three Jewels as such, even though these constitute the triple object of the central act of the Buddhist life, from which all other acts derive their significance, and without reference to which Buddhism itself is unintelligible.

The present work is designed to remedy this deficiency. Originally written as a series of articles for the *Oriya Encyclopædia*, it subsequently reached a much wider audience when published in book form. May this new Windhorse edition be the means of opening the eyes of many more people to the multi-faceted splendour of the Three Jewels.

Sangharakshita
Madhyamaloka
Birmingham
26 January 1998

Part One

THE BUDDHA

1

LIFE AND RECORDS

AN ACCOUNT of Buddhism necessarily begins with the Buddha. Though he is not regarded by his followers either as prophet or incarnation of God, from him as the perfectly Enlightened and boundlessly compassionate teacher of all sentient beings proceeds the unique message of the Path to Enlightenment, and it is therefore his figure, either in its original human form or in various idealized hypostases, which dominates the entire history of Buddhism. His spirit, active not only during eighty years of earthly life, but now and for ever, permeates all subsequent developments of the Teaching, giving guidance in the midst of doubt and indecision, support in moments of crisis, and a fresh impetus in times of stagnation and decay. As the eagle in ancient legend draws strength from gazing at the sun, so both the individual Buddhist and the whole vast spiritual, cultural, and social movement we call Buddhism again and again derive inspiration from the recollection of the exemplary life of that most serene, dignified, wise, and loving of the sons of men. 'How pleasant is thy shadow, O Śramaṇa!' cried Rāhula, the child of his humanity, and mankind itself might echo the exclamation.

Even if the Buddha is regarded merely from the historical point of view, his influence is unparalleled. Besides being the founder of Buddhism, a teaching that eventually won the allegiance of one-fourth of the human race, he reshaped Hinduism and profoundly modified Taoism, Confucianism, and Shintoism. Through Neoplatonism and Sufism respectively, Christianity and Islam received from him spiritual impulses which for centuries did much to temper the dogmatic harshness of these religions. Today the whole Western world is beginning to come under the influence of his teaching. Judged by these standards, Gautama the Buddha is the most conspicuous figure in the history of the human race.

But what do we actually know of his life? A handful of hard facts, a glittering mass of legends, and a body of abstruse disquisitions on his true nature, are practically all that remains. So far back in time does he stand, so high in attainment does he tower, that, as with some lofty mountain peak, the intervening depth of atmosphere, while enhancing the beauty of the spiritual colours of his career, would seem to blur the sharpness of the biographical outline. Yet despite the comparative paucity of biographical records as compared with doctrinal and disciplinary material in the Buddhist scriptures, we know considerably more about the Buddha than about either Jesus or Muhammad, while his historicity is indisputable.

Though no complete biography is found in the Tripiṭaka or 'Three Collections' of sacred traditions current in the early monastic communities, they do contain certain connected accounts of the Buddha's attainment of Enlightenment at Bodh Gaya and his *parinirvāṇa* at Kusinārā, as well as of the occurrences immediately preceding and succeeding these two great events. Incidents and anecdotes pertaining to the forty-five years in between are indeed not wanting, but the complete sequence is very difficult to determine with accuracy. Nevertheless, by having recourse to aesthetic and didactic, as well as to scientific, principles in the ordering of the vast material at their disposal, the ancient Buddhist writers were able to compile or compose five biographies of the Buddha.

Of these the mixed Sanskrit *Lalitavistara* or 'Extended [Account of the] Sports [of the Buddha]' – probably a Sarvāstivādin work which has undergone editing at Mahāyanist hands – is the most systematic. 'Its sonorous gāthas', says Dr Nalinaksha Dutt, 'are replete with bold imagery and its descriptive accounts in prose and poetry, through unrealistic, are calculated to produce faith and devotion for the Great Being.'[1] Even earlier is the *Mahāvastu* or 'Great Relation', a bulky and rather chaotic work, also in mixed Sanskrit, compiled from earlier materials probably 300 years after the parinirvāṇa and purporting to belong to the late Vinaya Piṭaka of the Lokottaravāda, a sub-school of the Mahāsāṁghika. Both these works depict the Buddha as an essentially transcendental being who, having gained perfection in previous lives, appears again among mankind out of compassion. Of more purely human interest, and even greater literary value, is the *Buddhacarita* or 'Acts of the Buddha' of Aśvaghoṣa, one of the supreme poets and dramatists of India, who flourished towards the end of the first century CE. Unfortunately the last fifteen chapters of this work, which was written in pure Sanskrit, have been lost in the original and are extant only in translation. A similar fate has befallen the whole of the *Abhiniṣkramaṇa Sūtra* or 'Discourse on the Great Renunciation', a work belonging to the Dharmaguptika – one of the eighteen early schools – and composed probably in mixed Sanskrit. Lastly there is the *Nidānakathā* or 'Connected Account' written in pure Pāli by way of introduction to the commentary on the *Jātaka* book and attributed to the eminent fifth-century Theravādin scholastic Buddhaghosa.

With the help of these biographies, as well as with that of the Pāli Tipiṭaka and such portions of its Sanskrit counterparts as are still extant, either in the original or in translations, it should be possible to give a sketch of the Buddha's career which would not be unacceptable even to the scientific historian. It will also be necessary to examine the significance of the legendary and mythological elements in which the traditional biographies abound, as well as to consider the metaphysical ponderings of the Buddhist doctors on the real nature of the Enlightened One. However, before dealing with his last life, in which he became the Buddha, we must direct our attention to those many former lives through which, as Bodhisattva, the Great Being struggled towards his goal.

2

THE BODHISATTVA CAREER

BUDDHISM TEACHES rebirth. Not, indeed, in the sense of an unchanging immaterial entity (*ātman*) transmigrating from one physical body to another, but in a deeper, subtler sense. Just as, in the present existence, a preceding becomes the condition for a succeeding mental state, so in dependence on the last thought-moment of one life arises the first thought-moment of the next, the relation between the two lives, as between the two mental states, being one of causal continuity. The illustration appropriate to the case is not that of a man who changes from one set of clothes to another, the man himself remaining the while unchanged, but rather that of a flame which, in its advance, feeds upon successive bundles of fuel.

Popular expositions of the Dharma, including discourses attributed to the Buddha, do indeed sometimes make use of such terms as *ātman* and *punarjanma*; but they are employed only by way of an accommodation to conventional modes of expression and are certainly not to be taken literally and made the starting point for a series of deductions about Buddhism. Advanced expositions make use of a more precise terminology. Instead of *ātman* they speak of *cittasantāna* or psyche-continuum (sometimes simply *santāna*), while *punarbhava*, 'again-becoming', replaces *punarjanma*, 'rebirth'.

To say that, at death, the psychical life ceases with that of the body is one extreme view; to say that any psychical element, such as an immortal soul, survives death unchanged is the other. Here, as elsewhere, Buddhism follows the middle path, teaching that the 'being' of one life is neither exactly the same as, nor completely different from, the 'being' of another life. Though consenting to speak in terms of rebirth, it precludes misunderstanding by pointing out that there is no one who is reborn.

Unless this is clearly understood, we are likely to be misled by those who, on the basis of a very superficial acquaintance with Buddhism, maintain either that the Buddha contradicted himself by teaching the *anātman* doctrine *and* rebirth, or that he taught one of them but not the other. We may also be in danger of wondering whether the accounts of the Buddha's successive lives as a Bodhisattva are not apocryphal!

This does not mean that we should fly to the opposite extreme and accept at face value the entire contents of the *Jātaka* books. As Rhys Davids has pointed out, only the verses of the Pāli *Jātaka* book belong to the Tipiṭaka. The 550 'birth-stories' are related in the commentary and are non-canonical.[2] The canonical birth-stories are found scattered throughout the *nikāyas* of the Sutta Piṭaka. In them the Buddha (or Bodhisattva, as he then was) is depicted not as a bird or animal, as in the tales of the *Jātaka* commentary, but invariably as a famous sage or teacher of olden time – which is what we should have expected. The non-canonical tales of the *Jātaka* book commentary, which have delighted and inspired hundreds of generations of Buddhists, need not therefore be dismissed as worthless. Whether or not pertaining to the psyche-continuum of Gautama the Buddha himself, they do illustrate, often in an extremely moving manner, how the urge to Enlightenment is immanent in all forms and spheres of life, from the humblest to the highest, and manifests whenever a kind and intelligent action is performed.

Moreover, whatever our doubts about the authenticity of this or that particular tale may be, we should not forget that the Buddha did claim the power of remembering his previous existences as far back as he wished. This power, technically known as *pūrvanivāsānusmṛti*, 'recollection of previous abodes', constitutes one of the *abhijñās* or 'superknowledges' attained by him on the night of his Supreme Enlightenment. It is attainable, albeit not to the same degree, by other beings also. In modern times – it is interesting to observe – attempts are being made, in various ways, to verify rebirth experimentally.[3] The attempt is of scientific rather than spiritual significance, as according to Buddhism the power of recollecting previous births, though developed in the higher stages of mental concentration, is not in itself a factor conducive to the attainment of Enlightenment.

All the *Jātakas*, canonical and non-canonical, in theory represent the Bodhisattva preparing himself for the attainment of Buddhahood by the practice of certain definite virtues afterwards called *pāramitās* or 'perfections'. In the earliest texts dealing with the subject, which are in Sanskrit, these are six in number: generosity (*dāna*), morality (*śīla*), patience (*kṣānti*), energy (*vīrya*), concentration (*samādhi*), and wisdom (*prajñā*). Four more were subsequently added to the list: skill in means (*upāya-kauśalya*), resolution (*praṇidhāna*), power (*bala*), and knowledge (*jñāna*). A later and less systematic list, apparently drawn up in imitation of the earlier one, is found in the Pāli literature of the Theravādins.

Each birth-story is designed to illustrate the Bodhisattva's practice of a particular perfection. In the well-known tale of the life in which he was Kṣāntivādin – 'Advocate of Patience' – for example, he preaches this virtue to a group of palace ladies, who in order to listen to the sermon leave their sleeping lord and master unattended. When the king wakes up and finds himself alone he is so enraged that he cuts off the preacher's limbs one by one, at the same time asking him, with each blow of the sword, whether he still advocates patience. Each time Kṣāntivādin replies that he does. In the yet more popular tale of the king of the Śibis the Bodhisattva sacrifices an equivalent amount of his own flesh in order to ransom the life of a bird, thus practising the perfection of generosity.

Most accounts divide not only Gautama's but any bodhisattva's career into three periods, each consisting of 10^{59} years. During the first he meets an Enlightened One (Buddhism teaches a plurality not only of lives but of inhabited worlds) and, inspired by his example, develops in his presence the Will to Enlightenment (*bodhicitta*), resolves to attain Supreme Buddhahood for the good of all, and receives from him an assurance (*vyākaraṇa*) of final success. By the practice of the perfection of giving he attains the 'joyful stage' (*pramuditābhūmi*), the first of the ten stages of spiritual progress through which a bodhisattva must pass. In the second period he practises the perfections of morality, patience, energy, concentration, wisdom, skilful means, and resolution, thus traversing six more *bhūmis* and attaining the seventh. These are the 'immaculate' (*vimalā*), 'illuminating' (*prabhākarī*), 'blazing' (*arciṣmati*), 'very difficult to conquer' (*sudurjayā*), 'face-to-face' (*abhimukhī*), 'far-going' (*dūraṅgamā*), and 'unshakeable' (*acalā*). In the third and last period he practises the perfections of power and knowledge, traverses the two remaining *bhūmis*, those of 'good thoughts' (*sadhūmatī*) and 'cloud of dharma' (*dharmameghā*), and becomes a Supreme Buddha for the benefit of all sentient beings.[4]

Though these and other similar details of the bodhisattva's career need not be understood too literally, or made articles of faith, once one has accepted the basic premise of 'again-becoming' they will seem neither fantastic nor improbable, and in outline at least should not be found difficult of acceptance. Buddhahood being in any case so hard of achievement it is but natural that the moral, intellectual, and spiritual equipment necessary to create a sound basis for its full realization and effective manifestation should take some time to accumulate and call for the energetic practice of virtues such as the *pāramitās* during not one but many lives.

In the case of 'our own' Buddha, as he is called, tradition tells us that countless ages ago, in another world-period, he was a brahmin named Sumedha who, perplexed by the problems of existence and determined to find a way out, renounced his wealth and became a forest-dwelling hermit:

> At that time Dīpaṇkara Buddha appeared in the world, and attained enlightenment. It happened one day that Dīpaṇkara Buddha was to pass that way, and men were preparing the road for him. Sumedha asked and received permission to join in the work, and not only did he do so, but when Dīpaṇkara came Sumedha laid himself down in the mud, so that the Buddha might walk upon his body without soiling his feet. Then Dīpaṇkara's attention was aroused and he became aware of Sumedha's intention to become a Buddha, and, looking countless ages into the future, he saw that he would become a Buddha of the name of Gautama, and he prophesied accordingly. Thereupon Sumedha rejoiced, and, rejecting the immediate prospect of becoming an Arahat, as the disciple of Dīpaṇkara, 'Let me rather', he said, 'like Dīpaṇkara, having risen to the supreme knowledge of the truth, enable all men to enter the ship of truth, and thus I may bear them over the Sea of Existence, and then only let me realize Nibbāna myself.'[5]

After practising the *pāramitās* and traversing the *bhūmis* in the manner and for the period already described, the Great Being, now on the threshold of Supreme Buddhahood, is born in the divine realm called 'Contented' (*tuṣitadevaloka*), whence descending into the womb of Māyādevī and being born in the Lumbinī garden he not only appears for the last time in the world of men but becomes accessible to historical inquiry.

3

THE LIFE

ACCORDING TO TRADITIONS current in the days of Aśoka, who ascended the throne of Magadha in 274BCE, the future Buddha was born at a spot midway between Kapilavastu and Devadaha. The dates given for the event in different Buddhist records vary considerably, but modern scholarship, working backwards from Aśoka, on the whole tends to place it at 563BCE. The Śākyas, the tribe or clan into which he was born, were a proud, independent people numbering perhaps 1,000,000 who inhabited nearly 2,000 square miles of territory at the foot of the central portion of the Himalayan Range, the northern part of the area now falling within the borders of Nepal and the southern forming part of India. Economically the Śākyas were a predominantly agricultural community; politically, like a number of other Northern Indian peoples in those days, they constituted a republic. Either at the time of the Buddha's birth or some later period his father Suddhodana, a well-to-do land-owning patrician, was serving a term as elected president of the public assembly at which was conducted the administrative and judicial business of the clan.

His mother dying shortly after his birth, Siddhārtha – 'The Accomplished One', as he was called – was reared by his maternal aunt Mahāprajāpati, Suddhodana having taken both sisters to wife. By contemporary standards the education he received was a good one, consisting mainly of a grounding in the ethics and traditions of the clan, training in manly sports and knightly exercises, and instruction in such brahminical lore as had by that time penetrated into Śākya territory. There is no evidence that he could read and write, and as in all 'primitive' communities such things as genealogies and ward-runes had to be learned by heart. The most significant event of his childhood was of the type loosely called mystical. Seated one day under a rose-apple tree, while his father was ploughing, he spontaneously experienced a state of purity, bliss, and peace so intense that years later, at a moment of supreme crisis, the recollection of it was able to exert a decisive influence upon the course of his career. Meanwhile he grew up enjoying all the comforts and luxuries, pleasures and amusements, proper to his age and class. According to his own subsequent confession he was a youth delicate to the point of effeminacy, being sheltered with white umbrellas, wearing costly apparel, and making use of garlands, perfumes, and cosmetics. He spent each season at a different spot, Suddhodana having placed at his disposal three mansions, one for the summer, one for the winter, and one for the rains. At each mansion lotus pools were made for him wherein bloomed blue or white or red lotuses. The rainy season, which he spent surrounded by female musicians, was in particular given up to pleasure, and for four months at a stretch he did not stir out of doors. Eventually, he was married, probably to more than one wife, and had a son. Yet despite so deep an enjoyment of worldly happiness he was not satisfied. The problem of existence tormented him. In particular he was obsessed by the pitiableness of the human predicament. Was there no way out for beings subjected to the miseries of birth, old age, disease, and death? Suddhodana, with whom he discussed the matter, was unable to answer his questions. He therefore resolved to follow the time-honoured practice of giving up family and possessions and going forth as a homeless wandering beggar in quest of Truth. In vain his father and foster-mother sought to dissuade him. One day, despite their tears and entreaties, he had his hair and beard cut off, donned the yellow robe, and went forth from the home into the homeless life.

Journeying south-east from Kapilavastu and penetrating into the jungles of what is now the province of Bihar, he came across the hermitage of Ārāḍa Kāḷāma, a noted sage, who agreed to accept him as a pupil. What Siddhārtha learned from him we are not told, though from the fact that on the practical side his teaching culminated in the realization of a superconscious state termed *ākiñcanyāyatana* or 'sphere of no-thing-ness' we may infer that the sage's teaching was a theosophy of the upanishadic type. Not satisfied with a merely theoretical grasp of the teaching, Siddhārtha applied himself to its realization, and in a short time succeeded in attaining whatever Ārāḍa Kāḷāma himself had attained. The noble-minded teacher, discerning his ability, thereupon invited him to share the leadership of the community. But feeling that beyond the sphere of 'no-thing-ness' there lay an even higher state, Siddhārtha refused to accept the generous offer and, instead, left Ārāḍa Kāḷāma's hermitage for that of Udraka Rāmaputra. With the help of this sage he attained an even higher state, that of *naivasaṁjñānāsaṁjñāyatana* or 'sphere of neither-perception-nor-non-perception'. But he felt that this too was not ultimate, and though his second teacher made the same offer as the first he resolved to continue his quest alone. Resuming his wanderings he passed through the kingdom of Magadha, and eventually reached a place called Uruvelā, on the outskirts of which he resolved to settle down. Thereafter followed six years of fearsome austerities. No ascetic, he subsequently declared, had outgone him in self-mortification, or was ever likely to outgo him. Nakedness, systematic reduction of food, exposure to extreme heat and extreme cold, retention of the breath until the body seemed on fire, together with every other repulsive and disgusting practice which the perverted ascetic imagination of the day had devised, did he compel himself to undergo in his search for Supreme Enlightenment. Yet the great effort failed. Eventually, when he was almost dead from exhaustion, he suddenly recollected his childhood experience under the rose-apple tree. Was this the way to Supreme Enlightenment, he wondered? Convinced that it was, he abandoned his austerities and started taking proper nourishment again. Five fellow ascetics, who had gathered around him in the hope of sharing the Truth when he gained it, now left him in disgust, feeling that he had given up the search and returned to a life of ease. Undismayed by their defection, however, and with strength renewed, the Bodhisattva seated himself on a heap of grass beneath a *pīpal* tree with the firm resolve not to stir from his seat until Supreme Enlightenment had been attained. Night fell. During the first watch, having traversed the four *dhyānas* (see p.101), he bent his purified and supple intelligence to the recollection of his former births, recalling in this way first hundreds, then thousands, and finally hundreds of thousands of previous existences. During the second watch, he saw with his superhuman divine vision beings vanishing from one state of existence and reappearing in another according to their good and bad deeds. During the third watch, having directed his mind to the destruction of the 'biases' (*āsravas*) towards sensuous experience (*kāma*), conditioned existence (*bhava*), and speculative opinions (*dṛṣṭi*), he realized the ineffable Truth and saw in its light the contingent and conditioned character of all mundane things whatsoever. In the resultant state of freedom and emancipation there arose the consciousness that rebirth had been destroyed and the higher life fulfilled. When dawn came a Supreme Buddha sat beneath the tree.

The next few weeks, which were spent at the foot of various other trees in the neighbourhood, were devoted to the full assimilation of the Truth he had discovered. During this period he had three visitors, a haughty brahmin who came and asked the characteristics of a brahmin in the course of the second week, and two travelling merchants, Trapuṣa and Bhallika, who turned aside from the road to pay their respects in the fourth week and who, after offering rice cake and honeycomb, took refuge in him and his Dharma, thus constituting themselves the first lay disciples. In the fifth week, after initial hesitation on account of its extreme abstruseness, he decided out of compassion to make known to mankind the Truth he had penetrated. His two former teachers having recently died, he determined to seek out his five fellow ascetics and preach first to them. Accordingly he set out on foot for the Deer Park near the ancient city of Benares, more than 100 miles away, where they were then residing. On the way he encountered a sceptical-minded Ājīvaka named Upaka to whom, in response to his enquiries, he declared that having gained knowledge by his personal exertions he had no teacher, being in fact himself the highest teacher, unequalled in the world of men and gods, the Supremely Enlightened One. Unconvinced, Upaka walked on. A week later the Buddha entered the Deer Park. Still thinking him a renegade from asceticism, the five ascetics agreed not to receive him with the customary remarks of respect. But so awe-inspiring was his demeanour that as he approached they involuntarily rose from their seats. It was only with much difficulty, however, that he succeeded in persuading them that, far from being a fallen ascetic, he was now the Supremely Enlightened One. Convinced at last, they consented to listen to his teaching. He thereupon preached to them his First Sermon, the *Dharmacakrapravartana Sūtra* or 'Discourse Setting in Motion the Wheel of Truth', which according to the unanimous testimony of the most ancient records consisted in a brief statement of the Middle Way, the Four Noble Truths, and the Noble Eightfold Path. One by one the five ascetics, beginning with Ajñāta Kauṇḍinya, realized the import of the teaching and received ordination from the Master, thus becoming the first bhikṣus. Further conversions followed. Yaśa, a rich young man of Benares, became a monk after a midnight talk with the Buddha, while his parents became lay disciples. Before long, fifty-four of Yaśa's friends, all belonging to prominent merchant families of the city, had followed his example. Including the Buddha, there were now sixty-one Arhants, or Enlightened beings, in the world.

The Master then took a step of extraordinary and far-reaching importance. Addressing the sixty Enlightened disciples, he declared,

> I am delivered, monks, from all fetters, human and divine. You, monks, are also delivered from all fetters, human and divine. Go ye now, monks, and wander for the gain of the many, for the happiness of the many, out of compassion for the world, for the good, for the gain, and for the welfare of gods and men. Let not two of you go the same way. Preach, monks, the Dharma which is lovely in the beginning, lovely in the middle, lovely at the end, in the spirit and in the letter; proclaim a consummate, perfect, and pure life of holiness. There are beings whose mental eyes are covered by scarcely any dust, but if the Dharma is not preached to them, they cannot attain salvation.[6]

He himself, he said, would go to preach at Uruvelā. Thirty pleasure-seeking young men whom he met on the way were converted to his teaching and received into the Order. Uruvelā was at that time an important centre of the Jaṭilas, or fire-worshipping ascetics, 1,000 of whom resided in the area under the leadership of the three Kāśyapa brothers. Although the Buddha stayed for a considerable time with Uruvelā Kāśyapa, the eldest brother, for whose benefit he performed extraordinary feats of supernormal power, the stubborn fire-worshipper could not be converted. Despite the wonders he saw, he persisted in thinking himself holier than the Buddha. Eventually the Buddha had to tell him bluntly that he was neither holy nor on the path to holiness. Converted at last, Uruvelā Kāśyapa, together with his 500 followers, was received into the Order. Nāḍi Kāśyapa with 300, and Gayā Kāśyapa with 200 adherents, followed suit. Leading the thousand ex-fire-worshippers to Gayā Head, a neighbouring promontory, the Buddha preached to them one of the most famous and magnificent of all his discourses, the *Āditya-paryāya Sūtra* or 'Fire Sermon'. At Rājagṛha, the capital of the kingdom of Magadha, whither he proceeded with his retinue of new followers, doubt arose in the minds of King Bimbisāra and the brahmins and householders of Magadha as to whether Uruvelā Kāśyapa had converted the Buddha or the Buddha Uruvelā Kāśyapa. Apprised of the facts of the case, they too took refuge in the Buddha, the Dharma, and the Sangha. King Bimbisāra, in fact, invited the Buddha and his disciples to lunch, after which he gifted to them the Veḷuvana or 'Bamboo Grove', a royal park situated outside the city gates. This was the first landed property to be donated to the Order. Meanwhile Aśvajit, one of the original five ascetics, had converted Śāriputra, a follower of Sañjaya Belaṭṭhiputra, who had in turn converted his friend Maudgalyāyana. Together with 250 companions, all followers of the same teacher, they came to the Bamboo Grove for ordination. As he saw them coming from afar the Buddha predicted that the two friends would be his chief pair of disciples. By this time so many converts had joined the Sangha that people started raising objections, saying that the Buddha had made parents childless, and wives to become widows, and that he was causing the destruction of families. They even made a gibing popular song about it. Telling the monks that the disturbance would die down after seven days, the Buddha gave them a stanza to chant in reply. Eventually all befell as he had predicted, and the circle of his adherents continued to expand.

At this point the story of the Buddha's life, which had hitherto marched with epic sublimity from climax to climax, starts breaking up into incidents and episodes the chronological order of which it is impossible to determine. Though it is not difficult, indeed, to arrange the more important events chronicled in the most ancient records in a quite plausible sequence, the result would pertain not so much to the life as to the legend of the Master. Only as we approach the very end of his ministry do we find ourselves, chronologically speaking, on as firm ground as at its beginning. Yet however unsatisfactory from the narrative point of view the material at our disposal may be, the largely unconnected anecdotes and episodes of which it consists convey a definite unity of impression. Even making due allowance for pious exaggeration, in depth and extent of influence the Buddha was evidently, during his own lifetime, the most successful propagandist the world has ever seen, and the picture which jigsaw-puzzle-wise emerges is that of a vigorous spiritual movement in process of constant expansion, adaptation, and consolidation. If the events up to and immediately after the Enlightenment form as it were a single narrative line climbing graph-like from peak to peak of achievement, those of the remaining forty-five years suggest a number of lines radiating from a common centre of force. Though prose or verse narrative may suffice for the first, only painting, with its power of depicting a number of episodes simultaneously, could do justice to the second. Geographically, the area of the Buddha's personal influence in north-eastern India formed a rough triangle based upon Campā in the east and Kośāmbi in the west, with Kapilavastu as the apex. Politically it included the kingdoms of Kosala, Magadha, and Anga, in each of whose capitals the Order had important foundations, and republics such as those of the Śākyas, the Kāḷāmas, the Mallas, and the Licchavis. In terms of present-day political geography the area covered comprises, approximately, distances 450 miles from east to west, by over 200 from north to south; from west of Allahabad in the Uttar Pradesh, to east of Bhagalpur in Bihar. Within this triangle, perhaps 50,000 square miles in extent, the social and cultural – to say nothing of the spiritual – influence of the Buddha was ubiquitous. Bimbisāra and Prasenajit, the rulers of Magadha and Kosala respectively, were his adherents, as were most of the leading republican families. Members of the wealthy trading class, like Anāthapiṇḍada and Viśākhā, both of whom built hostelries for the Order at Śrāvastī, declared themselves his followers and contributed lavishly to the cause. Cultured brahmins, whether ritualists or free-thinkers, were in regular communication with him, and though not always converted to the Teaching were evidently aware of its prestige and popularity. On his travels, which lasted for nine months of the year, the Buddha came in close personal contact not only with wandering ascetics of various types but also with peasants, artisans, shopkeepers, and robbers, with young and old, men and women, rich and poor, learned and ignorant. Men of all castes, from the lordly *kṣatriya* to the humble *śūdra*, poured into the Sangha, there to lose their separate designations, being thereafter reckoned simply 'monks who are sons of the Śākyan' (*śākyaputra-śramaṇas*). So extraordinary was the Master's influence, that rival teachers, at a loss to account for his success, alleged that he charmed and attracted people by means of spells.

In a sense they were right. The fascination of the Buddha's personality was unequalled. Diehard adherents of this or that sectarian teacher, after seeing him only once, behaved as if bewitched. Though sublime in his dignity, he was eminently approachable, combining aristocratic aloofness and democratic cordiality, freedom and reserve. So awe-inspiring was his presence that kings grew nervous as they approached, yet so compassionate that the broken-hearted fled to him for refuge as though by instinct. Fearlessness, equanimity, self-confidence, and energy were among his most outstanding characteristics. Whether expounding the Teaching to the dull-witted, or dealing with recalcitrant followers, his patience was unfailing. Practical difficulties connected with the organization and administration of the Sangha he met in a manner which suggested that Enlightenment did not exclude common sense. Moreover, as numerous episodes attest, he was not without a sense of humour. Yet despite these and many other human qualities he was at the same time so very much more than human that even his closest and most advanced disciples felt that in his true nature he transcended their understanding. Like the great ocean, the Tathāgata was unfathomable.

Fortunately the relative chronology of what, historically speaking, are the three most outstanding episodes of the Master's public career is clear from internal evidence, and with these we must bridge the gap between the end of the beginning of his ministry and the beginning of the end. The first centres on his return to Kapilavastu. Though at first displeased to see him begging – as was his custom – from door to door, Suddhodana eventually gave ear to his son's teaching and became a convert. Ānanda and Devadatta, both cousins of the Buddha, joined the Order, as did a number of other young Śākyans. Rāhula, sent by his mother to claim his inheritance, received instead of any mundane patrimony the gift of the Dharma, being admitted into the fellowship as a novice by Śāriputra and Maudgalyāyana. Several of the Buddha's admonitions to Rāhuḷa survive in the Scriptures. The scene of the second episode, which took place more than twenty years later, is the Licchavi capital Vaiśālī. Apparently on a recent visit to Kapilavastu the Buddha had refused the request of Mahāprajāpati, his foster-mother, that women be allowed to go forth into the homeless life. She therefore cut off her hair, donned the saffron-coloured robes, and as though to present him with a *fait accompli* trudged with a number of other Śākyan women to Vaiśālī.

But for all her tears the Buddha refused to admit her to the Order. Only on the intercession of Ānanda, who by that time had become his personal attendant, did he finally relent. It is with reference to this episode that writers on Buddhism represent the Buddha as declaring that women having been admitted to the Order it would last in its integrity for 500 years instead of for 1,000. A closer examination of the text[7] does not bear out this interpretation. What the Buddha in effect said was that the eight special conditions he had imposed upon Mahāprajāpati were designed to prevent such a deterioration, which otherwise in the nature of things was bound to take place. Whatever lowering of standards might subsequently have occurred in the Sangha, there is no evidence whatever to suggest that it was in any way connected with the presence in it of women. The last episode, or rather series of episodes, took place in and around Rājagṛha in the closing decades of the Buddha's earthly life. Devadatta, who had already instigated Ajātaśatru to seize the throne of Magadha from his father Bimbisāra, suggested that the Buddha, being old, should make over the leadership of the Sangha to him and live in retirement. This suggestion the Buddha sternly rejected. Making use of his influence with Ajātaśatru, Devadatta thereupon plotted to kill the Master. First he hired assassins to lie in wait for him, then himself rolled down upon him a huge boulder, a splinter from which wounded him in the foot, and finally released against him a mad elephant. All these attempts miscarried. Having failed either to assume leadership of the Sangha or to remove the Buddha, Devadatta tried to create a schism and win over at least a section of the Order to his own side. But proving unsuccessful in this attempt also, he eventually died in despair. After his death the Buddha declared that Devadatta had come to grief because of evil desires and evil friends, and by his having come to a stop on the Way because he had attained the lower psychic powers.

During the last six months of his life the Buddha sojourned at fourteen different places, beginning with the Gṛdhrakūṭa or 'Vulture's Peak' at Rājagṛha, and ending with the Sāl Grove of the Mallas at Kusinārā, where he attained parinirvāṇa. Aware that it was his last tour among his disciples, he missed no opportunity of instructing and admonishing them. At eleven out of the fourteen places he delivered a 'comprehensive religious discourse' which, since it occurs so many times, and under such circumstances, may be regarded as constituting the essence of his teaching. 'Such and such is right conduct (*śīla*),' the texts in brief report him as saying,

> ... such and such is meditation (*samādhi*), such and such is wisdom (*prajñā*). Great becomes the fruit, great the advantages of meditation, when it is set round with upright conduct. Great becomes the fruit, great the advantage of wisdom, when it is set round with meditation. The mind set round with wisdom is set quite free from the biases (*āsravas*), that is to say, from the bias towards sensuous experience (*kāma*), towards conditioned existence (*bhava*), towards speculative opinions (*dṛṣṭi*), and towards ignorance (*avidyā*).[8]

Before the Buddha left Rājagṛha, Ajātaśatru, who was planning the destruction of the Vajjians, sent his minister to enquire whether the attempt would be successful. Recalling the seven conditions of welfare he had once taught them, the Master declared that so long as these conditions were observed by the Vajjians they would not decline but prosper. After the minister's departure he called together all the bhikṣus in the neighbourhood and taught them 'seven times seven conditions of welfare, less one', observing which the Sangha might be expected not to decline but to grow. During the last rainy season retreat, which he spent at Beluva, a village near Vaiśālī, the Master fell ill; but thinking it would not be proper to pass away without addressing the disciples and taking leave of the Order he suppressed the sickness by sheer force of will and carried on. Shortly afterwards Ānanda hinted at the desirability of some final instructions regarding the Order. This suggestion the Buddha flatly repudiated. It was enough that he had taught the Dharma; he did not imagine that he led the Sangha or that it was dependent on him. Let Ānanda and the rest be lamps unto themselves, refuges unto themselves; let them take the Dharma as a lamp, the Dharma as a refuge. Such true disciples, practising mindfulness with regard to body, sensations, moods, and ideas could, either then or after he was dead, attain the very topmost height. But they should be willing to learn! At Vaiśālī, again calling the monks together, he exhorted them, in language reminiscent of the charge to the first sixty Arhants, to make themselves masters of the truths he had taught, to practise them, meditate upon them, and spread them abroad,

> in order that pure religion may last long and be perpetuated, in order that it may continue to be for the good and happiness of the great multitudes, out of pity for the world, to the good and the gain and the weal of gods and men![9]

Bidding farewell to the pleasant groves and shrines of Vaiśālī, the Buddha, accompanied by a great number of monks, walked by easy stages to Pāvā, taking between two and three months to complete the journey and preaching as he went.

At Pāvā, at the hands of Cunda the metal-worker, he partook of his last meal, presumably in the forenoon. Unfortunately, some of the mushrooms with which he was served were poisonous, and the meal brought on a severe attack of dysentery. Nevertheless the Buddha pressed on to Kusinārā, though twice on the way he felt tired and had to rest. But physical debility did not prevent him from preaching. Pukkusa, a young Mallian, who had stepped aside from the road after seeing the Buddha resting at the foot of a tree, was converted as the result of a short discussion, and sending home for a pair of robes of cloth-of-gold robed the Buddha in one of them and Ānanda in the other. The Master also found time to think of Cunda the metal-worker, warning Ānanda that he was not to be allowed to suffer remorse or blame himself on account of the last meal. Eventually the party reached the Sāl Grove of the Mallas at Kusinārā. Here, between two sāl trees, with its head to the north, there stood a stone couch. On this the Buddha lay down. As he did so untimely blossoms rained down upon him from the branches above. Ānanda, in his devotion, took this for an act of worship, and was delighted. But even at such a moment the Buddha would not tolerate sentimentality, and firmly reminded him that true worship of the Tathāgata consisted in following his teaching. Ānanda then enquired what they were to do with his remains. But more firmly and earnestly still the Master exhorted him that the monks should devote themselves to their own spiritual growth, leaving to the lay followers the honouring of his dead body. Despite such exhortations, however, Ānanda was so moved at the thought of the imminent departure of his beloved master that he went aside and wept, and had to be sent for by the Buddha who, after comforting him, predicted his speedy Enlightenment and praised him to the assembled brethren. He was then dispatched to inform the Mallas of Kusinārā that the parinirvāṇa would take place during the third watch of the night. The first watch was accordingly taken up with the visits of these republican folk, who came in large numbers to pay their last respects. In order to save time Ānanda introduced them family by family. During the second watch came Subhadra, a wandering ascetic, who, having heard that the Buddha was about to pass away, pleaded for an interview. Ānanda was unwilling that the Tathāgata should be troubled at such a time; but overhearing their conversation the Buddha ordered the man to be admitted. After a short discussion, in the course of which the Master roundly declared that true saints were found only where the Āryan Eightfold Path was found, and nowhere else, he too was converted and received into the Order. The third watch of the night was devoted to the brethren. After telling Ānanda that, after his death, they were to regard the Dharma and the Vinaya as their teacher, he urged them to declare whatever doubt or misgiving they had in their mind as to the Buddha, or the Dharma, or the Sangha, or the Path, or the Method. But none had any doubt, and the Buddha declared that even the most backward of them was assured of Enlightenment. He then addressed them and said, 'Behold now, brethren, I exhort you, saying: "Impermanent are all component things. With mindfulness strive on."' These were his last words.

4

THE LEGENDS

MODERN WRITERS on Buddhism in general believe that the traditional accounts of the Buddha's life consist of a substratum of historical fact upon which have been superimposed successive layers of 'legendary' material, and that their task is to separate the one from the other – it being assumed as self-evident that 'legendary' is synonymous with 'fictitious'. In adopting this procedure they are only partly correct. Though we have followed them to the extent of giving, in our short sketch of the Buddha's career, only such facts as are generally allowed to have survived the shakings of their sieve, this concession has been made only as a matter of convenience, not on principle. Far from being all of one kind, those elements in the traditional biographies which are dismissed as legendary are on the contrary found, on analysis, to comprise at least three distinct categories of material. To the first category belong episodes which are legendary in the common acceptation of the term, that is, which though represented as historical did not really take place; to the second, episodes which are treated as untrue because they violate certain scientific notions of what is possible and what impossible; to the third, those which, though presented in the form of external, historical events, in fact symbolize spiritual truths and experiences. A few examples of each of these categories, all of which are capable of subdivision, will help to make the distinction perfectly clear and demonstrate that the 'life' of the Buddha ought not always to be so sharply divided from the 'legend' as the learned have commonly supposed.

To the first category belong legends, or legendary elements, which are traceable to simple exaggeration, to interested invention, or to misattribution. Of these the first is the most innocent and easily detectable. In contrast to the Greek, the classical Indian mind was constitutionally prone to extravagance and exaggeration, especially when inflamed by religious devotion. This gave rise, for example, in the case of Buddhism, to a pronounced tendency to augmentation of the number of persons in attendance on the Buddha or converted as a result of his preaching. Thus if 1,250 monks are mentioned by an earlier text one of later date, dealing with the same episode, is sure to increase the number to at least 12,500. So much a habit does this multiplication of zeros become among the redactors of the canonical literature that in one of the 'Perfection of Wisdom' texts the Lord is represented as taking by way of example 'a mother who has many children – five, or ten, or twenty, or thirty, or forty, or fifty, or one hundred, or one thousand'.[10] This tendency to numerical exaggeration, as well as to prolixity and discursiveness of all kinds, permeates the vast bulk of Buddhist canonical literature to so great an extent that the student may be pardoned for mistaking it for a characteristic of Buddhism itself. That this is by no means the case is demonstrated by the history of Buddhism in China, where the Ch'an or Dhyāna School in particular, reacting not against Indian Buddhism so much as against distinctively Indian modes of expression, supplies the corrective by creating, out of indigenous resources, a terser and more compact form of expression for the same spiritual truths.

As easily detected, though less innocent and less amenable to correction, are the legends attributable to interested invention. The 'interest' is often a nationalistic one. To this subdivision may be assigned those accounts, made so much of by certain modern writers belonging to the countries concerned, of the Buddha's personal visits to Sri Lanka and Burma. For these visits there is not a shred of evidence. Yet to such an extent can scholarship be vitiated by national prejudice that even writers of repute insist on according these pious fictions the status of indubitable historic facts. Were they presented simply as an expression of an understandable wish for a closer link with the person of the Buddha than that which history vouchsafes, little objection to these legends could be raised: they have their parallels in the belief that Christ visited Britain and in the pure Arabian descent alleged by some Indian Muslims. But when in all seriousness they are made the basis for a claim to spiritual pre-eminence in the Buddhist world they cannot be allowed to pass uncontradicted.

By misattribution, the third and last subdivision of the first category, is meant the relating about the Buddha of an incident which actually happened not to him but to some other person, usually a disciple. One of the most striking examples of this type of 'legend' is found in the Vinaya Piṭaka's account of how Yaśa, one of the earliest converts (see p.17), abandoned home one night after seeing his dancing-girls asleep in various unseemly and disgusting attitudes.[11] This story the *Nidānakathā* relates of the future Buddha! It is also referred to in the *Mahāvastu*,[12] besides being recounted at length in Aśvaghoṣa's *Buddhacarita*,[13] where it forms one of the most admired passages in that noble poem. Some may, of course, argue that the episode was transferred from the Master's life to the disciple's. But against this must be weighed the fact that what appear to be the oldest and most authentic accounts of the Bodhisattva's renunciation make no mention of it whatever.

The second category of legendary material includes all incidents in which the Buddha is represented as exercising supernormal powers, such as clairvoyance, clairaudience, and levitation, or as holding converse with non-human beings, *devas, brahmās, māras*, etc. Brought up as most of them were under the overt or covert influence of eighteenth-century rationalistic and nineteenth-century materialistic and agnostic modes of thought, the older generation of orientalists naturally discarded these incidents as pure invention, assuming it to be self-evident that in a universe governed by natural law they could not have taken place. Their modern counterparts are usually not so rash. Scientific thinking is now much less biased towards materialism than it was, and few scientists would be prepared to dogmatize on the limits of the possible. Some, indeed, are seriously investigating, by means of standard procedures, a variety of phenomena now classified under the heading of ESP. Rhine's experiments in this field are well known. Unfortunately, however, due partly to the fact that in many cases the works of the older orientalists are still in circulation, and partly to the operation of a sort of cultural time-lag, whereby at least half a century elapses before an idea or discovery gets into general circulation, works on the Buddha and Buddhism continue to reflect modes of thought that have been definitely discredited. Even as late as 1948 there could appear a scholarly compilation from the Pāli Canon that deliberately excises all references to the 'supernatural'.[14] This is not to say that tales of the Cock Lane Ghost variety do not appear in Buddhist literature, or that every miracle and marvel reported in the Tripiṭaka is deserving of unlimited credence. One must follow a middle path between credulity and scepticism. Besides, it must not be forgotten that unlike Christianity Buddhism does not regard the 'miracles' of its founder as establishing either the truth of his teaching or the uniqueness of his personal spiritual attainments. Psychic powers such as those exhibited by the Buddha are natural, not supernatural, and can be developed by anyone willing to practise the appropriate exercises. But they do not lead to liberation and Enlightenment. In the same way, devas and brahmās, however superior to humanity they may be, still belong to the natural world, and are subject to its laws. Though the showing of respect to them is traditional in most Buddhist lands, it is well understood that this practice does not conduce to the attainment of the ultimate goal of the Teaching. Once all these points are borne in mind it should not be difficult for us to adopt a more truly scientific attitude towards this category of 'legendary' material, not only so far as the traditional lives of the Buddha are concerned, but in regard to Buddhist literature generally. Even though unable to accept at their face value all 'legendary' episodes of this type, we are no longer justified in rejecting even the most absurd of them on *a priori* grounds. The Buddha's greatness had, perhaps, dimensions of which modern knowledge has as yet taken no cognizance.

True as this is of the second, it is still more true of the third and last category, consisting of those legends the significance of which is really not historical at all, but psychological and spiritual. Far from being either devotional effusions or flights of poetic fancy these legends in fact make up a symbolical biography of the Buddha no less important than the historical narrative with which, in the traditional biographies, it is interwoven, and upon the main episodes of which it constitutes a spiritual-cum-metaphysical commentary of the highest value. To disengage the symbolical from the historical elements is not always easy, however. The compilers of the traditional biographies do not seem to have made so absolute a distinction between fact and symbol as people do now, nor to have made it with such rigorous consistency, so that although some episodes are clearly historical, and some symbolical, others would seem capable of being not only either but both. But with such differences as these we are not now concerned. A systematic study of the symbolical biography of the Buddha, though one of the most fruitful works that could be undertaken, would require excursuses into Buddhist thought and spiritual practice, as well as into modern psychology, more extensive than are possible here. All we propose to do, therefore, is to cite a few representative episodes which, even if not self-evidently symbolical, are at least sufficiently simple to require the minimum of interpretation to establish our point.

The story of the Four Sights, of how Siddhārtha, issuing from his father's mansion, encountered for the first time an old man, a sick man, a corpse, and a monk, is recounted by all the traditional biographies and occurs in most modern works. But though no episode is better known than this, few are less likely to be factually true. Its authenticity has indeed often been challenged, usually on the grounds of inherent improbability. How, it is asked, would it have been possible to keep a young man as ignorant of life as the story suggests? Is it really credible that until his twenty-ninth year Siddhārtha knew nothing of old age, disease, and death? Could he conceivably have never till then set eyes on a wandering mendicant, when saffron robes and begging-bowls were to be encountered at every street corner? These objections are unanswerable, and from the historical life of the Buddha the episode must certainly be deleted. But this does not mean it should be altogether discarded, or relegated to literary limbo along with Ossian and the Decretals of Constantine. From a passage in the *Aṅguttara-Nikāya,* which evidently constitutes the psychological basis of the story of the Four Sights, we can see that this episode belongs not to the historical but to the symbolical biography of the Buddha.

> Then, O monks, did I ... think thus, 'an ignorant, ordinary person, who is himself subject to old age, on seeing an old man is troubled, ashamed and disgusted, extending the thought to himself. I too am subject to old age, not beyond the sphere of old age, and should I, who am subject to old age, not beyond the sphere of old age, on seeing an old man be troubled, ashamed, and disgusted?' This seemed to me not fitting. As thus I reflected on it, all the elation [*mada*, lit. 'intoxication'] in youth utterly disappeared.[15]

The same is then repeated of sickness and death. As E.J. Thomas pertinently remarks,

> It is easy to see how the above account can have been developed into the story of his actually meeting these objects, but not how, if the story is a real biographical event, it can have been converted into this abstract form.[16]

With the *Aṅguttara-Nikāya* account before us, it becomes obvious that the compilers of the traditional biographies, or the oral sources on which they drew, after objectifying the psychological experience projected it into the world of external events in the vivid and colourful form of the well-known episode. Whether this was done of deliberate intent, for pedagogical reasons, or whether the minds of some early Buddhists were so constituted as to apprehend the spiritual truth of the Buddha's life more easily in concrete images and pictures than in psychological abstractions, it is perhaps fruitless to inquire. But that such transpositions did occur the present instance demonstrates.

Another well-known episode which is in reality the objectification of a psychological experience is that which took place immediately before the Great Enlightenment, when Māra launched against the tranquil figure beneath the bodhi tree his army of lusts, hatreds, and fears. The legends give long and vivid descriptions of this tremendous attack. Demoniacal figures, some monstrously deformed, swirl round the Bodhisattva with frightful noises in a vain attempt to disturb his meditation by swinging clubs, hurling rocks and uprooted trees, shooting arrows, and spitting flame. A detonation of truth in the Bodhisattva's unconscious mind had clearly exploded thousands of emotional ideas and impulses. This does not mean, of course, that he might not have actually 'seen' the fragments of his own exploded unconscious spread out before him in the form of menacing or alluring shapes. All that we are not to imagine, as generations of less instructed Buddhists have perhaps imagined, is that Māra and his host appeared on the scene in gross material bodies. Vividly as they can at times be perceived, the basic reality of such externalized mental phenomena is psychological.

Also connected with the period of the Enlightenment, though its symbolism is more recondite, is the Mucalinda episode. During the third week after the Great Awakening, relate the traditional biographies, there came a great storm. For seven days and seven nights it rained. In order to protect the Buddha from the downpour, Mucalinda, the serpent king, wrapped his coils seven times round him and sheltered him with his hood. When the storm had subsided he appeared before the Buddha in the form of a beautiful sixteen-year-old youth and respectfully saluted him.[17] Some, of course, give a purely naturalistic explanation of this episode, regarding it as an instance of that remarkable power over animals which holy men often possess. But it must not be forgotten that the legends relating to the weeks (four in earlier, seven in the later accounts) spent by the Buddha in the neighbourhood of the bodhi tree immediately after the Enlightenment are concerned mainly with his spiritual experiences. In any case the appearance of the nāga king, an obviously symbolical motif, should put us on our guard against naturalistic explanations. The nāgas inhabit the depths of the ocean, where they dwell in marvellous palaces in which are heaps of priceless jewels and other treasures. They represent the upsurging energies of the unconscious, not in their negative destructive aspect (symbolized by Māra and his host) but in the positive creative aspect which makes available to the conscious mind treasures of beauty, insight, and understanding it did not dream it possessed. They are the forces of artistic and religious inspiration in general. Their king, Mucalinda, is the *kuṇḍalinī* or 'coiled-up' power, the latent spiritual energy which, according to a well-known system of yoga, resides in the lowest of the seven chakras or psychic centres in the human body. His wrapping himself seven times round the Buddha, laying one coil upon another (as frequently depicted in art), indicates the ascent of this energy through all these centres. The storm (which lasts for *seven* days) is the shower of bliss that descends into every part of the body as soon as the *kuṇḍalinī* reaches the topmost chakra. As for the beautiful youthful form finally assumed by Mucalinda, it represents the purely spiritual body into which the Buddha's exalted realization has transmuted the energies of his human personality, while the serpent king's bowing before him signifies the perfect serviceability of that body as the instrument of the Enlightened mind. All the symbols occurring in this episode are met with again and again in Buddhist literature, especially in Tantric works, one of the characteristics of which is to make systematic use of symbolism in connection with spiritual exercises and experiences. Further research will probably establish the fact that not only the

Mucalinda episode but other incidents taking place immediately after the *sambodhi* represent not historic events but a symbolical unfolding of different aspects of the Buddha's Enlightenment.

For a simple example of a 'legendary' episode with a metaphysical rather than a psychological significance we shall have to go back to the Buddha's birth. In the traditional biographies symbolism here reigns supreme. Among other marvels it is related how the Bodhisattva, as soon as he was born, took seven steps, at each of which a lotus sprang up to support his foot. Much could be said, of course, on the significance of the number of steps taken. At the moment, however, we are concerned with the lotuses. These beautiful flowers, it is well known, bloom with petals unstained by the mud and water out of which they grow. Hence in Buddhist literature (as at *Sutta-Nipāta* 71), and in Indian religious works generally, the lotus represents the state of living 'in the world, but not of it'. This being so, it is understandable that it should have been adopted as a symbol of their doctrine by those who, from an early period, perhaps even during the Buddha's own lifetime, regarded him not as a human but as a purely transcendental being who underwent the ordinary experiences of life in appearance only. Lotuses spring up as he takes his first seven steps to prevent him making direct contact with the earth, thus emphasizing that he was of transcendental origin from the very outset of his earthly career, being in truth not the product of this world but the irruption into it of transcendental reality in the form of an eternally enlightened personality.

5

PHILOSOPHICAL INTERPRETATIONS

TO THE EXTENT that it keeps in touch with living experience Buddhist thought is always in the making. In the course of its development it resembles a great river which, having taken its rise high in the mountains, winds through thousands of miles of field, forest, and desert, receiving hundreds of tributaries on the way, until at last it comes to the end of its long journey and plunges into the sea. None of the doctrines of Buddhism, perhaps, is so novel that it is not foreshadowed, however faintly, in earlier teachings, and none so antiquated as to be incapable of further development. These remarks apply with particular force to our present subject. Nearly a thousand years after the parinirvāṇa the efforts of generations of saints and sages to fathom the Master's true nature culminated in the doctrine of the *trikāya* or 'Three Bodies' of the Buddha. Though other Indian schools of major importance also contributed to its development,[18] this doctrine was given full and definitive expression by the Yogācārins, or 'Practitioners of Yoga'.[19] As elaborated by them, it is one of the finest flowers of Buddhist thought, combining profound philosophical meaning with the richest spiritual and artistic significance, and unless it is properly understood the *raison d'être* of much that is most precious in the tradition is likely to remain obscure. This does not mean that we cannot understand the trikāya doctrine without tracing it through the successive phases of its development, or following up every one of its numerous ramifications. What is essential is a grasp of the basic principle of the doctrine; once this is grasped the rest will follow.

Though comparatively simple, the principle on which the trikāya doctrine is based is perhaps best made clear with the help of an illustration. Three people are looking at a flower. One is a child, one a botanist, and one a poet. All that the child sees is an object of a certain shape with a pleasing bright colour. The botanist, while not failing to observe its shape and colour, sees that the flower belongs to a particular species, thrives best at a certain time, place, etc. The poet, though his eyes are as keen as the child's, and though he knows as much about botany as the botanist, is not so preoccupied with the colour of the flower or the formation of its leaves and petals. He sees that the flower is alive, joyously alive, even as he is alive, and that there works through the frail perfection of its leaves and blossoms the same spirit of life whose creative impulse he feels pulsing in the depths of his own being. Despite their great differences of vision, however, the child, the botanist, and the poet still all see the same flower, not three different flowers. The child's seeing is mere visual perception. This the botanist also has; but as he looks at the flower there comes into operation a faculty higher than perception – understanding – which enables him to see deeper into the reality of the flower than the child could. The poet has both perception and understanding, but when *he* looks at the flower there comes into operation a faculty higher than either, intuition, which enables him to see deepest of all, and not only to see but to feel, and even to become one with what he sees and feels.

In the same way, an ordinary person, a *yogin*, and one possessing *prajñā* or wisdom, look at the Buddha. The first, beholding either with his physical eyes (if a contemporary) or with his earthbound intelligence (if he merely hears or reads about the Buddha), perceives or forms the idea of a human, historical person subject – like himself – to the laws of time, space, and causation. He sees a Buddha whose existence is separated from his own by hundreds or thousands of years or miles, a Buddha who is born, grows old, and dies. In other words he sees the *nirmāṇakāya*, the first of the Three Bodies of the Enlightened One. Some canonical texts designate the body as the *rūpakāya*, or 'form body'; but when the Yogācārins systematized the trikāya doctrine they popularized the term *nirmāṇakāya*, 'created body' or 'body of transformation', found in other texts, probably because it reflected the widely current view that what appeared to be the Buddha's physical body was in reality a purely spiritual presence created by Absolute Compassion and projected into the world for the benefit of all sentient beings. In the present context it makes no difference which term is used, since even those holding transcendentalist views admitted that the Buddha's human body was perceived *as though* it was in all respects material. Most people, including even Buddhists, make use only of their physical senses and their earth-bound intelligence. It is but natural, therefore, that the Buddha's *nirmāṇakāya* should be more widely known and better understood than his other bodies.

When the yogin looks at the Buddha it is with attention withdrawn from the senses, so that sense impressions are stopped and the external world no longer perceived. Unwholesome emotions such as greed, hatred, anxiety, ennui, and perplexity have been suppressed and the grosser forms of mental activity suspended, so that equanimity and concentration alone are present. In other words, the yogin sees not in the ordinary waking state but in the superconscious state of *samādhi*. Where the ordinary person sees the *nirmāṇakāya*, therefore, he sees the *sambhogakāya*, the second of the Three Bodies of the Enlightened One. According to one explanation the *sambhogakāya*, or 'body of mutual enjoyment', is so called because the vision of it is enjoyed by the bodhisattvas, those highly advanced beings who in both this world and other higher realms of existence practise the Six or Ten Perfections, including *dhyāna-pāramitā*, the perfection of concentration. According to another it is the body 'enjoyed' by the Buddha himself as a result of all the good deeds he had performed and the knowledge he had accumulated during his countless lives as a bodhisattva. These explanations do not exclude each other. Inasmuch as a literal translation fails to convey the full meaning of the term, *sambhogakāya* is also rendered as 'body of bliss' or 'glorious body'. The latter rendering is perhaps the best. The yogin, in his meditation, has transcended time and space, at least in the form that they are known to us, for he has transcended the mind which perceives things under the form of these two great categories. At the moment of his meditative experience, therefore, he sees the Buddha as actually present before him in that higher, wider, more spiritual dimension of space (or rather, of consciousness) which has been called 'the beyond within'. He sees him in a glorious form which, though human, is infinitely more majestic, brilliant, and beautiful than any mortal frame. This form is adorned with the thirty-two major and eighty minor 'marks', two standard sets embodying an ancient Indian conception of ideal beauty which the Buddhists, at an early date, took over from traditions concerning the *mahāpuruṣa* or superman and applied to their own more spiritual purposes. All yogins do not, of course, perceive the *sambhogakāya* Buddha in the same way. The brilliance of his form, seemingly made up of pure radiance, may be either dazzlingly white or suffused by a particular colour – red, blue, green, or golden yellow. His expression may be peaceful, fascinating, stern, or even (according to Tantric tradition) terrible. There are also a variety of *mudrās*, or postures of the hands, each of which has a meaning. One of the most important *sambhogakāya* forms is Amitābha, 'Infinite Light', also known as Amitāyus, 'Infinite Life'. These names indicate the universality of the *sambhogakāya*, the spiritual activity and influence of which are unlimited as regards both space and time. According to some sources, he exercises jurisdiction over 10,000,000,000 worlds, for the spiritual progress of all the sentient beings in which he is responsible. The *sambhogakāya* Buddha is not, however, identical with the God of the theistic religions, being not the creator of the universe but only the teacher of its inhabitants, and to regard the trikāya doctrine as involving some kind of theistic development within the Mahāyāna is one of the most pernicious errors of which a student of Buddhism can be guilty. Other *sambhogakāya* forms are Vairocana, 'The Illuminator', Ratnasambhava, 'The Jewel-Born', Amoghasiddhi, 'The Unobstructed Success', Akṣobhya, 'The Imperturbable', and Vaidūryaprabha, 'Blue Radiance'. Despite what may appear to be the contrary testimony of Buddhist iconography, none of these forms is subject to spatial limitation in the ordinary sense, nor are they perceived in quite the same way as we perceive external objects or mental pictures. In the earlier stages of meditation Buddha-forms may indeed be perceived in this manner, and perceived very vividly; but these are usually images released from the subconscious mind, not glimpses of the *sambhogakāya*. Since the Yogācārins stressed the importance of meditation, and emphasized that a comprehensive view of reality should pay adequate attention to the nature of the world as perceived by the yogin in a state of *samādhi*, they were naturally more highly aware of the existence of the *sambhogakāya* than the followers of schools that emphasized either psychological analysis or dialectics. Historically, indeed, the contribution of the Yogācārins to the trikāya doctrine consists in their clearly distinguishing the *sambhogakāya* from the other *kāyas* and recognizing it as an independent body.

When one who possesses *prajñā* in its distinctively Buddhist sense of insight into the painful, transitory, and insubstantial nature of all conditioned things looks at the Buddha he sees him as the unconditioned Absolute Reality. As Buddhist thought developed, Truth or Reality naturally acquired a number of designations, according to the different angles from which it was viewed. Some of these, such as *śūnyatā*, or 'the voidness', indicated its transcendence over the world or phenomena; others, like *dharmadhātu*, 'realm of truth', its characteristic of totality and all-embracingness. *Tathatā*, 'suchness', revealed its unique indefinable essentiality; *tathāgatagarbha* its mysterious immanence. *Ālaya-vijñāna*, 'store consciousness', recognized it as the principle of potentiality, *nirvāṇadhātu*, 'sphere of extinction', viewed it as the support of the emancipated mind, while *bhūtakoṭi*, 'pinnacle of existence', drew attention to its aspect of consummation and completion. Reality may also be thought of as fully realized by the Buddha and therefore as revealed in and through him. It is this aspect which is known as the *dharmakāya*, 'body of truth or reality', or 'essential body', the third of the Three Bodies of the Enlightened One. Though the trikāya doctrine was systematically formulated long after the parinirvāṇa, the fact that there existed beyond the Buddha's human personality an unconditioned ineffable essence which constituted his true being was recognized from the beginning. Says the Master in the *Pārāyana-vagga* of the *Sutta-Nipāta*, one of the oldest portions of the Theravāda Pāli Canon:

> There is no measuring of man,
> Won to the goal, whereby they'ld say
> His measure's so: that's not for him;
> When all conditions are removed,
> All ways of telling are removed.[20]

Similarly, in the *Saṁyutta-Nikāya* he declares of himself:

> Since a Tathāgata, even when actually present, is incomprehensible, it is inept to say of him – of the Uttermost Person, the Supernal Person, the Attainer of the Supernal – that after dying the Tathāgata is, or is not, or both is and is not, or neither is or is not.[21]

Again, to the same effect, in the *Majjhima-Nikāya*:

> That material shape, that feeling, that perception, those impulses, that consciousness by which one, in defining the Tathāgata, might define him – all have been got rid of by the Tathāgata, cut off at the root, made like a palm-tree stump that cannot sprout again. Free from reckoning by material shape, feeling, perception, the impulses, consciousness is the Tathāgata; He is deep, immeasurable, unfathomable, as is the great ocean. 'Arises' does not apply, nor does 'does not arise', nor 'both arises and does not arise', nor 'neither arises nor does not arise'.[22]

The same idea is adumbrated in the great Mahāyāna sūtras, especially in those belonging to the *Prajñāpāramitā* or 'Perfection of Wisdom' corpus, where the bodhisattva is time and again urged to contemplate the Buddha not under his conditioned but under his unconditioned aspect. A passage from the *Vajracchedikā* bearing on this theme concludes with the well-known stanzas:

> Those who by my form did see me,
> And those who followed me by voice,
> Wrong the efforts they engaged in,
> Me those people will not see.
>
> From the Dharma should one see the Buddhas,
> From the Dharmabodies comes their guidance.
> Yet Dharma's true nature cannot be discerned,
> And no one can be conscious of it as an object.[23]

In another passage from the same corpus the Buddha makes it clear that inasmuch as the *dharmakāya* constitutes his true personality this alone should be the object of the bodhisattva's recollection:

> How does a bodhisattva develop the recollection of the Buddha? He does not attend to the Tathāgata through form, or feeling, etc. For form, feeling, etc., have no own-being. And what has no own-being, that is non-existent.... A Tathāgata further should not be attended to through the thirty-two marks of a Superman,... nor should he be attended to through the effulgence of his halo, or through the eighty minor characteristics. And that for the same reasons as before.[24]

All these texts indicate that the *dharmakāya* is impersonal. This is denied, however, by Dr D.T. Suzuki, who in one of his early works maintains that it is personal.[25] This in effect nullifies the distinction between the *dharmakāya* on the one hand and the two remaining *kāyas* on the other. The texts which he quotes from the *Gaṇḍavyūha Sūtra* seem really to mean that inasmuch as it constitutes their ultimate reality whatever is predicated of the *nirmāṇakāya* and the *sambhogakāya*, including love, will, and intelligence, is indirectly predicated of the *dharmakāya*. In dealing with the trikāya doctrine, however, one must beware of being led astray by words. The *dharmakāya* is not impersonal in the sense that it utterly and completely excludes personality, for that would be to identify it with one of two opposite terms, whereas the truth of the matter is that, being non-different from Absolute Reality, the *dharmakāya* transcends all opposites whatsoever.

Having distinguished the *kāyas* one from another for purposes of exposition it is now necessary for us to reintegrate them into a living whole. The child, the botanist, and the poet of our illustration did not see three different flowers. They saw one flower. The difference lay in the greater or lesser extent to which they succeeded in penetrating into its reality and seeing it as it really was. In the same way the ordinary man, the yogin, and one possessing *prajñā* all see the same Buddha. All see the *dharmakāya*. But so gross is the ordinary man's perception, so darkened his mind by unwholesome emotions and erroneous views, that, like one almost totally blind who sees instead of the sun only a faint glimmer of light, he sees not the *dharmakāya* but the *nirmāṇakāya*. The yogin's perception is more refined. Disciplined by long practice of meditation, his mind has become freed from the grosser veils. When he looks at the Buddha through the subtle veils that remain the *dharmakāya* appears as the *sambhogakāya*. One with *prajñā* has removed all veils. He sees the Buddha as he really is. He sees the naked *dharmakāya*. Between him and the Buddha there is no difference. He has become the Buddha. That this is the correct interpretation of the trikāya doctrine is borne out by an important passage in *The Awakening of Faith in the Mahāyāna*, a Chinese work traditionally believed to have been translated from a Sanskrit original by Aśvaghoṣa. After saying that the *dharmakāya* has two aspects the text proceeds:

> The first one depends on the phenomena-particularizing consciousness, by means of which activity [the *dharmakāya*] is conceived of by means of the mind of common people (*pṛthagjana*), *Śrāvakas* and *Pratyekabuddhas*. This aspect is called the Body of Transformation (*nirmāṇakāya*).... The second aspect of the *Dharmakāya* depends on the activity-consciousness (*karma-vijñāna*) by means of which the activity is conceived by the minds of bodhisattvas while passing from their first aspiration (*cittotpāda*) stage to the height of bodhisattvahood. This is called the Body of Bliss (*sambhogakāya*).[26]

Needless to say, it should not be thought that there is a hard and fast line of distinction between one *kāya* and another any more than there is between one colour in a rainbow and the next. Between the respective perceptions of the ordinary person, the yogin, and the one possessing *prajñā* there are innumerable gradations of perception. *Nirmāṇakāya* therefore merges into *sambhogakāya* and *sambhogakāya* into *dharmakāya* by imperceptible degrees. As actually three in number, the *kāyas* are no more than points abstracted from a line at regular intervals, like the inches marked on a foot-rule. This should help us remember that in the trikāya doctrine we have to deal not with an abstract metaphysical speculation but with an attempt to explain systematically the deepening spiritual experience of the devotee of the Buddha in his quest for Absolute Reality.

Part Two

THE DHARMA

6

APPROACHES TO BUDDHISM

IN THE *Udāna*[27] the Buddha relates the Parable of the Blind Men and the Elephant. A number of men, blind from birth, are asked to feel the body of an elephant and then describe the beast. Those who felt the head declared it to be a pot, those who grasped the ear said it was a winnowing-basket, those who handled the tusk opined it was a ploughshare, and so on. Eventually, each one vehemently maintaining his own opinion, they began to quarrel and fight. The parable illustrates not only the one-sidedness of the sectarian teachers of the Buddha's own time, in connection with whom it was originally told, but also the wide divergences that can be noticed between the different approaches to Buddhism adopted by modern writers.

Until very recently three approaches were most common. They may be termed respectively the sectarian, the fundamentalist, and the encyclopedic. The basic error of the sectarian approach is that it mistakes the part for the whole. Quite early in the history of Buddhism, perhaps within a century of the parinirvāṇa, there arose within the Buddhist community circumstances which eventually led to the formation of different schools. Though differing on various doctrinal and disciplinary points, these schools shared a common tradition which united them to a far greater extent than their points of difference divided them. As time went on, however, and they started occupying different geographical centres, not only in India but throughout Asia, their differences gradually grew more pronounced. The result is that instead of consisting of one version of the Dharma only, Buddhism now comprises a number of different versions laid as it were side by side and overlapping in varying degrees. To identify Buddhism with one particular version, on whatever grounds, is ridiculous. As Dr Edward Conze says (we have quoted his words elsewhere, but they bear repetition),

> The doctrine of the Buddha, conceived in its full breadth, width, majesty and grandeur, comprises all those teachings which are linked to the original teaching by historical continuity, and which work out methods leading to the extinction of individuality by eliminating the belief in it.[28]

Unfortunately, some corners of the Buddhist world have not yet awoken to the truth of these words. Books, pamphlets, and articles continue to be produced which naïvely present a single branch as the whole tree. This is not to say that the branch is not a noble branch, nor that individual accounts of the different Buddhist schools are not needed. We refer to something quite different: the practice of presenting, as complete accounts of Buddhism, what are in fact expositions of the tenets of one school based on a highly selective reading of a single branch of the canonical literature, usually the Pāli Tipiṭaka. Some writers go to the extreme of explicitly repudiating as 'not the pure Dharma' all Buddhist traditions but their own. Despite occasional absurdities of this kind, however, the sectarian type of approach to Buddhism is fortunately on the wane. Throughout the Buddhist world the conviction is steadily gaining ground that so far as the Dharma is concerned the truth, to apply the Hegelian dictum, is the whole.

The fundamentalist approach is concerned with what the Buddha 'really' said. It has two forms. The first to some extent coincides with the sectarian approach which, in one of its forms, maintains even in the face of abundant internal evidence to the contrary that the Pāli Tipiṭaka consists entirely of the *ipsissima verba* of the Buddha. The second, the intellectually respectable form, is a product of modern scholarship, largely non-Buddhist. By means of textual criticism, comparison with archaeological and epigraphical evidence, etc., it endeavours to separate the passages belonging to earlier from those belonging to later strata of the canonical literature. Broadly speaking, this attempt has met with some success. The fundamentalist desires, however, a greater degree of certainty than the nature of the subject allows. Even if it is possible to isolate the most ancient texts, the problem of the relation of these to the oral tradition which preceded them and of this to the Buddha's own utterances remains insoluble. It is doubtful whether any known Buddhist text contains a line which preserves the Dharma in the same language or dialect in which it was originally expounded by the Buddha. The more strictly scientific methods are applied, the greater likelihood there seems to be that the fundamentalist will eventually be left with nothing but the Buddha's 'noble silence'. Some, indeed, horrified by the void confronting them, have sought to fill it with their own arbitrary constructions of what they imagine the Buddha 'really' taught. Both forms of fundamentalism commit the mistake of assuming that the Teaching is bound up with a certain form of words, and that unless these are known it cannot be properly understood. Though such an approach is ultimately self-destructive, as we have shown, it has recently been adopted by at least one earnest writer on Buddhism. However, instead of pursuing the approach to its logical conclusion, the Buddha's silence, he stops short at those parts of the Pāli Tipiṭaka he believes to be the most ancient and then reverts to the naïve form of fundamentalism with regard to them.

The encyclopedic approach emphasizes breadth rather than depth of knowledge. It tends to confuse knowledge *about* Buddhism with knowledge *of* Buddhism. It is concerned more with facts than with principles, tries to see from without instead of feeling from within. For a century it has profoundly influenced, if not dominated, the world of non-traditional Buddhist scholarship. Since it is not an isolated phenomenon, but has its roots deep in the soil of the modern scientific outlook, whose general tendencies it exemplifies within its own special field, this approach is likely to remain important for some time to come. Provided its limitations are understood, and any mischief to which they might give rise guarded against, this is not necessarily a bad thing for Buddhism. Such scholarship has accomplished much useful work. Moreover, during the last decade it has been leavened and enlivened, in the case of one or two well-known writers, by elements of sympathy and understanding which were originally lacking. Nevertheless, this does not alter the basic fact that, owing to the vast extent of Buddhist literature, which includes thousands of works regarded as canonical, besides innumerable non-canonical works, its aim of achieving complete factual knowledge about Buddhism and from this inferring its nature is impossible of attainment.

The ideal approach to Buddhism incorporates elements from the sectarian, the fundamentalist, and the encyclopedic approaches, shorn of their imperfections. It has for basis an insight into the Dharma derived from the actual practice of a system of spiritual discipline which, owing to the specialized nature of such techniques, is necessarily that of a particular school – Japanese Zen, Tibetan Mahāmudrā, or the Thai 'Sammā Arahaṁ' method. Despite this fact, it will be vividly aware and warmly appreciative of the multiple richness of the Buddhist tradition, and however firmly it may grasp a particular thread will never lose sight of its connection with the whole fabric. While accurately distinguishing earlier formulations of the Teaching from later ones, and even preferring the former for introductory purposes, it will not commit the mistake of treating the age of a formulation as the sole criterion of its spiritual authenticity, nor consider the Dharma to be limited to its verbal expressions. Depth will not, however, exclude breadth. Besides keeping abreast of developments in the field of non-traditional Buddhist studies, the ideal approach to Buddhism will not only take all Buddhism for its province but will enforce its conclusions by drawing upon as wide a range of scriptural reference as possible. Above all, it will be concerned to exhibit the living spirit of Buddhism.

7

THE ESSENCE OF THE DHARMA

MANY STUDENTS of Buddhism are at first staggered by the vastness of the field before them and bewildered by the abundance of material. This is natural. Like Christianity and Islam, Buddhism is not only a teaching but a culture, a civilization, a movement in history, a social order, in fact a whole world in itself. It comprises systems of philosophy, methods of meditation, rituals, manners and customs, clothes, languages, sacred literature, pagodas, temples, monasteries, calligraphy, poems, paintings, plays, stories, games, flower-arrangements, pottery, and a thousand other things. All this is Buddhist, and often immediately recognizable as such. Whether it be a stone Buddha seated cross-legged in the jungles of Anuradhupura, a Tibetan sacred dance, a cup of tea between friends in Japan, or the way in which a bhikṣu answers a question in London, everything is invisibly signed with the same mysterious seal. Sometimes it floats with the clouds between heaven and earth, shines in the rainbow, or gurgles over pebbles in the company of a mountain stream. 'Looked at, it cannot be seen; listened to, it cannot be heard.'[29] Sooner or later, however, the student tries to identify it. He wonders what it could be that gives unity to all these diverse expressions, so that however remote in space and time, and however different their respective mediums, one perfectly harmonizes with another, creating not the dissonance that might have been expected but 'a concord of sweet sounds'. Eventually a question shapes itself in his mind, and at last he enquires, 'What is the essence of the Dharma?'

The best answer to this question would be the 'thunder-like silence' with which Vimalakīrti, in the Mahāyāna sūtra that bears his name, answered the bodhisattva Mañjuśrī's question about the nature of Reality. Can we describe even the colour of a rose? But this apparently negative procedure the student would not find very helpful. Concessions must be made. Buddhism is essentially an experience. 'An experience of what?' Before answering this second question let us try to explain why, of all the words in the dictionary, 'experience' is the first term on which one falls back when compelled to abandon the 'thunder-like silence'. Unlike thought, experience is direct, unmediated; it is knowledge by acquaintance. Hence it is characterized by a feeling of absolute certainty. When we see the sun shining in a clear sky we do not doubt that it is bright; when a thorn runs beneath our fingernail we do not speculate whether it is painful. In saying that Buddhism is essentially an experience we do not suggest that the object of that experience in any way resembles the objects of sense-experience, nor even that there is an object at all. We simply draw attention to its unique unconceptualized immediacy. The relation between sense-experience and the one with which we are now concerned is merely analogical. For this reason it is necessary to go a step further and complete our definition by saying that the essence of the Dharma, of Buddhism, consists in a *spiritual* or *transcendental* experience. This is what in traditional terminology is called Enlightenment-experience.

Apart from conveying an impression of the subject having now been lost sight of in the clouds, the mere addition of these adjectives is inconclusive. They themselves need definition. But inasmuch as this will involve the use of terms even more abstract, more remote from concrete experience, such definition will set up a process of conceptualization as a result of which the reflection of Enlightenment-experience in our minds will be in danger of complete distortion, like the moon's reflection in a pond the surface of which the wind has chopped into waves. Concepts had therefore better be treated as symbols, the value of which lies not in their literal meaning so much as in their suggestiveness. They should be handled in the spirit not of logic but of poetry; not pushed hither and thither with grim calculation like pieces on a chessboard, but tossed lightly, playfully in the air like a juggler's multicoloured balls. Approaching the subject in this spirit we may define Enlightenment-experience as 'seeing things as they (are *yathābhūtajñānadarśana*)'. This is the traditional definition. Here also, it will be observed, the use of the word 'seeing' (*darśana*) – which primarily denotes a form of sense-perception – emphasizes not only the directness and immediacy of the experience but also its noetic character. Enlightenment-experience is not just a blind sensing of things, but, as the English word suggests, the shining forth of a light, an illumination, in the brightness of which things become visible in their reality. Such expressions should not mislead us into thinking that there is any real difference between the subject and the object of the experience, between the light and the things illuminated (which disposes of the second question raised above). Were it not for the fact that all words indicative of existence have for Buddhism a disagreeable substantialist flavour, it might even be preferable not to speak of Enlightenment as an experience at all but as a state of being. Fortunately other ways of surmounting the difficulty are available. The *Avataṁsaka Sūtra*, for instance, depicts the world of Enlightenment-experience as consisting not of objects illuminated from without but entirely of innumerable beams of light, all intersecting and intersected, none of which offers any resistance to the passage of any other. Light being always in motion, this striking similitude has the additional advantage of precluding the notion that Enlightenment is a definite state in which one as it were settles comfortably down for good, instead of a movement from perfection to greater perfection in a process in which there is no final term, the direction of movement alone remaining constant.

If spiritual or transcendental experience is a state of seeing things as they are, its opposite, mundane experience, wherein all unenlightened beings are involved, must be one of seeing them as they are not. The cause of this blindness is twofold. Being a creature of desires, man is concerned with things only to the extent that they can be made to subserve his own ends. He is interested not in truth but in utility. For him things and people exist not in their own right but only as actual or possible means of his own gratification. This is the 'veil of passions' (*kleśāvaraṇa*). Usually we do not like to acknowledge, even to ourselves, that our attitude towards life is often no better than that of a pig rooting for acorns. Motives are therefore rationalized. Instead of admitting that we hate somebody, we say he is wicked and ought to be punished. Rather than admit we enjoy eating flesh, we maintain that sheep and cows were created for man's benefit. Not wishing to die, we invent the dogma of the immortality of the individual soul. Craving help and protection, we start believing in a personal God.

According to the Buddha, all the philosophies, and a great deal of religious teaching, are rationalizations of desires. This is the 'veil of (false) assumptions' (*jñeyāvaraṇa*). On the attainment of Enlightenment both veils are rent asunder. For this reason the experience is accompanied by an exhilarating sense of release. The Buddha compares the state of mind of one gaining Enlightenment to that of a man who has come safe out of a dangerous jungle, or been freed from debt, or released from prison. It is as though an intolerable burden had at last been lifted from his back. So intense is this feeling of release from pain, suffering, conflicting emotions, and mental sterility and stagnation that many of the older canonical texts speak of the Enlightenment-experience exclusively in terms of freedom or emancipation (*vimukti*). One of them represents the Buddha himself as saying that even as the great ocean had one taste, the taste of salt, so his teaching had one flavour, the flavour of emancipation.[30] Besides a psychological aspect, *vimukti* has an intellectual and an existential aspect. In the first place it is a freedom from all theories and speculations about Reality; and in the second, from any form of conditioned existence whatever, including 're-becoming' as a result of karma. The freedom into which one breaks through at the time of Enlightenment is not limited and partial, but absolute and unconditioned.

This introduces an aspect of Enlightenment-experience which is not always properly understood. Freedom, to be really unconditioned, must transcend the distinction between conditioned and unconditioned, *saṁsāra* and *nirvāṇa*, bondage and liberation, all of which are really mental constructions and, as such, part of the 'veil of assumptions'. Therefore there can in the ultimate sense be no question of escaping from the conditioned to the Unconditioned as though they were distinct entities. Or, to speak paradoxically, in order to be truly free one has to escape not only from bondage but from liberation, not only from saṁsāra into Nirvāṇa but from Nirvāṇa back into saṁsāra. It is this 'escape' or descent that constitutes the *mahākaruṇā* or 'Great Compassion' of the Buddha, which is in reality his realization of the non-duality of the conditioned and the Unconditioned as that realization appears from the viewpoint of the conditioned. The Enlightenment-experience is therefore not only one of illumination and freedom but also of infinite and inexhaustible love, a love which has for object all sentient beings, and which manifests as uninterrupted activity in pursuit of their temporal and spiritual welfare.

8

DOCTRINAL FORMULAS

WHILE IT IS POSSIBLE to lose sight of the spirit of Buddhism among the multifariousness of its forms, it is no less possible to lose the spirit by repudiating the forms prematurely. The Buddha Amitāyus, 'Infinite Life', bears in his hands a jar containing the nectar of immortality. Jar without nectar is useless, but nectar without jar to contain it will only be spilled and wasted. After exhibiting as clearly as possible the spirit of Buddhism we have therefore to relate it to its doctrinal embodiment, as well as to indicate the origin, true nature, and proper function of that embodiment.

As already related, it was out of compassion that the newly Enlightened Lord decided to make known to mankind the Truth he had penetrated (see p.16). Again, when a few months later he sent forth the sixty Enlightened disciples he charged them to go forth and proclaim the Dharma 'out of compassion for the world' (see p.17). This love or compassion, which as we have just seen constitutes with illumination and freedom the essence of Buddhism, brings the Enlightened into communication, even into communion, with the unenlightened mind. The medium of this communication is the formulated Dharma. This consists in the first place of words and concepts. But the fact that these were not invented by the Buddha, and can be traced in the records of pre-Buddhist teachings, does not justify such sweeping conclusions as 'the Buddha was influenced by the Upanishads' or 'Buddhism is an offshoot of Hinduism'. One might just as well maintain that Shakespeare 'copied' his plays from obscure early Elizabethan dramatists on the grounds that he made use of the same words and drew upon the same general stock of ideas as they did. Whatever words and concepts constitute the formulated Dharma, it is in fact essentially a medium for the communication to mankind of a unique and ineffable experience, the Buddha's experience of illumination-freedom-love, as well as an attempt to induce all who heard the words and understood the concepts to participate in it themselves by having immediate and vigorous recourse to such methods as he in his wisdom could devise. As such the Dharma is not an end in itself but a means to an end. In the *Majjhima-Nikāya* the Buddha compares his teaching to the raft used for crossing a great stretch of water, roundly declaring that to burden oneself with it after its work is done is sheer foolishness.[31] The comparison is doubly apposite. It brings out not only the more obvious point to which reference has just been made, but also the subtler one that although the Dharma is only a means it is an indispensable means. The point is important. Only too often do those with a merely theoretical understanding of the instrumental value of the Dharma assume themselves to be thereby exempted from the necessity of having effective recourse to it as the veritable Means of Enlightenment. This is to abandon the raft before one has even started crossing the water. A middle path should be followed. One must understand that a collection of sticks only constitutes a raft through the existence of the further shore, and it is only by means of the raft that the further shore can be actually reached. Spirit and letter are interdependent. Divorced from the living spirit of the Master's teaching, the letter of the Dharma, however faithfully transmitted, is dead, a thing of idle words and empty concepts: separated from its concrete embodiment in the letter, the spirit of the Dharma, however exalted, lacking a medium of communication is rendered inoperative. In writing about Buddhism one should therefore be careful to pay equal attention to both aspects. The ideal account would in fact show spiritual experiences crystallizing into concrete doctrinal and disciplinary forms and these resolving themselves back into spiritual experiences. Full justice would then be done both to the letter and to the spirit of the tradition.

What is true of the whole is no less true of its parts. For reasons mainly mnemonic and pedagogic, much of the recorded Dharma has come down to us in the shape of stereotype formulas and numbered lists of doctrinal terms. Thus we have the Three Characteristics (*tri-lakṣana*), the Four Āryan Truths (*catur-āryasata*), the Five Groups (*pañca-skandha*), the Six Bases (*ṣaḍāyatana*), the Seven Factors of Enlightenment (*sapta-bodhyaṅga*), the Āryan Eightfold Path (*ārya-aṣṭāṅgika-mārga*), the Nine Transcendental States (*nava-lokottara-dharma*), the Ten Perfections (*daśa-pāramitā*), the Twelve Links (*dvadaśa-nidāna*), the Thirty-Seven Wings of Enlightenment (*bodhi-pakṣyā-dharma*), and hundreds more. After the parinirvāṇa of the Buddha the drawing up of such lists, especially of mental states, became almost an obsession with a section of his followers, and though a reaction eventually set in, Indian Buddhism was hardly ever free from this tendency. The result is that having been compiled under such auspices almost the whole of the Hīnayāna and much of the Mahāyāna canonical literature has come down to us in an artificial, stereotyped form which, as one can see from short passages which proved unamenable to such treatment, is often at variance with the spiritual vitality of the message it enshrines. This is not to say that, given the conditions under which it had to be transmitted, the Dharma could have been handed down in any other manner, or that we should not feel profoundly grateful to the compilers and codifiers who gave it such an unattractive but durable shape. Yet for the student of Buddhism, and even more acutely for the writer, the existence of so many doctrinal formulas does constitute a problem. What is one to do with them all? Some writers, of course, ignore them, and give an arbitrary account of what they imagine the Buddha taught. Others, like the author of *Atthārasarāsī Dīpanī*,[32] which purports to be an aid to meditation, include as many as possible without giving a thought to what they really mean. The first procedure is justifiable only if, like the Buddha, one has oneself crossed to the Other Shore, and can speak out of the depths of one's own Enlightenment-experience; the second, if one is compiling a glossary of Buddhist terms. Once again a middle path should be pursued. For the student of Buddhism to try to understand the Dharma without having mastered at least all the more important doctrinal terms would be like a pianist attempting to play the Moonlight Sonata who had never bothered to practise any scales. Nevertheless scales are not sonatas, and the student should not commit the mistake of thinking that knowing by heart the doctrinal categories of Buddhism in Pāli or Sanskrit or any other language is the same thing as a true understanding of the Dharma. The balanced writer on Buddhism follows a similar course. While not obtruding doctrinal formulas ostentatiously on the reader for their own sake, he does not seek in his expositions to eschew the use of them altogether. The principal formulas he will delineate with precision and clarity, drawing attention to their importance for the history of Buddhist thought. At the same time instead of treating them so literally that they become as it were solid and opaque he will enable them to fulfil their true function by refining them to so high a degree of transparency that through them the radiance of the Enlightenment-experience shines with the minimum of obstruction.

9

COSMOLOGY

ONE OF THE MOST important doctrinal categories is that which divides all *dharmas*, as the Abhidharma tradition terms the ultimate elements of existence (reckoned by different schools as 172, 75, 84, or 100 in number), into two groups, that of *saṁskṛta-dharmas*, compounded or conditioned elements of existence, and that of *asaṁskṛta-dharmas*, elements which are uncompounded and unconditioned. The first of these, which comprises by far the larger number of terms, constitutes the whole phenomenal universe or cosmos of Buddhism. As this provides the background against which the formulated Dharma unfolds we shall attempt a rough sketch map of it before turning to consider, in a subsequent chapter, the 'marks' which are attached to it and which express its true nature. The second group, that of the unconditioned *dharmas*, includes Nirvāṇa. This topic will also be dealt with.

So far as grand outlines are concerned, the most striking fact about Buddhist cosmology is the extent to which it dwarfs the conceptions of the Semitic religions on the subject and the degree to which its vision of the universe resembles the one disclosed by the modern telescope. Until recently the Christian world believed that the universe consisted of seven concentric spheres, one within another like Chinese ivory balls, with the earth in the centre and the sphere of the fixed stars at the circumference, and further that this universe, which had been created by the fiat of the Almighty about 4,000 years BCE (some chronologists succeeded in working out the exact date) had an extension in space of about 10,000 miles. The corresponding Buddhist notions are by contrast of overwhelming sublimity. To begin with, the phenomenal universe is declared to be without perceptible limit in space or perceptible first beginning in time. Here *perceptible* is the operative word. As the list of the Fourteen Inexpressibles (*avyākṛtavastūs*), one of the oldest doctrinal formulas, makes clear, the fact that the universe is not finite, either in space or in time, does not mean that it is infinite, or even that it is either both or neither.[33] Analysis reveals all these alternatives as self-contradictory, or, as we shall see later, space and time are not objective realities external to consciousness but part of the conditions under which it perceives things. However far in space one may go, therefore, in any direction, it is always possible to go still farther, for wherever one goes the mind goes too.

The Scriptures try to convey some conception of the inexhaustible vastness of space not by means of calculation but imaginatively. According to one similitude, even if a man were to take all the grains of sand in the river Ganges and, travelling north, south, east, or west, go on depositing one sand-grain at the end of every period of years equal in number to all the sand-grains, even after exhausting the whole river Ganges he would be no closer to reaching the end of space than he was at the beginning. As even the most unimaginative reader of popular modern works on astronomy has probably felt, the contemplation of vistas such as these is not without effect on the mind. Growing up as they did with the transcendent immensity of space for background, the Dharma and its followers through the ages naturally developed a breadth and freedom of outlook which would have been impossible within the stuffy confines of the dogmatic Christian world-view.

Their awareness of the dimensions of the phenomenal universe did not, however, cause them to overlook what were, in comparison, matters of detail. Besides being of unimaginable breadth and depth, the cosmos mirrored in the Scriptures is filled with millions of world systems, each one containing ten thousand worlds. These world systems, which are described as disc-like, are distributed through space at unthinkably vast intervals. They resemble what modern astronomy terms spiral galaxies, consisting of thousands of millions of stars rotating round a common centre. The world system Buddhists called the *sahā-loka* or 'world of tribulation' corresponds in part to the Milky Way, somewhere upon the outer fringes of which exists the solar system wherein our own earth 'spins like a fretful midge' among its sister planets. The Scriptures reveal a number of other details also. Many worlds are inhabited by intelligent living beings who, according to the Mahāyāna sūtras, have Buddhas of their own from whom they hear the same Dharma that Śākyamuni Buddha preaches to the beings of the *sahā-loka*. As might be expected, there is much traffic of Buddhas and bodhisattvas to and fro between different world systems. Though these details are not necessarily untrue even if understood literally, they clearly indicate the universality of the Dharma, which can be practised wherever living beings endowed with intelligence are found, and the omnipresence of the Enlightenment-mind, which manifests wherever conditions are favourable.

As space is plotted out by the world systems so time is measured in *kalpas*. A kalpa is a length of time equivalent to the life-period of a world system, from its initial condensation to its final destruction by water, fire, or wind. Scholastics with a penchant for mathematics later on tried to work out a figure for this enormous stretch of time, and though the results they arrived at often differed they all agreed it amounted to thousands of millions of years. The Buddha, perhaps more wisely, had been content with a simile. Suppose, he said, there was a cube of solid rock four leagues square, and at the end of every century a man were to come and stroke it once with a fine piece of Benares muslin – the rock would be worn away before the kalpa came to an end.[34] Each kalpa is divided into four 'incalculable' kalpas corresponding to different phases of the involution and evolution of the world system and the progress and deterioration of the human race; each incalculable kalpa into twenty 'intermediate' kalpas, and each intermediate kalpa into eight *yugas* or 'ages'.

As the scale of events decreases and we come to what are, geologically speaking, our own times, certain discrepancies between Buddhist traditions and current scientific notions begin to appear. This hardly ever amounts to flat contradiction. Taking into account as it does the existence not only of the material universe but also of the subtle spiritual counterpart from which, by a process analogous to that of condensation, it emerged, Buddhism interleaves with the facts of science a set of spiritual facts of its own discovery. Thus while in no way denying the animal descent of man as a physical organism, it makes it clear that the emergence of *homo sapiens* is due to the conjunction of a descending spiritual order of personal existence with an ascending biological one. (This is the true meaning of the popular Tibetan belief that human beings are descended from the bodhisattva Avalokiteśvara and a female monkey.)

At the same time, we cannot ignore the fact that the Scriptures make a number of statements on geography, anatomy, and physiology, and other scientific subjects, that are plainly wrong. The Buddha, or whoever compiled and edited his words, was more concerned with the spiritual reality of his message than with the factual truth of the scientific references embedded in the language and culture which were his medium of communication. The statement 'King Charles was beheaded two hours after sunrise' is not invalidated by the fact that it is the earth, not the sun, which moves. Some modern readers are outraged by Buddhaghosa's account of the digestive processes and the internal organs. Yet, far from being dependent on fifth-century misunderstandings of the subject, the spiritual exercises the great Theravādin commentator describes can just as well be practised on the basis of the most advanced scientific knowledge of human physiology. In any case, there is nothing in Buddhism that hinders us from discarding whatever obsolete science the Scriptures may contain, for while all schools held the Buddha to be omniscient as regards the Path and the Goal, the Tripiṭaka, unlike the Bible and the Koran, was never revered as being of divine origin, verbally inspired and hence infallible.

Before deciding that a given scriptural text is unscientific, however, we should make quite sure that we really know to what order of existence it pertains. Ridicule has often been poured on Buddhist geography, with its 'islands' and 'oceans' and its many-tiered Mount Sumeru, the abode of the gods, rising from the centre of the map. But despite the fact that Sumeru was sometimes identified with a particular peak in the Himalayan Range, it is clear that this apparently fantastic picture is meant as a description not of this earth only, but of a number of intersecting planes of existence the common axial principle of which is symbolized by Mount Sumeru, and of which our earth, represented by Jambudvīpa, 'The Rose-Apple Island', constitutes one plane.

This brings out the point that whereas the universe of science exists only in space and time, that of Buddhism exists also in depth. This depth is not physical but spiritual. According to ancient traditions basic to all schools, the phenomenal universe as distinct from the limited physical universe consists of three planes or spheres of existence (*lokas*), each 'higher' and subtler than the preceding one. First there is the *kāma-loka* or 'plane of desire' in which are included, besides the universe known to science, the various worlds inhabited by spirits, infernal beings, and the lower, earthbound orders of deities. Next comes the *rūpa-loka* or 'plane of (subtle) form', which is inhabited by higher orders of deities imperceptible to ordinary human sense whose consciousness, though dissociated from 'matter', is still bound up either with one or with many spiritual forms. These deities are of various degrees of luminosity. Finally in the *arūpa-loka*, the 'formless plane', dwell deities of the highest orders of all who, being free even from spiritual form, represent various dimensions of pure but still mundane consciousness. They are naturally of even greater luminosity. Like the first, the second and third planes are divided into a number of sub-planes, and their inhabitants distinguished by different names. Some of these names are indicative of the type or degree of radiance emitted by the class of deity concerned. Despite the detailed classifications found in some works, the higher one goes in the hierarchy of deities the more careful one should be not to think too literally in terms of groups and classes, for here, even more than with lower forms of existence, the ascent is continuous rather than by discrete steps, the lower being transformed into the higher mode of being without perceptible break.

One classification, or rather principle of classification, however, is too relevant to be omitted. It is well known that through the practice of concentration the yogin attains certain superconscious states known as *dhyānas* (Sanskrit) or *jhānas* (Pāli). These are divided into two groups, a lower and a higher. Each group is in turn divided into four, the successive grades constituting the first group being distinguished according to the psychological factors variously present, and the classes which make up the second group (the psychological factors of which are those of the fourth lower *dhyāna*) being differentiated according to their respective objects. What concerns us here is the fact that the *dhyānas* comprising the first group are known collectively as *rūpa-dhyānas* and those comprising the second group as *arūpa-dhyānas*. There is thus a correspondence between *dhyānas* and *lokas*, the one representing the psychological, the other the cosmological aspect of existence. A *loka* is attained, and its inhabitants are seen, when the yogin succeeds in entering the corresponding *dhyāna*. This means that, existentially speaking, *dhyāna* is prior to *loka*, or that, as the first verse of the Pāli *Dhammapada* teaches, consciousness precedes and determines being. (The double meaning of the word *saṁskāra*, which may stand either for the formative psychological factors or for things formed – in the latter case being equivalent to *saṁskṛta-dharma* – may conceal a reference to this idea.) Moreover, space and time being correlative, as soon as he attains a particular *loka* the yogin also begins to experience a new timescale. The Abhidharma tradition explains this by means of a table according to which the life-term in the *loka* of the deities called 'the four great kings' is 9,000,000 years, one day and night being equivalent to 50 years of human life, and so on up through the *lokas* as far as the plane of the supreme Brahmās, the highest deities of all, whose life-term is 16,000 kalpas. Since ultimately it is consciousness that determines both space- and time-perception, and since the entire phenomenal universe exists nowhere save in space and time, it is evident not only that consciousness determines being but that in essence being is consciousness. In the language of the first verse of the *Dhammapada* the elements of existence are not only mind-preceded (*manopubbaṅgamā*) and mind-determined (*manoseṭṭhā*) but also made up or composed of mind (*manomayā*). Here is the germ of the doctrine, set forth in Mahāyāna sūtras such as the *Laṅkāvatāra* and *Sandhinirmocana*, and systematized by the Yogācāra School, that all conditioned things – world systems, planes, deities, and even Buddhas (as *The Tibetan Book of the Dead*, for example, explicitly teaches) – are in truth merely phenomena of the eternally radiant unconditioned reality of Absolute Mind. The tantras express the same idea when, reverting to geographical symbolism, they identify Mount Sumeru with the spinal column in the human body.

10

THE WHEEL OF LIFE

THE LAWS in accordance with which individualized consciousness determines conditioned being are covered by the compendious term *karma*, while the actual process is elucidated in the complex of teachings pictorially represented in Buddhist art by the 'Wheel of Life' (*bhavacakra*).

So far as its usage in connection with Buddhism is concerned, the word karma is often employed in a gravely erroneous manner. Some writers make it mean not only action, its literal meaning, but the result of action, for which Buddhist literature reserves separate terms such as *karma-vipāka* and *karma-phala*. Others use it in the sense of fate or destiny, sometimes even going so far as to maintain that according to Buddhism whatever happens to us, whether pleasant or painful, comes about as the result of previous karma. The confusion must be cleared up before the different types of karma are enumerated.

Though having the literal meaning of action, karma in this context invariably means act of volition. Thus we get the important equation karma = *cetanā* (volition) = *saṁskāras* ('formative' or rebirth-producing psychological factors). As opposed to Jainism, Buddhism maintains that involuntary actions, whether those of body, speech, or mind, do not constitute karma and therefore cannot bring about the results accruing to karma. This does not mean that such actions produce no results at all: the unintentional dropping of a brick on our own toes hurts no less than if we had done it deliberately, perhaps more so. It only means that unwilled actions do not modify character. The confusion arises because the fact that according to Buddhism there is a relation of 'cause' and 'effect' between karma, or act of will, and *karma-vipāka*, the fruit of that act in the form of pleasant or painful experience, has led some unwary students to jump to the conclusion that the law of karma and the law of cause and effect are synonymous. Karma (or more correctly karma and *karma-vipāka*) is only one particular type of cause-effect relation. The *Nikāya/Āgama* discourses represent the Buddha as repeatedly condemning the doctrine of fatalism and as declaring that though he teaches that every willed action produces an experienced effect he does not teach that all experienced effects are products of willed action or karma.

This important distinction is elaborated in the formula of the five *niyamas*, or different orders of cause-effect or conditionality obtaining in the universe. They are *utu-niyama*, physical inorganic order; *bīja-niyama*, physical organic or biological order; *mano-niyama* (non-volitional) mental order; *karma-niyama*, volitional order; and *dharma-niyama*, transcendental order. To distinguish effects produced by one *niyama* from those produced by another is not always easy. Some effects, in fact, can be brought about by any *niyama*. Suppose there is a man suffering from fever. The complaint may be due to a sudden change of temperature (*utu-niyama*), to the presence of a germ (*bīja-niyama*), to mental strain or worry, or to tension due to experiences taking place in the *dhyānas* (*mano-niyama*), to the fact that in a previous life he had harmed someone (*karma-niyama*), or to chemical and cellular changes occurring in the body consequent upon transcendental realization (*dharma-niyama*).

This doctrine has an important practical bearing. Critics of the Dharma sometimes allege that Buddhists are indifferent to human suffering, and take no steps to relieve it, because their religion teaches them to regard it as the result of past karma. However true this may be of Hinduism, which generally inclines to a fatalistic view of karma, or even of some less instructed Buddhists in Asian lands, the accusation certainly does not hold good in respect of the Buddha and his teaching. Buddhists are urged to make every effort to remove disease, privation, and want in all their ignoble, soul-crippling, life-destroying forms because not being Enlightened they cannot know by which *niyama* they have been brought about. Only after making every attempt to remove a certain condition, and finding that although other circumstances are favourable an unknown factor frustrates all our efforts, are we entitled to apply the method of residues and conclude that the condition is due to karma. In any case, it would be a mistake to regard the *karma-niyama* or any other *niyama* as an absolutely self-contained system. Despite the contrary impression sometimes created by modern Theravādin writers, the five *niyamas* not only all act one upon another, but are collectively acted upon and influenced by the higher and wider containing reality of the Universal Consciousness (*ālaya-vijñāna*).[35] Unless this is borne constantly in mind, the drily analytic manner in which such writers tabulate and chart the workings of karma may make us feel that we have to do not with the heart-throbs of a living human mind and character but with an intricate piece of dead mechanism.

The different types of karma are described in the Abhidharma literature with a wealth of illustrative detail. Here we shall be briefly concerned only with the broad principles of classification. These are seven in number. Karmas may be grouped in accordance with their ethical status, the 'door' through which they act, the appropriateness of the resultant experiences, their time and relative priority of taking effect, the nature of their function, and the plane of existence on which they mature. Of these principles, the first is the most important, since this constitutes the basis of the rest. From the point of view of its ethical status or quality a volition (including its concomitant mental factors) is either wholesome (*kuśala*) or unwholesome (*akuśala*). Unwholesome volition is that rooted in greed (*lobha*), hatred (*dveṣa*), and delusion (*moha*) – another primitive formula – and wholesome volition that rooted in the opposite of these passions, that is to say rooted in contentment, love, and mental pellucidity. Each of these two types of volition can act either directly through the 'door' of the mind (the terminology is not to be taken too literally) or indirectly through the door of body or the door of speech.

On this fact are based two of the most important ethical findings of Buddhism. First, that a man will reap the consequences not only of what he has intentionally said and done, but also of what he has deliberately thought, or allowed himself to think, without giving it overt expression in word or deed. One who, in the vigorous language of the New Testament, looks at a woman to lust after her, not only has already committed adultery with her in his heart but, under the operation of the *karma-niyama*, will one day suffer the consequences of adultery. This does not quite mean that we are no less answerable for a passing dirty thought than for the actual unwholesome deed.

Volitions admit of varying degrees of intensity. A volition that fulfils itself in word or deed is generally stronger than one that does not, and a strong will obviously produces greater results than a weak volition. Whether wholesome or unwholesome, however, a mind-volition of the degree of intensity that normally results in word or deed or both will, even if denied overt vocal or bodily expression, undoubtedly bring about the same pleasant or painful experiences that the actual performance of the deed would have done. The point is illustrated by a number of charming traditional anecdotes, like that of the Chinese pilgrim about the old woman who worshipped a dog's tooth thinking it was the Buddha's, or the Zen story of the monk who carried a pretty girl across a stream and then forgot her while his more strait-laced companion 'carried' her in his mind all the way back to the monastery. Tales such as these, which generations of Buddhists have found more illuminating than pages of psychological analysis, link the first with the second of the two important ethical findings based on the relation between volition and 'doors'.

On account of this second finding Buddhist ethics has been described as an ethics of intention. Words and deeds are wholesome or unwholesome, it says, not in themselves, but according to whether they are the expression of wholesome or of unwholesome volitions. Despite its formidable lists of rules, therefore, Buddhist ethics consists essentially in the cultivation of a morally healthy mental attitude towards life. The rules, whether those prescribed for the monk or those prescribed for the layman, merely represent the normal behaviour pattern of one in whom such an attitude is predominant.

Both ethical status and doors enter into the third principle of classification, that according to the appropriateness of the resultant experiences. In the *Cūḷa-* and *Mahā-kammavibhaṅga Suttas*, or Lesser and Greater Discourses on the Analysis of Volitions,[36] the Buddha makes it clear that those who are given to the taking of life, cruelty, anger, envy, avarice, and pride, all of which are acts rooted in unhealthy volitions, will be reborn in states of suffering, or, if reborn as men, will be short-lived, diseased, ugly, despised, poor, and of mean descent. Contrariwise, those whose acts of body, speech, and mind are the opposite of these, being rooted in healthy attitudes, will be reborn in the blissful higher planes of existence, or, if reborn as men, will be long-lived, healthy, handsome, respected, wealthy, and of distinguished family. Other texts give further examples of this type of correspondence. One declares stupidity to be the result of mental indolence, and intelligence of a desire to learn. In the case of this principle of classification one should be careful not to pervert the Buddha's teaching by arguing that, for example, poverty is invariably the punishment for 'bad' and riches the reward of 'good' karmas performed in past lives, for this would be to fall a victim to the very misunderstandings that we have tried to clear up at the beginning of the section.

With regard to time and relative priority of effect, the fourth and fifth principles, the classification of karmas is in each case a fourfold one. A karma may ripen in the very life in which it was performed, in the next life, in a succeeding life, or, owing to the preponderance of 'counteractive' karma or to its being too weak, it may never ripen. The classification according to priority of effect refers not to the effects of karma in general but only to one kind of effect, that which we call rebirth, or, more correctly, rebecoming. From this point of view karmas are classified as 'weighty', 'death-proximate', 'habitual', and 'residual'. The *dhyānas* are all reckoned as healthy weighty volitions. Matricide, parricide, killing an Arhant, wounding a Buddha, and creating a schism in the Sangha, together with erroneous opinions of the type negating the very possibility of a life dedicated to the attainment of Enlightenment, are all unhealthy weighty volitions. Death-proximate karma is the healthy or unhealthy volition occurring immediately before death, which may be the reflex of some previously performed healthy or unhealthy karma, or of something connected with it, or of a sign indicating the future plane of existence. Habitual karma is a healthy or unhealthy volition either repeatedly performed or performed once and repeatedly reflected upon. Authorities on the Abhidharma agree that as a factor determining the nature of the next rebirth a weighty karma, whether healthy or unhealthy, invariably takes precedence over death-proximate and habitual karmas. In the absence of a weighty karma, the determining factor is either a death-proximate or a habitual karma, the order of precedence being here a matter of dispute. Residual karma is a healthy or unhealthy karma not included in the previous three classes which has been performed once and which can determine rebirth only if it has been repeatedly reflected upon.

Karmas are also fourfold according to function, the sixth principle of classification. From this point of view they are either 'reproductive', 'supportive', 'counteractive', or 'destructive'. The first function produces the psychophysical 'personality' of the next birth and maintains it for the period of its existence; the second produces no effects of its own, but supports and strengthens those of a reproductive karma; the third, on the contrary, weakens the results of a reproductive karma; the fourth destroys them and produces effects of its own. Reproductive karma is likened to sowing seed, supportive to manuring and irrigating the field, counteractive to a hailstorm that spoils the crop, and destructive to a fire that consumes it and leaves only ash.

Though enumerated one after another, the thirty-two types of karma so far described are not mutually exclusive, for we have to deal not with a machine made up of a limited number of cogs and wheels, each with its own separate function, but simply with a play of healthy and unhealthy volitions that can be looked at from various points of view as represented by the principles of classification.

With regard to the plane of existence on which they mature, the seventh and last such principle, four classes of karma are distinguished: unhealthy volitions maturing in the four lowest, subhuman *kāma-loka* planes, namely those of the anti-gods (*asuras*), revenants (*pretas*), animals, and infernals, all of which are planes of misery; healthy volitions maturing in any one of the seven higher *kāma-loka* planes, namely the human plane, where 'joy and pain are woven fine', and the six lowest divine realms, where there is only joy; healthy volitions (namely the four *rūpa-dhyānas*) maturing according to their degree of intensity in any one of the twelve higher divine sub-planes of the *rūpa-loka*, where from the fourth sub-plane upwards even joy is transcended; and healthy volitions (the four *arūpa-dhyānas*) maturing in the four sub-planes of the *arūpa-loka*. Counting the human plane and each of the three lowest *kāma-loka* planes (omitting that of the *asuras*) separately, and reckoning all the divine planes, lower and higher, as one plane, we get the *pañca-gati* or five 'goings' of sentient beings according to their karma as depicted in the five principal segments of the Wheel of Life. A sixth segment is often made by dividing that of the gods into two and allotting one half to the *asuras*.

According to the *Divyāvadāna* or 'Divine Heroic Feats [of the Buddha and his Disciples]', one of the best-known *avadānas* of the Sarvāstivādins, the original model of the Wheel of Life was painted over the gateway of the Veḷuvana Vihāra at Rājagṛha on the personal instructions of the Master, who indicated exactly how the work should be done. Whether or not of so ancient an origin, it undoubtedly figures on the wall of one of the rock-cut monasteries of Ajaṇta, and is still well known in Tibet, where it is often depicted inside temple porches for the edification of the faithful.

The Wheel consists of four concentric circles. Working from centre to circumference, the first circle, which constitutes the hub of the Wheel, contains three animals representing the three poisons: a dove (or cock) for lust (*lobha*), a snake for hatred (*dveṣa*), and a pig for delusion (*moha*), each biting the tail of the one in front. They represent different aspects of egocentric volition which, whether in its subtle healthy or its gross unhealthy forms, keeps going the whole process of conditioned existence. The second circle is divided into two equal segments, one white and one black. In the former, human beings whose volitions were healthy joyfully ascend into the realm of the gods; in the latter, those whose volitions were unhealthy plunge terrified headlong into hell. The third circle is divided into six segments, one of each of the six classes of sentient beings already described. At the top is the realm of the gods, next (in clockwise order) the *asuras*, then the animal kingdom,[37] at the bottom the infernal regions, after that the plane of the *pretas*, and finally the human world. In each sphere of existence the bodhisattva Avalokiteśvara, representing the omnipresence of Absolute Compassion, appears in a differently coloured Buddha-form with insignia appropriate to the needs of its inhabitants. As a white Buddha he plays the melody of impermanence on a lute to the long-lived gods, as a green one brandishes at the warlike *asuras* the flaming sword of knowledge, which alone wins the true victory, as a blue one shows the animals a book, as a smoke-coloured one showers the infernal beings with ambrosia, as a red one regales the *pretas* with food and drink, and as a yellow one bears among men a staff and begging-bowl, symbolical of the holy life which they alone of the different classes of sentient beings are fully capable of leading.

The fourth and outermost circle of the Wheel is divided into twelve segments, each representing one of the *nidānas* or 'links' in the process of the *pratītya-samutpāda* or 'conditioned co-production' of the so-called individual stream of consciousness-volition as, appearing now in one, now in another of the six spheres, it twists round and round in the vortex of conditioned existence. The first two segments (again counting in clockwise order from the top) depict a blind man with a stick and a potter with wheel and pots. These represent *avidyā* and the *saṁskāras* ('ignorance' and the 'formative' psychological factors), which together constitute the karma-process of the past life and in dependence on which arises the result-process of the present life. This result-process is covered by the next five segments, which respectively depict: a monkey climbing a flowering tree; a boat with four passengers, one of whom is steering; an empty house with six apertures; a man and woman embracing; and a man with an arrow stuck in his eye. The monkey is *vijñāna*, consciousness; not in the widest acceptation of the term, but in the narrower sense of the initial flash of consciousness arising in the mother's womb at the moment of conception in dependence on the last flash of consciousness of the previous life. This *paṭisandhi* or 'relinking' consciousness, as it is technically called, is neither the same as nor different from the *cuti-citta* or 'death-consciousness' by which it is conditioned. Hence it does not constitute an unchanging, transmigrating entity. Though the requisite physical factors are present, in the absence of the relinking consciousness no conception can take place. The boat and its four passengers are the *skandhas*, the five 'groups' or 'heaps' into which Buddhism analyses the psychophysical personality. These are *rūpa* or body (the boat) and *vedanā* or feeling, *saṁjñā* or perception, the *saṁskāras* or volitional mental phenomena, and *vijñāna* or consciousness (the four passengers: consciousness is steering). They will be dealt with in Chapter 12. The empty house with six apertures stands for the six sense-organs (*ṣaḍāyatana*), mind being reckoned as the sixth, while the man and woman embracing represent contact (*sparśa*) in the sense of the mutual impingement of the sense-organs and the external world. The man with the arrow stuck in his eye depicts feeling (*vedanā*), whether pleasant, painful, or neutral. The eighth, ninth, and tenth segments of the circle show a woman offering a drink to a seated man, a man gathering fruit from a tree, and a woman great with child. These represent the karma-process of the present life. The woman offering drink to the seated man symbolizes thirst or craving (*tṛṣṇā*), the man gathering fruit from the tree grasping (*upādāna*), and the woman great with child 'becoming' (*bhava*) or conception. Though the Theravādins include the last of these three links in the karma-process of the present life, it ought really to be reckoned as the first link of the result-process of the next life. According to the

Sarvāstivādins, who interpret the word differently, it refers to the *antarabhava* or period of 'intermediate existence' between two lives of which the *Bardo Thödol,* known in the West as *The Tibetan Book of the Dead,* paints a vivid picture. The eleventh and twelfth segments, representing the two links which constitute the result-process of the next life, show a woman in childbirth and a man carrying a corpse to the cemetery on his back. The first obviously illustrates birth, the second (old age, disease, and) death.

Thus after being divided into karma-processes and result-processes the twelve *nidānas* of the *pratītya-samutpāda* are distributed over the past life, the present life, and the future life. Herein it should be noted that ignorance and the formative psychological factors, the karma-process of the past, coincide with craving, grasping, and becoming, the karma-process of the present. Likewise consciousness, name and form, the six sense-organs, contact, and feeling, the result-process of the present, correspond with birth and death, the result-process of the future. In each life karma-process and result-process go on simultaneously, the result-process of the preceding coexisting with the karma-process of the succeeding existence. The karma-process in a way resembles the *Wille* and the result-process the *Vorstellung* of Schopenhauer's philosophy. To summarize the message of the twelve segments: sentient existence consists of activities set up through spiritual ignorance; as a result, beings take rebirth as psychophysical organisms equipped with sense-organs by means of which they establish contact with the external world and experience pleasant, painful, and neutral sensations; developing a craving for the pleasant sensations, they try to cling on to the objects that produce them, which leads (according to the Theravādins) to fresh conception in a womb or (according to the Sarvāstivādins) to the plane of intermediate existence; in consequence of this they again have to undergo birth, old age, disease, and death.

Finally, peering over the rim of the outermost circle a fearsome monster wearing a headdress of skulls is shown clasping the Wheel with all its circles and segments in his teeth and between his arms and legs. This is Death or Impermanence. Outside the Wheel above the monster's head, floating on clouds to the right, the Buddha compassionately points out to sentient beings the way of release from conditioned existence.

The details of the Abhidharma discussion of karma and the *pratītya-samutpāda*, a few of which have just been given, should not be allowed to obscure the great truth of which they are both expressions, namely that, on the level of individuality, consciousness precedes and determines being, and that being is therefore in essence consciousness. Consciousness-volition is of two kinds, individual and collective. As Takakusu, using a slightly different terminology, puts it:

> Individual action-influence creates the individual being. Common action-influence creates the universe itself.[38]

The Wheel of Life is the objectivization of the lust, hatred, and delusion in the mind of man. A modern writer, Ben Shahn, seems to have understood this more clearly than some scholars of Buddhism.

> In a monastery near the border of Tibet – where I went hoping it might be over the wall – I found a portrait of myself. Someone in saffron told me that it was called the Wheel of Life, the Round of Existence, but it was myself, exact and representational. There were all the many aspects of myself painted crude and clear: the pig, the lion, the snake, the cock, all animals, angels, demons, titans, gods and men, all heaven and hell, all pleasures and pains, all that went to make me, and all as it were, within the round of myself, within the wall, exactly as I had found it. All that I could be was within the enclosure of myself, all that I could do would only turn the Wheel around and around. There was no way out. I would go on and on, now up, now down, never ceasing, never changing. The mechanism was perfect. I had achieved perpetual motion: immortality.[39]

Hui Neng (Wei Lang), the sixth patriarch of the Ch'an or Dhyāna School in China, had given the same idea profounder and more succinct expression centuries earlier.

> The idea of a self (ātma) or that of a being is Mount Meru. A depraved mind is the ocean. Kleśa (defilement) is the billow. Wickedness is the evil dragon. Falsehood is the devil. The wearisome sense objects are the aquatic animals. Greed and hatred are the hells. Ignorance and infatuation are the brutes.[40]

The universe referred to here, and depicted in the Wheel of Life, is of the kind known as an impure Buddha-field. As previously described (see p.36), a *sambhogakāya* Buddha exercises jurisdiction over and is responsible for the spiritual progress of the inhabitants of one world system, which is therefore known as his Buddha-field. Such fields (*kṣetras*) of influence are of two kinds, pure and impure. An impure Buddha-field, like the one to which our own earth belongs, is inhabited by beings of all the six classes of existence. A pure Buddha-field contains only two of them, namely gods and men, and the conditions under which they live are infinitely more favourable to the attainment of Enlightenment than those of an impure Buddha-field. Some pure Buddha-fields come into existence as a result of the collective karma of divine and human beings of more than average spirituality; others are willed into existence by a particular bodhisattva who, out of compassion for sentient beings, vows to establish for their benefit a Pure Land whereof, after his Enlightenment, he will himself be the presiding Buddha. Both kinds of pure Buddha-field arise in dependence on a consciousness that, whether individual or collective, is not merely healthy but spiritually pure, for which reason they are not regarded as included in the three great planes of existence, the *kāma-loka*, the *rūpa-loka*, and the *arūpa-loka*, but as it were standing apart from and outside them all. As the *Vimalakīrti-nirdeśa* declares:

> If one wishes to reach the Pure Land, he must purify his mind. In accord with the purity of his mind, so will the Buddha-field be pure.

Just as the impure mind, whether healthy or unhealthy, creates impure Buddha-fields, so the pure mind creates Buddha-fields that are pure. In the words of the *Avataṁsaka Sūtra*:

> All the Buddha-fields rise from one's own mind and have infinite forms;
> Sometimes pure, sometimes defiled, they are in various cycles of
> enjoyment and suffering.

Nevertheless it should not be thought that the six spheres of existence depicted in the Wheel of Life, and the various Pure Lands described in the Scriptures, are no more than figurative expressions for what in essence are purely subjective mental states. The 'objective' world we perceive, with all its seas and mountains, trees, houses, and human beings, is in reality a state of mind. Contrariwise, what is in reality a state of mind can appear as an objectively existing world which those who inhabit it or, more precisely, those who have been or who are in the mental state correlative to it, can actually experience and perceive.

11

THE NATURE OF EXISTENCE

NOW THAT WE HAVE explored the universe of Buddhism as it exists in space, time, and spiritual depth, as well as seen the way in which consciousness is involved in a process of perpetual objectification of itself to itself as one or another modality of sentient being, it is time to consider the 'marks' which attach to all conditioned existence and which express its true nature.

Besides provisionally distinguishing between *saṁskṛta-* and *asaṁskṛta-dharmas,* the conditioned and the Unconditioned, Buddhism, like the great metaphysical idealisms of the West, also distinguishes the conditioned as it exists in reality from the conditioned as it appears, that is, as presented to the senses and interpreted by the unenlightened mind. In reality conditioned existence is painful (*duḥkha*), impermanent (*anitya*), insubstantial (*anātman*), and ugly (*aśubha*). Owing to our habitual self-centredness and our deeply-rooted attachments, however, we imagine it to be pleasant (*sukha*), permanent (*nitya*), substantial (*ātman*), and beautiful (*śubha*), thus falling a victim to what are known as the four *viparīyāsas* or (mental) 'perversities'. Of course, most religious people, including even those who are nominally Buddhists, profess to regard the world as a vale of tears, a house of sorrow, a 'battered caravanserai' in which man passes but one night and moves on; but observing them in the affairs of daily life one will be able to detect little difference, if any, between their behaviour and that of their admittedly worldly brethren, and it will soon transpire that the principles on which their actions are based, and which therefore constitute the real though concealed mainspring of their being, are usually the very opposite of the ones professed. They, no less than other men, live as though the world was on the whole a pleasant enough place, as though whatever they acquired could never be taken away from them, and as though they were going to live for a few centuries at least, if not for ever. Everyone will smile at the portrait, and perhaps recognize himself in it; but none but will continue to act as before. This is because the mental perversities are not just a matter of incorrect information, like thinking that the Buddha was born in China, but attitudes as deeply rooted almost as sentient existence itself. According to the Buddha's teaching they can be extirpated only by prolonged systematic meditation on the fact that the world as we know it is unreal. As an ancient and famous verse incorporated in the *Vajracchedikā Sūtra* exhorts us:

> As stars, a fault of vision, as a lamp,
> A mock show, dew drops, or a bubble,
> A dream, a lightning flash, or cloud,
> So should one view what is conditioned.[41]

In order to assist such meditation, sūtras like the *Laṅkāvatāra* and *ācāryas* like Asaṅga and Vasubandhu not only multiply such similes but explain them elaborately. Conditioned things are like stars, for instance, because having no real existence they cannot be got at or grasped; because they are insignificant in comparison with Absolute Reality, even as the stars in comparison with the vastness of space; and because when the Truth is realized it is no more possible to discern them than it is to see the stars after the sun has risen. In their zeal to uproot the *viparyāsas* both sūtras and *ācāryas* sometimes went to the extreme of declaring that the world was not only unreal but absolutely non-existent. According to the older and more widely accepted tradition, however, systematic meditation on the unreality of the world does not involve impugning its existence but consists in viewing it simply as painful, transitory, and insubstantial. These are the three 'marks' or 'characteristics' (*lakṣaṇas*) of conditioned existence with which we are now concerned. They correspond with the first, second, and third of the four mental perversities. The *locus classicus* of this most important doctrinal formula is *Dhammapada* verses 277–9, according to which the vision – by means of wisdom (*prajñā*) – that all *saṁskāras* are *anitya*, all *saṁskāras duḥkha*, and all *dharmas anātman*, constitutes the Path of Purity (*viśuddhi-mārga*). As the third characteristic applies not only to the conditioned but also to the Unconditioned, in this case the all-inclusive term *dharma* is used instead of the word *saṁskāras*, which denotes only the conditioned. Sometimes a fourth *lakṣaṇa*, 'Nirvāṇa alone is peace', is added to the original set of three. This obviously applies only to the Unconditioned. For convenience of exposition we shall review the marks attaching to conditioned existence, and their corresponding mental perversities, not in the traditional order but in that of the ugly, the impermanent, the insubstantial, and the painful.

Aśubha, which means not only ugly but also horrid, disgusting, repulsive, or impure, is best understood by referring to the word from which it is derived by the addition of a negative prefix. *Śubha*, literally 'purity', really means beauty, though beauty of the spiritual rather than of the sensuous order. It is pure beauty in the Platonic and Neoplatonic sense of something shining in a world of its own above and beyond concrete things, which are termed beautiful only so far as they participate in its perfection. When Buddhism insists that all conditioned things are *aśubha*, it does not mean that we have to regard a flower, for instance, as essentially ugly, but only that in comparison with the beauties of a higher plane of reality those of a lower plane are insignificant. Beauty and ugliness are relative terms. We cannot really see the conditioned as *aśubha* until we have seen the Unconditioned as *śubha*. Similarly, within the conditioned itself, in order to see the ugliness and impurity of objects belonging to a lower plane it is necessary to ascend, in meditation, to one which is higher. This is the significance of the well-known episode of the Buddha's cousin Nanda and the heavenly nymphs:

> The Lord said to the venerable Nanda: 'You admit it is true that without zest you fare the Brahma-faring, that you cannot endure it, and that, throwing off the training, you will return to the low life. How is this?'
>
> 'Revered sir, when I left my home a Śākyan girl, the fairest in the land, with hair half combed, looked back at me and said: "May you soon be back again, young master." Revered sir, as I am always thinking of that, I have no zest for the Brahma-faring, can't endure it, and, throwing off the training, will return to the low life.'
>
> Then the Lord, taking the venerable Nanda by the arm, as a strong man might stretch out his bent arm or might bend back his

outstretched arm, vanishing from the Jeta Grove, appeared among the Devas of the Thirty-Three. At that time as many as five hundred nymphs were come to minister to Sakka, the lord of devas, and they were called 'dove-footed'. The Lord asked the venerable Nanda which he thought the more lovely, worth looking at and charming, the Śākyan girl, the fairest in the land, or these five hundred nymphs called 'dove-footed'.

'O, revered sir, just as if she were a mutilated monkey with ears and nose cut off, even so the Śākyan girl, the fairest in the land, if set beside these five hundred nymphs called "dove-footed", is not worth a fraction of them, cannot be compared with them. Why, these five hundred nymphs are far more lovely, worth looking at and charming.'[42]

The Heaven of the Thirty-Three Gods is only two *kāma-loka* sub-planes above the world of men; but regarded even from this level the loveliest human face is repulsive. The *rūpa-loka* sub-planes, corresponding to the four *rūpa-dhyānas*, are higher still. Viewed from these levels the five hundred nymphs called 'dove-footed' are ugly. Thus objects are *śubha* in comparison with those of a lower plane, and *aśubha* in comparison with those of a higher plane of existence.

The type of meditation exercise that will help one to realize this personally by ascending into the *dhyānas* and actually seeing the lower ranges of conditioned existence as *aśubha* differs according to temperament. The *lobhacaritra* or 'passionate temperament', which tends to concentrate on the bright side of life ignoring the dark, and in which greed and attachment therefore predominate, will find the *aśubhabhāvanā* helpful. This method consists in contemplating the ten progressive stages of decomposition of a corpse. The *dveṣacaritra* or 'malevolent temperament', which sees the bad side of everything, and in which aversion predominates, on the contrary will be helped by concentrating on discs of pure bright beautiful colours such as those of flowers. One of passionate temperament should never begin by concentrating on attractive objects, which in his case will stimulate greed, nor one of malevolent temperament on repulsive objects, which in him will excite hatred, and greed and hatred are hindrances to meditation. On attaining the *rūpa-dhyānas*, however, both see the *rūpa-loka* as beautiful and the *kāma-loka* as, in comparison, ugly.

Unfortunately, the specific function of those practices which focus attention on the repulsive and disgusting aspects of existence, as well as their special relation to one type of temperament, is not always understood even by Buddhist writers, some of whom appear to believe that according to Buddhism ugliness is real and beauty unreal and that one progresses in the spiritual life merely by seeing more and more ugliness and less and less beauty everywhere and at all levels of existence. As a well-known Sri Lankan Thera remarked to the writer once when shown an album of Tibetan religious paintings, 'I'm afraid that being a monk I'm not allowed to appreciate beauty.' Such strange misunderstandings, though current in some modern Theravādin circles, are easily refuted even from the Pāli scriptures. Addressing a non-Buddhist recluse the Buddha says:

> Now, Bhaggava,... certain recluses and brahmins have abused me with groundless, empty lies that have no truth in them, saying: 'Gotama the recluse and his brethren have gone astray. For Gotama the recluse teaches this:
>
> "When one reaches up to the Release, called the Beautiful, and having reached it abides therein, at such a time he regards the Whole (Universe) as ugly."'
>
> But I never said that, Bhaggava. This is what I do say: 'Whenever one reaches up to the Release, called the Beautiful, then he knows indeed what Beauty is.'[43]

However necessary a negative approach may be at first for those of passionate temperament, it is clear from this notable passage that, in principle, awareness of beauty, the positive factor, predominates in the Buddhist spiritual life over awareness of ugliness, the negative one. In the absence of any awareness of and delight in the 'beauty' of the Unconditioned all our efforts to convince ourselves rationally that conditioned existence is *aśubha* are likely to remain unfruitful, with the result that despite our protestations we shall continue to wallow in the mire of the *kāma-loka*. The failure to appreciate this fact is one of the reasons for the spiritually moribund condition of most parts of the Theravādin Buddhist world today.

'Sabbe sankhārā aniccā.' The characteristic of all conditioned things being impermanent, the first *lakṣaṇa* according to the traditional order, and the second *vipariyāsa*, occupies a position as it were intermediate between the characteristics of *anātman* and *duḥkha*, the one

representing a higher, the other a lower, degree of generality of the same truth. For this reason, personified Impermanence, and not Insubstantiality or Pain, is the monster shown clutching the Wheel of Life in murderous fangs and claws. The idea thus concretely expressed is not, of course, peculiar to Buddhism: in one form or another it is a commonplace of all higher religious and philosophical thought, as well as the oft-recurring theme of poets and mystics in every age and clime. What distinguishes the Buddhist treatment of it from that of other teachings is the relentless thoroughness with which it pursues, explores, and exhausts the topic. In traditional Christianity, only the more remarkable and catastrophic changes in human life, in history, and in nature were ever taken into consideration. Towards the end of the medieval period the crudely macabre vision of the Dance of Death, representing the transitoriness of mortal joys, haunted the imagination of the age; but however much a prey to worms sublunary things might be, for medieval thought all above the sphere of the moon rested in immutable perfection. Bodies might rot, but then, as now, the soul was a simple, incorruptible, and immortal substance.

No such exceptions to the law that all conditioned things are impermanent have ever been recognized by Buddhism, for it sees clearly that whatever has a beginning must also have an end. Whether in the physical universe without or the psychic world within, nothing is so huge or so minute that it can escape the clutches of the demon Impermanence. Already we have seen revealed as the cosmological background of Buddhism infinite space and infinite time wherein universes unnumbered rise into existence, persist, and disappear, the life period of each one covering thousands of millions of years (see pp.56–7). At the opposite end of the cosmic scale Buddhism shoots a penetrating glance at the tiniest conceivable unit of 'matter', the so-called atom, and sees not a microscopic billiard ball, static, homogeneous, and eternal, but a continuously changing dance of forces about a common centre. Again, plunging into the spiritual depths of the universe, instead of everlasting abodes of eternally redeemed or eternally tormented spirits it beholds mental states objectified as perceptible worlds which, even though enduring for thousands of aeons, are still finite as the healthy or unhealthy volitions that first conjured them into being. Heaven, the ultimate goal of so many faiths, since it is a mode of contingent and hence of transitory existence is accounted no more than a pleasant interlude in a pilgrimage fundamentally of more serious import.

Deep as such insights into the impermanence of the conditioned go, and destructive as they are of cherished delusions, there is yet one which penetrates deeper still and destroys what, by reason of the natural resistance of the human mind, is the greatest delusion of all. Turning from the physical to the psychical, and focusing its gaze within, the Eye of Enlightenment pierces the depths of the human personality itself. Where common sense posits a real 'I', idealist philosophers the residual self, and theologians an immortal soul, that undeceivable Eye beholds not any such unchanging entity but, instead, an uninterrupted flow of mental events which, themselves arising in dependence on conditions, in turn function as conditions for the arising of further states.

For Buddhism, no less than for modern physics and psychology, all the apparently stable and solid material and mental objects in the universe are in reality temporary condensations of energy. Hence despite what some have assumed the use of such words as 'states' and 'elements' to mean, seeing conditioned things as impermanent does not consist in conceiving them as chopped up into bits (which would raise the artificial problem of how the bits were to be joined together again), but rather in seeing them as so many phases of one or the other of two pure, absolutely continuous, interdependent streams of energy which can be locked up in the atom, in the one case, and trapped in the individual mind, in the other. Whether the energy which is the reality of 'matter' and the energy which is the reality of 'mind' are ultimately one energy Buddhism does not at this stage of its analysis enquire. But according to some of the later developments in Buddhist thought, material is reducible to mental energy and both to the transcendental outpourings of the ineffable Void.

'*Sabbe dhammā anattā.*' From the impermanence of the conditioned to its insubstantiality is a short step; so much so that to penetrate at all deeply into the former is ultimately to find oneself in the midst of the latter. Like other doctrinal formulas, that of the three marks is by no means best understood when understood most literally, and it would be well to remind ourselves that in it we have to deal, not with three distinct properties of the conditioned, but rather with so many ways of penetrating into its true nature. One of the most convenient methods of making the transition from *anitya* to *anātman* is by considering the notion of change. We say 'the leaf changes from green to red.' In terms of the traditional grammatical-cum-logical analysis this is a sentence/proposition predicating in a certain subject/substance the succeeding of one attribute by another. Such an analysis implies that *in some sense* it is possible for a substance to exist without its attributes – that a leaf can hang on a tree without being red or green or yellow or blue or any other colour. In *what sense* this is possible has not always been clear, though. Quite a number of philosophers have treated what is evidently a purely linguistic convention, useful enough as a means of facilitating the acquisition of a language, as a real distinction between things. An extraordinarily large number of philosophical and religious doctrines are in fact based on this fallacy, including the conception of God as Absolute Being (that is, as being abstracted from all particular existent things), of the individual as embodying an immortal soul or changeless self independent of the sum total of psychophysical states, the dogma of the Trinity (unity of Godhead or substance distinct from plurality of persons), and the dogma of transubstantiation (change of the substances of bread and wine into the flesh and blood of Christ while their accidents remain unchanged). Other philosophers sought to evade the obvious difficulties of realism by maintaining that the distinction between a substance and its properties is conceptual; that it exists, but only in thought.

Buddhism, however, goes to the root of the matter and declares that, as modern studies in the subject have established, a phenomenon viewed dynamically is the totality of 'its' conditions and viewed statically the totality of its parts, and that over and above these conditions and parts no phenomenon exists. Abstracted from its green and red colour a leaf is not an independent entity but only a name. When it changes its colour what really happens is that, as the traditional formula would have it, in dependence on a green leaf a red leaf arises. This does not mean that the green leaf and the red are discrete, much less still that one is the 'cause' of the other, for the change from green to red is a continuous process. What it really means is that while the first *lakṣaṇa* affirms only that all conditioned things change, the second *lakṣaṇa*, penetrating far deeper, affirms that there is nothing which changes. To abstract the 'thing' which is changed from the process of change itself and set it up as an independent entity upon which change impinges as it were from outside is fallacious. The difference between *anitya* and *anātman* can also be expressed by saying that whereas according to the former the conditioned changes, according to the latter it *is* change – the implied distinction between subject and predicate, substance and attribute, being merely verbal. Further, since the change is continuous we are not to think of conditioned *dharmas* as entities lying as it were in a row side by side. They are in fact only so many sections marked off in the continuum of conditioned existence. In other words, the existence of the *dharmas* into which Buddhism resolves the so-called personality is in the final analysis as much nominal as that of the personality itself. This understanding receives explicit formulation in the doctrine of the twofold *nairātmya*, of *pudgalas* and of *dharmas*, advanced by the Mahāyāna to counteract the pluralistic realism of the Sarvāstivāda, an influential early Hīnayāna school, which while agreeing that personality, as a congeries of conditioned *dharmas*, exists only nominally, maintained that the substance of these *dharmas* persists unchanged through the three periods of time. Such a position, as its critics saw, and as from the positiveness of their denials we may infer even the Sarvāstivādins felt, logically results in a species of substantialism. Occasional deviations of this kind apart, Buddhist thought as a whole adhered faithfully throughout the long course of its development to the strict nominalism inherent in its doctrine of insubstantiality, for which reason it was able not only to root out from the minds of its true followers the last vestige of attachment to self, but also to remain free from the sort of confusions which arise from the uncritical assumption that the structure of reality must conform to linguistic usage.

The meaning of *anātman* is by no means exhausted, however. As we have seen, not only the conditioned, but also the Unconditioned, is insubstantial. But in what does its insubstantiality consist? Conditioned things are *anātman* because they are no more than the totality of their conditioned parts or functions and because, when they change, there is nothing which changes apart from the process of change itself. But the Unconditioned, the *asaṁskṛta* or uncompounded, is by definition impartite and unchanging. How, then, can it too be designated as *anātman*? On the face of it the term cannot be used in the same sense in both cases. The Unconditioned is *anātman* in the sense that it is *niḥsvabhāva* or devoid of determinate nature. It cannot be pointed out as this or that. All descriptions, such as that it is eternal and blissful, are true in the conventional sense only. In reality it is ineffable. Consequently it cannot be defined as existent, nor as non-existent, nor as both existent and non-existent, nor yet as neither existent nor non-existent. Carried to its logical conclusion, this means that it cannot be defined even as the Unconditioned, for such a definition limits it to being something other than the conditioned. Just as freedom, in order to be truly free, must liberate itself from the freedom that is opposed to bondage, so the Unconditioned, to be really such, must transcend the opposition between what is conditioned and what is not.

At this point the insubstantiality of the conditioned and the insubstantiality of the Unconditioned overlap. As we have already seen, the *dharmas* into which analysis resolves the so-called *pudgala* have themselves ultimately only a nominal, not a real, existence. Conditioned existence is in reality a pure continuum. The more deeply we fathom this continuum the more we realize that its true nature, too, is ineffable and that even as by penetrating into *anitya* we ultimately emerge in the midst of *anātman*, so by knowing the conditioned in its depth we know also the Unconditioned. Thus although at the level at which the two orders are seen as different *anātman* is used in one sense for the conditioned and in another for the Unconditioned, at the level where this difference is seen to be nominal the two kinds of insubstantiality resolve themselves, on sufficiently deep analysis, into a third, a profounder, kind. For *anātman* in this wider and deeper sense of the indescribable 'thusness' (*tathatā*) which constitutes the ultimate reality of both conditioned and unconditioned *dharmas* Mahāyāna thought generally appropriates the term *śūnyatā*, literally 'voidness'. Nirvāṇa, the fourth or supplementary *lakṣaṇa*, broadly coincides with the Unconditioned as cessation of the conditioned and hence as the goal of the aspiration of those to whom the surface of conditioned existence appears as permanent, pleasant, and real.

'Sabbe sankhārā dukkhā.' Though all the characteristics present difficulties to those who seek to understand Buddhism from a point of view other than its own, it is with regard to the statement that all conditioned things are suffering – corresponding to the second *viparyāsa* and the first Āryan Truth – that they are apt to become most acute. On account of this characteristic do its critics complain that Buddhism is morbid, pessimistic, cynical, a lover of the shady side of the street, the enemy of harmless pleasures, an unfeeling trampler on

the little innocent joys of life. At the same time they are confounded by the indisputable fact that the peoples of Buddhist lands seem happy; and often the more Buddhist the more happy. Some try to explain the anomaly as simply a case of Far Eastern cheerfulness breaking in through the Indian gloom of Buddhism; others dismiss it with irritation as a sheer perversity. In either case the critics remain uncomfortably aware of a plain contradiction between what they represent as the pessimistic principles of Buddhism and its optimistic practice. According to them, apparently, Buddhism being a pessimistic teaching its followers ought always to look sad.

In reality Buddhism is neither pessimistic nor optimistic. If compelled to label it in this way at all we should borrow a word from George Eliot and call it melioristic, for though asserting that conditioned existence is suffering it also maintains, as the third Āryan Truth teaches, that suffering can be transcended. The mistake of the critics lies in assuming that according to Buddhism the conditioned is painful *under all circumstances and from all points of view.* Despite the loftiness of its thought, however, Buddhism is not so absurdly remote from ordinary human life as to deny that for the average man a glass of beer, an evening with his girlfriend, or a new car, are pleasant things. What it does is to point out that life also contains a number of undeniably unpleasant things, which nobody would ever pretend were enjoyable, such as old age, disease, death, being separated from what we like and associated with what we dislike. The latter make up the dark, painful side of existence which most of us do our best to ignore, and it is because we act in this ostrich-like fashion, not because, as sometimes alleged, it considers pain more real than pleasure, that Buddhism recommends various spiritual exercises which by bringing this dark side of life more prominently into view will give us a less one-sided picture of existence. Having done this, it goes a step further and points out that the pleasant things and the painful things, the sweet and the bitter experiences of life, are interconnected, so that it is impossible to enjoy the one without having to suffer the other.

This is not to say merely that a glass of beer may result in a headache, a girlfriend prove unfaithful, or a ride in a new car end in hospital, though of course all these things may happen. Pleasure and pain can be connected in much subtler ways than this. The repressed awareness that we are enjoying ourselves at someone else's expense, as nearly always is the case, gives rise to an unconscious sense of guilt that spoils the enjoyment. Pleasant things are tied up with worry and anxiety, because we are afraid of losing them. Enjoyable experiences, whether of body or mind, strengthen our attachment to the psycho-physical personality that is the basis as much for suffering as for enjoyment. Moreover, pleasures differ not only in kind but in degree of intensity, and what was once pleasant may become less pleasant, or insipid, or even positively painful, in comparison with something more pleasant, or within the context of a wider range of experience. Vajrayāna tradition recognizes four stages of bliss: that arising from the senses (*ānanda*), from the *dhyānas* (*paramānanda*), from the attainment of Nirvāṇa (*viramānanda*), and from the realization of the non-duality of the conditioned and the Unconditioned (*sahajānanda*) – literally 'congenital', i.e. innate or natural bliss.[44] On experiencing the bliss of a higher degree one naturally loses interest in that of a lower degree of intensity. Thus although not maintaining the absurd thesis that all conditioned things are painful under all circumstances and from all points of view, Buddhism certainly does most vigorously maintain that no conditioned thing can be pleasant under all circumstances and from all points of view.

It goes even further than this. It maintains that even if one could cut out from the variegated web of life the bright parts of the pattern, leaving aside the dark, and assemble them into a single blaze of unmitigated brightness, the resultant experience would not even then be one of unmixed enjoyment. In the depths of the heart there would remain a void which no conditioned thing, but only the Unconditioned, could fill. This profound truth is echoed at a lower, theistic level of thought by St Augustine's famous apostrophe:

> Thou hast made us for Thyself, and our hearts are restless until they find rest in Thee.

It is illustrated by Goethe's great and complex philosophical poem *Faust*, wherein the hero promises his soul to Mephistopheles if he can give him one permanently satisfying experience:

> And heartily
> When thus I hail the Moment flying:
> 'Ah still delay – thou art so fair!'
> Then bind me in thy bonds undying.
> My final ruin then declare.

Knowledge, love, wealth, power, fail to pass the test. Like Māra in the Scriptures, Mephistopheles has at his disposal only conditioned things. The Unconditioned, which alone can satisfy the deepest longings of the human heart, is beyond his power, and Faust therefore never pronounces the word that would seal his doom. What the third *lakṣaṇa* really means is, in positive terms, that Nirvāṇa alone is peace, and negatively that conditioned things are painful because we seek in them that absolute bliss which only the Unconditioned can bestow and have, therefore, inevitably to experience disappointment and frustration.

To learn to see the conditioned as ugly, impermanent, insubstantial, and painful, instead of as the opposite, is not, of course, the work of a day. It can thus be seen only by means of *prajñā* or wisdom, a purely transcendental faculty that does not spring into existence all at once or by accident, but which has to be systematically nurtured, cultivated, and developed on the twofold basis of an ethical life expressive of healthy mental attitudes, and a purified, concentrated, and meditative consciousness. These categories, the first and second of which are covered by the terms *śīla* and *samādhi* respectively, together constitute the three great stages underlying all more detailed subdivisions of the Path to Enlightenment. Before we can proceed to discuss either the path in general, or the stages of which it consists, it will be necessary to make the acquaintance of the pilgrim.

12

THE HUMAN SITUATION

EXCEPT IN THE SENSE in which all things are unique, Buddhism, unlike the Semitic faiths, does not regard man as an absolutely unique being brought into existence by means of a special creative act and endowed by his divine maker with an immortal soul the possession of which constitutes an unbridgeable difference between him and all other creatures and entitles him to exploit and torture them for his own benefit and amusement. On the contrary it regards him as one manifestation of a current of psychophysical energy manifesting now as a god, now as an animal, revenant, tortured spirit, or titan, and now as a man, according to whether its constituent volitions are healthy, unhealthy, or mixed. Thus Buddhism does not think of sentient beings in terms of separate forms of life, one absolutely discrete from another, so much as in terms of separate currents of psychical energy each of which can associate itself with any form. Energy is primary, form secondary. It is not that man wills, but rather that will 'mans'. To state the position in this way should suffice to lay the dust raised by those according to whom Buddhism does not really teach that a man can be reborn as an animal, but only as a lower type of man dominated by a certain trait of which a particular animal is the generally recognized symbol, as the fox of cunning and the sparrow of lust. Putting as they do the cart before the horse, such misunderstandings are neither right enough to be wrong nor wrong enough to be right. According to Buddhism a man is not, strictly speaking, reborn as an animal; neither is he reborn as a man, nor as a god. What is 'reborn', in the sense of becoming temporarily linked to an appropriate form, is the continuously changing stream of psychical energy. If during the span of human life this stream consisted mainly of volitions connected with food and sex, or if the thought occurring at the moment of death was of the same low type, the consciousness arising in dependence thereon at the moment of rebirth (or, more properly, of reconception) will be an animal consciousness, and it will therefore arise in an animal womb. Apart from the exceptional cases of a yogin who has mastered the art of consciousness-transference or a bodhisattva who, out of compassion, chooses to be reborn on a subhuman plane, the idea of a human or spiritual consciousness imprisoned in an animal body is foreign to the Buddha's teaching. Besides failing to grasp the principle that sentient beings exist primarily as energy, and only secondarily as form, those for whom the Buddhist doctrines of karma and rebecoming involve any such idea are perhaps unconsciously motivated by the desire of somehow safeguarding the uniqueness of man. It is hardly necessary to elaborate the point that while Judaism, Christianity, and Islam, with their dogma of an irreducible difference between man and all other living things, condone and even encourage cruelty to animals, Buddhism, on account of its doctrine of psychical continuity, has ever taught that they should be treated with gentleness and compassion.

Though man is not unique in the sense of being at every level of his existence discrete from all other living things, human life does according to Buddhism possess a distinctive significance. For one thing, it is comparatively rare. For every one human being there exist thousands of mammals, millions of insects, and perhaps thousands of millions of microbes – not to speak of unnumbered gods, titans, revenants, and tormented spirits. Works of edification often ask us to reflect on this fact, realize the advantages of being born with a human body, and resolve to make the best possible use of the opportunity. The weight of the advice derives from the fact that, besides being comparatively rare, the human estate occupies a position of centrality in relation to the other modalities of sentient existence. In fact it is in this centrality that the distinctive significance of human life mainly consists. Probably because of the difficulty of representing all the aspects of a truth simultaneously, the place which is allotted in the third circle of the Wheel of Life to the realm of men does not bring this fact out. From our present viewpoint a truer picture would be one which depicted man at the centre, with gods and titans in the north, tormented spirits in the south, animals in the west, and revenants in the east.

The centrality which such an arrangement would illustrate is twofold. Firstly, the human state is central in relation to pleasure and pain. While the tormented spirits experience pain without pleasure, the gods experience pleasure without pain. Man experiences both. Consequently he is neither so intoxicated with the one, nor so stupefied by the other, as to be incapable of directing his attention from the conditioned to the Unconditioned. He experiences enough suffering to make him discontented with the former, and enough enjoyment to generate in him a desire for the latter. Secondly, the human state is central in relation to karma and *karma-vipāka*. Karma, it will be remembered, means healthy or unhealthy volition, while *karma-vipāka* means the result thereof in the form of pleasant or painful experience. Only in the case of man is the balance between the two approximately equal; he both reaps what he sowed in past lives and sows what he must reap in future lives. All other forms of sentient existence are states of passive experience; they reap, but do not sow. The gods enjoy happiness corresponding in degree to the *dhyānas* which they had attained during their lives on earth as men; the titans suffer the results of jealousy, animals of mental indolence, tormented beings of violent hatred, and revenants of inordinate greed. Not that volition is entirely absent. In the case of the gods the uninterrupted experience of pleasure may give rise to an attachment so strong that, unless there is a balance of reproductive karma pertaining to the world of men still outstanding from the previous human birth, the next 'relinking' (*pratisandhi*, Pāli *paṭisandhi*) of the stream of consciousness concerned may take place on an appropriate subhuman plane. In the case of the *asuras*, animals, and revenants the painful experiences of frustration, oppression, and want that they respectively undergo are apt to occasion feelings of hatred so violent that, as a result, they are reborn either on an even lower sub-plane of the same state or among the tormented spirits. As for the tormented spirits, they can only sink deeper and deeper into hell. In other words in all the non-human planes of sentient existence conditions are such that unhealthy volitions are very much more likely to arise than healthy ones. Once involved in them, therefore, the stream of consciousness can only with extreme difficulty escape from the ever-accelerating process of deterioration, decline, and downfall. Animals and revenants can, indeed, be helped through contact with human beings, especially if the latter are spiritually advanced; but for tormented spirits the only hope lies in the actual descent to their own plane of a bodhisattva who, by preaching the Dharma to them, will provide a support for healthy volitions which, on the expiry of their term of life in hell, can function as conditions for rebirth on higher planes of existence. This dark picture throws into relief the greater freedom of action enjoyed by man, who, since he is provided with occasions for both healthy and unhealthy volitions, has facility of access to both the planes above and the planes below his own. Moreover, inasmuch as the state of concentrated wholesome volition called *samādhi* can function as a condition for the development of *prajñā* (wisdom), and *prajñā* for the attainment of *vimukti* (freedom), he also has access to the Unconditioned.

Basically, the twofold centrality of his position, in relation to pleasure and pain, and in relation to karma and *karma-vipāka*, consists in the fact that, one or two classes of quasi-exceptional cases apart, it is only when supported by a human body that the stream of consciousness can evolve to the point at which it is able to function as a basis for the manifestation of the Absolute Consciousness that constitutes Enlightenment. The distinctive significance of human life resides in the fact that by virtue of its mundane centrality in relation to the other forms of sentient existence it is analogous to the transcendental centrality of Buddhahood. A reference to our re-arrangement of the six segments of the third circle of the Wheel of Life will bear this out. The re-arrangement forms a sort of mandala. Snellgrove defines a mandala as

> A circle of symbolic forms ... one symbol at the centre, which represents absolute truth itself, and other symbols arranged at the various points of the compass, which represent manifested aspects of this same truth.[45]

Thus there is not only a general correspondence, in the Hermetic sense, between the realm of conditioned and the realm of unconditioned existence, but also a particular, indeed a special, correspondence between the human condition and Buddhahood. This correspondence is the foundation of all such affirmations as 'I am the Buddha' and 'I am Vajrasattva' – or whatever other Buddha-form it is occupies the centre of the mandala. These affirmations, which occur in certain Mahāyāna sūtras, in many systems of Vajrayāna meditation, and in the sayings of Zen masters, may legitimately be made only in profound *samādhi*, in connection with which they can induce a state of consubstantiation between the yogin and the transcendental form on which he is meditating. Used indiscriminately, they are extremely dangerous. A purely theoretical concept of Buddhahood may, in effect, be superimposed upon the ego, with disastrous results. For this reason Buddhism generally prefers to speak the language not of identity but of analysis and change.

In the terms of this safer and in a way stricter language the so-called individual being is analysed into his constituent parts or, more accurately, his constituent events. According to the oldest and best-known analysis these events are of five types, technically known as 'groups' or 'heaps' (*skandhas*): (1) form (*rūpa*), (2) feeling (*vedanā*), (3) perception (*saṁjñā*), (4) mental phenomena (*saṁskāras*), and (5) discriminating consciousness (*vijñāna*). They are here spoken of as five types of event in order to emphasize the fact that, as most English renderings of the term fail to make clear, each of the *skandhas* (Pāli *khandhas*) represents not an unchanging 'thing' but rather a congeries of related processes, as well as to guard against creating the impression that the individual being can be analysed into the five *skandhas* much as a table, for instance, is analysed into four legs and a top.

(1) *Rūpa* or form consists of the four great elementary qualities (*mahābhūta*) together with a number of derived or secondary qualities (*upādāyarūpa*). The former are enumerated as earth, water, fire, and air, by which are meant not the popular elements bearing those names but the forces of cohesion, undulation, radiation, and vibration. About the exact number of the secondary qualities there are differences of opinion between the various schools, the Theravādins enumerating twenty-three or twenty-four and the Sarvāstivādins and Vijñānavadins only eleven, but they may be said to comprise on the whole

> the objective constituents of perceptual situations (colours, sounds, etc.) and the 'sensitivities' (*rūpaprasāda*) of the sense organs which are manifested to a person himself by a mass of bodily feeling and to others through certain visual and tactual senses.[46]

The fact that such items as masculinity (*puruṣendriya*), femininity (*strīndriya*), and gesture (*kāyavijñāpti*) are listed among the secondary qualities of *rūpa* should cause us to beware of thinking of this term as 'matter' in either the popular or the philosophic usage of the term.

(2) *Vedanā* or feeling, in the sense of the affective colouring which saturates a particular content of consciousness, is of five kinds, pleasant (*sukha*), painful (*duḥkha*), and neutral (*upekṣā*), the first and second being either bodily (*kāyika*) or mental (*caitasika*), and the third only mental. It covers, thus, not only sensation, or hedonic feeling, but also emotion, which can be not only hedonic but also ethical and even spiritual. Pleasant and unpleasant mental feeling are termed respectively *saumanasya* or joy and *daumanasya* or sorrow. It is of interest to observe that while the latter can be hedonic only, the former possesses a positive ethical value and can be not only 'healthy' in the technical sense (see p.63) but even karmically neutral. *Upekṣā* has an even wider connotation. It can mean not only hedonic indifference, both sensational and emotional, but also that positive state of spiritual balance or equanimity in respect of worldly things which plays so vital a part in the attainment of Supreme Enlightenment, being in fact reckoned, in this higher sense, as one of the seven *bodhyaṅgas* or 'Enlightenment-factors'.

(3) *Saṁjñā* (Pāli *saññā*) or perception is of six kinds, one for each of the five senses and one for the mind. Its function is twofold, consisting in the referring of a particular feeling to its appropriate basis, whether to one of the five physical senses or to the mind, as well as the awareness of the characteristics, real or imaginary, by which an object either of sense or thought is, or may hereafter be, recognized. It may also be either general or specific, the latter kind being that wherein a certain salient feature of perception is made the sole or at least the principal content of consciousness.

(4) By the *saṁskāras* (Pāli *saṅkhāras*) are meant, in this context, not conditioned things in general (see p.55), nor the formative psychological factors (see p.68), but all mental phenomena whatsoever, with the exception of *vedanā*, *saṁjñā*, and *vijñāna*. As such the term corresponds to what are known, in the Abhidharma classification, as the *caitta-dharmas* (Pāli *cetasika-dhammas*) or 'mental concomitants' (here including *vedanā* and *saṁjñā*, separately enumerated in the five-*skandha* classification) which come or tend to come into operation with the arising of a particular type of consciousness. These mental concomitants are forty-six in number according to the Sarvāstivādins, fifty-one according to the Vijñānavadins, and fifty-two according to

the Theravādins. Despite minor differences of enumeration and classification, the list is substantially the same for all three schools. Each distributes the mental concomitants into various categories according to whether they arise in conjunction with all types of consciousness, healthy, unhealthy, and neutral, or in conjunction only with healthy and neutral, or only with unhealthy, states of consciousness. The Sarvāstivādins and Vijñānavadins reckon an additional category consisting of those mental concomitants which cannot, according to them, be included in any of the categories already mentioned.

(5) *Vijñāna* (Pāli *viññāṇa*) or discriminating consciousness is according to the Sarvāstivādins in itself only one, though sixfold in function inasmuch as it arises in dependence on the contact of the six sense-organs, including the mind, with their respective objects. The Theravādins, however, distinguish from the ethical point of view eighty-nine types of consciousness, twenty-one being karmically healthy, eleven karmically unhealthy, and fifty-five karmically neutral. The Vijñānavadins, who continue and develop the Abhidharma tradition of the Sarvāstivādins, count eight *vijñānas*. The two extra ones are the *kliśto-mano-vijñāna* or 'defiled mind-consciousness' and the *ālaya-vijñāna* or 'store consciousness', which occupies an important place in the philosophy of this school. All three schools agree in regarding every 'unit' of consciousness as momentary (*kṣaṇika*) and as arising in dependence on a certain complex of conditions.

From this fivefold Buddhist analysis of the individual being, of which only a sketch has here been given, it is obvious that corresponding to the term 'man' (*pudgala*), or to such terms as 'being' (*sattva*), 'living being' (*jīva*), and 'self' (*ātman*), there exists no unchanging substantial entity but only an ever-changing stream of physical and psychical (including mental and spiritual) events outside which no such entity can be discerned. Hence there can be no such thing, either, as human nature in the sense of a fixed and determinate quality or condition holding good of such an entity at all times and places and under all possible circumstances. Human nature is in reality a no-nature. Though capable of unspeakable wickedness man is not, for that reason, essentially and by very definition a miserable sinner, as some believe; neither is he 'in reality' a stainless immortal spirit, as supposed by others. Man is in fact indefinable.

This is the very conclusion reached from similar premises by the French existentialist Jean-Paul Sartre. Explaining what Existentialism means by speaking of man as the being whose existence comes before its essence, he says:

> If man as the existentialist sees him is not definable, it is because to begin with he is nothing. He will not be anything until later, and then he will be what he makes of himself. Thus, there is no human nature, because there is no God to have a conception of it. Man simply is. Not that he is simply what he conceives himself to be, but he is what he wills, and as he conceives himself after already existing – as he wills to be after that leap towards existence. Man is nothing else but that which he makes of himself. That is the first principle of Existentialism.[47]

It is also the first principle of Buddhism. In Buddhism, however, the range of possibilities of conditioned existence open to man by virtue of his 'central' position in the universe is incomparably wider than that envisaged by Existentialism. Moreover, in Buddhism the principle possesses an infinitely greater depth. As we have already seen, the mundane centrality of human life in respect of other forms of sentient existence is analogous to the transcendental centrality of Buddhahood. This means that man can not only make of himself whatever he wants to be but also cease altogether from making himself anything whatsoever. Existentialism goes as far as to assert that human nature is a no-nature. Buddhism, however, proclaims that this no-nature is Buddha-nature. Man realizes 'his' Buddha-nature when the energy of which 'he' is the expression no longer craves manifestation in any other form of conditioned existence.[48] Since this happens neither automatically nor instantaneously but by pursuing a regular sequence of steps with energy and determination over a certain period of time we again come back to the Path.

13

THE STAGES OF THE PATH

THIS SUBDIVISION of the Dharma, being the central one and pragmatically the most valuable, ought to be the clearest and simplest. In fact, however, it is often the most complex, not to say complicated. Such a state of affairs has come about due principally to two causes. Firstly, formulations of the Path as consisting of a specific set of moral and spiritual qualities or a particular sequence of steps and stages are so numerous, so rich in variety, and withal so often seemingly divergent, that what the Path is *in principle*, apart from all such formulations, is as much lost sight of as the original central trunk of the banyan tree amid the vast proliferation of supporting stems. Secondly, each school of Buddhism has tended to interpret the Path, not only in terms of the common doctrinal tradition, but also in accordance with its own distinctive tenets. In this account we shall be concerned with what the Path is in principle and with the formulation that seems to exhibit that principle with the greatest distinctness.

Man, as we have seen, is by nature indefinable. Human life represents a transformation of energy in dependence on which any other transformation of energy, mundane or transcendental, can arise. This is not to say that it is possible for any one such transformation to arise in immediate dependence on any other. As when a seed produces a flower, or when rough ore is smelted into gold and the refined metal wrought into an ornament, a number of intermediate steps connect the beginning with the end of the process. In the case of conditioned sentient existence the transformation takes place through the operation of the laws in accordance with which individualized consciousness determines being, that is to say, through karma and *karma-vipāka*, while the intermediate steps are the twelve *nidānas* depicted in the outermost circle of the Wheel of Life. In the case of the higher evolution from a mundane to a transcendental consciousness the laws governing the process are represented by the technical terms *mārga* and *phala*, 'path' and 'fruit', the intermediate steps being set forth in the negative and positive counterparts of the twelve *nidānas*.

These two sets of terms, that is to say karma and *karma-vipāka* on the one hand, and *mārga* and *phala* on the other, correspond respectively to the first two and the second two of the Four Noble Truths. In the formula of the Truths, however, the sequence is not deductive from cause to effect, but inductive from effect to cause. Thus karma corresponds to the second Noble Truth, the cause of suffering (*duḥkha-samudaya*), in this case craving (*tṛṣṇā*), and *karma-vipāka* to the first Noble Truth, namely suffering (*duḥkha*); similarly, *mārga* corresponds to the fourth Noble Truth, the way (*mārga*) leading to the cessation of suffering, i.e. to Nirvāṇa. More philosophically speaking, karma and *karma-vipāka*, the first two Noble Truths, and the arising of the twelve *nidānas* from ignorance to old age, disease, and death, represent a process of reaction in a cyclical order between two opposites, such as pleasure and pain, virtue and vice, healthy and unhealthy mental states, as a result of which what is popularly termed 'the world' or saṁsāra comes into existence. *Mārga* and *phala*, the second two Noble Truths, and the non-arising of the twelve *nidānas* from ignorance to birth, old age, disease, and death, represent not merely the counter-process of cessation, through which 'the world' or saṁsāra passes out of existence, disappears, or is annihilated, but also a process of reaction in a progressive order between two things of the same genus, the succeeding factor augmenting the effect of the preceding one, through or by means of which the gross, turbulent, and mutually conflicting energies inherent in saṁsāra are progressively refined, transmuted, and transformed into the state of harmonious and beneficent activity popularly termed Nirvāṇa.

This process of reaction *in a progressive order* constitutes the basic principle of the Path taught by the Buddha as distinct from the various formulations wherein, for pedagogical reasons, the principle is given concrete expression. As the embodiment of this 'spiral' principle, moreover, and not because it represents a 'golden mediocrity' of the Aristotelian type or a half-hearted spirit of compromise, the

Path receives its primary designation as the Middle Path or Way (*madhyama-mārga*). In the *Nidāna-vagga* of the *Saṁyutta-Nikāya* the number of intermediate steps that connect the samsaric beginning with the nirvanic 'end' of the process whereby mundane mind is transformed into transcendental mind appear as a series of positive counterparts to the negative process of the cessation of the twelve *nidānas*.

In the canonical passage referred to the twelve factors constituting what may be termed the positive and progressive aspect of the *pratītya-samutpāda* are enumerated three times, once in descending and twice in ascending order. According to the latter mode of enumeration there is causal association of *saddhā* with *dukkha*, *pāmojja* with *saddhā*, *pīti* with *pāmojja*, *passaddhi* with *pīti*, *sukha* with *passaddhi*, *samādhi* with *sukha*, *yathābhūtañāṇadassana* with *samādhi*, *nibbidā* with *yathābhūtañāṇadassana*, *virāga* with *nibbidā*, *vimutti* with *virāga*, and *khaye ñāṇa* with *vimutti*.[49]

(1) *Dukkha* (Sanskrit *duḥkha*) or suffering. This is not only the first member of the nirvanic but according to our present text the last of the samsaric series, here replacing the more usual *jarāmaraṇa* or old age and death. As the second of the two *nidānas* which make up the result-process of the future life it corresponds to *vedanā* or feeling, the last of the five *nidānas* constituting the result-process of the present life (see p.68). It also corresponds to the first Noble Truth or, more generally, to 'the world' as presented to the senses and the mind. Upon the attitude that we take up towards it depends our future fate. If we react with craving (*tṛṣṇā*), the first *nidāna* of the action-process of the present life, then we become once again caught up in the process of reaction in a cyclic order between opposites, and the Wheel of Life continues to revolve. If we refuse to react in this manner and respond instead with a healthy mental attitude we are carried out of saṁsāra into the process of reaction in a progressive order between two counterparts or complements, at the 'end' of which lies Nirvāṇa. *Vedanā* in general and *dukkha* in particular thus represent the point of intersection of the two different orders of reaction. It is the point of choice and decision, a choice, moreover, that confronts us not on two or three momentous occasions only but every instant of our lives.

Theoretically, of course, a total annihilation of craving, with a consequent instantaneous realization of Nirvāṇa, is possible at any time. In practice it is impossible. Whenever such cases seem to occur they will be found, on examination, to be the result of prolonged preparation. Nor might it be advisable to attempt a really instantaneous total destruction of craving even if this could be achieved. As with a sudden slamming on of brakes when the train is going at full speed such an achievement is likely to result in a derailment. What is needed is a smooth and gradual application of brakes. However quickly, or however slowly, they may be applied, the mechanical process of application consists of a certain number of stages. In the present series the first of these stages is represented by the second *nidāna*. In causal association with *dukkha* arises

(2) *Saddhā* (Sanskrit *śraddhā*) or faith. Though the Indian term is by no means equivalent to 'belief' in the Christian sense of accepting as literally true statements about God, the Fall of Man, the Virgin Birth, etc. for which there is no evidence, we have nevertheless rendered it by 'faith' in order to emphasize its definitely emotional character. *Saddhā* is, in fact, the healthy counterpart of *taṇhā* (Sanskrit *tṛṣṇā*), thirst or craving. It develops when, as the result of our experience of the painful, unsatisfactory, and frustrating nature of samsaric existence, we begin to 'place the heart' (the literal meaning of the verb with which *saddhā* is connected) not so much on the conditioned as on the Unconditioned. At first this is no more than a vague intermittent stirring of the emotions, hesitant and confused. But as it grows stronger, and as its object comes more clearly into focus, it develops into *saddhā* proper, that is to say into faith in the Buddha, the Dharma, and the Sangha, the first being primary, the other two secondary. Taken in this more definite sense *saddhā* may be defined as the heartfelt acknowledgement of the fact that the historical personality Gautama is the Buddha or Enlightened One, grounded firstly on the intuitive response that arises out of the depth of our heart by reason of the affinity existing between his actual and our potential Buddhahood, and secondly on the sensible evidence and rational proofs of his Enlightenment afforded us by the records of his life and teachings. When by following the Dharma we experience for ourselves the successive stages of the Path this faith, without losing its emotional character, becomes consolidated into confidence. At the stage with which we are now concerned *saddhā* expresses itself as generosity (*dāna*) and ethical behaviour (*sīla*), which as we shall see later, are the first two *pāramitās*. Through the practice of these virtues the mind is purged of its feelings of guilt, repentance, and remorse, and thus a

healthy mental attitude is created. In causal association with *saddhā* arises

(3) *Pāmojja* (Sanskrit *prāmodya*) or satisfaction and delight. Negatively this is the feeling experienced on becoming aware that one has nothing with which to reproach oneself as to morals. As such it is equivalent to the possession of an easy conscience. Positively it is the feeling of cheerfulness and content that arises in a man's mind out of his awareness that he is following the path of virtue. In Buddhism great importance is attached to this state. A mind that is disturbed by the recollection of a breach of moral precepts is incapable of concentration, so that the way to further progress is barred. Meditation masters such as Chih-I, the founder of the Chinese Tien-t'ai School, therefore recommend that before embarking on the practice of *dhyāna* one who has been guilty of any such lapse should undergo various observances, including confession, repentance, ritual worship of the Buddha, and the ceremonial recitation of sūtras, for a certain number of days, weeks, or months, or until such time as his mind is freed from the burden of guilt and again feels fresh, clear, and light.[50] Whether induced in the former or in the latter manner, *pāmojja* represents a blending (*modanā*) of the various elements in the emotive aspects of concentration, because the absence or resolution of the conflicts which arise whenever a man's behaviour fails to accord with his own ethical ideals inevitably promotes a sense of unity, harmony, and integration. As this develops and grows stronger, in causal association with *pāmojja* arises

(4) *Pīti* (Sanskrit *prīti*) or interest, enthusiasm, joy, rapture, ecstasy. This *nidāna*, the development of which marks the transition from the *kāma-loka* to the *rūpa-loka* or in other words to a level of consciousness higher than that of the 'normal' waking state, arises naturally and spontaneously in the course of meditation practice as methodical concentration on a given object becomes more and more intense. Just as in the case of the previous *nidāna* the absence of any conflict between one's ethical ideals and one's actions produces a feeling of satisfaction and delight, so *pīti* represents the much greater sense of relief which comes about as the result of the liberation of the emotional energies which had been locked up in the deep-seated conflicts of the unconscious mind. Guenther therefore quite rightly speaks of it as 'a driving and even overwhelming emotion'.[51] As, by a sort of psychological chain-reaction, greater and greater quantities of energy

are released, *pīti* becomes more and more transporting. Tradition therefore distinguishes a number of different degrees of *pīti*. In the words of the *Aṭṭhasālinī*,

> Rapture is of five kinds: the lesser thrill, momentary rapture, flooding rapture, all-pervading rapture and transporting rapture. Of these, the lesser thrill is only able to raise the hairs of the body; the momentary rapture is like the production of lightning moment by moment; like waves breaking on the seashore, the flooding rapture descends on the body and breaks; [when all-pervading rapture arises, the whole body is completely surcharged, blown like a full bladder or like a mountain cavern pouring forth a mighty flood of water;][52] the transporting rapture is strong, and lifts the body up to the extent of launching it in the air.[53]

From these descriptions it is evident that far from being only mental, *pīti* is accompanied by a variety of physical innervations. It is this that distinguishes it from *sukha*, the next *nidāna* but one. Hence before *sukha* can arise, in causal association with *pīti* arises

(5) *Passaddhi* (Sanskrit *praśrabdhi*) or calmness, repose, tranquillity, serenity. When the energies which in the process of liberation were experienced as *pīti* have been, as it were, exhausted, the accompanying physical innervations subside and in the ensuing mood of relaxation the attention is first disengaged and then wholly withdrawn from the body and its concerns. Consequently there also takes place a subsidence of feeling, in the sense of pleasurable sensation, and a subsidence of the perception and motivation derived therefrom. *Passaddhi* is therefore spoken of as twofold: that of the mind (*citta*) and that of the body (*kāya*) – here not the physical body but the mental factors of feeling (*vedanā*), perception (*saññā*), and motivation (*saṅkhāra*) collectively. It would be a mistake, though, to regard *passaddhi* as a merely passive state. Not only does it tranquillize consciousness and the mental factors but also, by easing strain and tension, bring about in them a condition of functional lightness, plasticity, adaptability, readiness, and directness. *Passaddhi* is thus a state of extreme refinement and delicacy of feeling, in causal association with which therefore arises

(6) *Sukha* or bliss. Though the word has a very wide range of meaning, including that of pleasurable bodily sensation, it stands in this context for the apparently causeless feeling of intense happiness

that wells up from the depths of his being when, the physical innervations associated with *pīti* having subsided, the meditator is no longer aware of the physical body. When discussing *vedanā* or feeling we saw that the term covers not only sensation, or hedonic feeling, but also emotion, which can be not only hedonic but ethical and spiritual. In the terms of this *sukha* may be defined as non-hedonic spiritual happiness. The author of the *Aṭṭhasālini*, according to whom *pīti* belongs to the *saṅkhāra-khandha* and *sukha* to the *vedanā-khandha*, endeavours to exhibit the true meaning of the present *nidāna* by contrasting it with *pīti* by means of an apt similitude.

> A man who, travelling along the path through a great desert and overcome by the heat, is thirsty and desirous of drink, if he saw a man on the way, would ask, 'Where is water?' The other would say, 'Beyond the wood is a dense forest with a natural lake. Go there, and you will get some.' He hearing these words would be glad and delighted and as he went would see lotus leaves, etc., fallen on the ground and become more glad and delighted. Going onwards, he would see men with wet clothes and hair, hear the sound of wild fowl and pea-fowl, etc., see the dense forest of green like a net of jewels growing by the edge of the natural lake, he would see the water lily, the lotus, the white lily, etc., growing in the lake, he would see the clear transparent water, he would be all the more glad and delighted, would descend into the natural lake, bathe and drink at pleasure and, his oppression being allayed, he would eat the fibres and stalks of the lilies, adorn himself with the blue lotus, carry on his shoulders the roots of the mandālaka, ascend from the lake, put on his clothes, dry the bathing cloth in the sun, and in the cool shade where the breeze blew ever so gently lay himself down and say: 'O bliss! O bliss!' Thus should this illustration be applied: The time of gladness and delight from when he heard of the natural lake and the dense forest till he saw the water is like rapture [*pīti*] having the manner of gladness and delight at the object in view. The time when, after his bath and drink he laid himself down in the cool shade, saying, 'O bliss! O bliss!' etc., is the sense of ease [*sukha*] grown strong, established in that mode of enjoying the taste of the object.[54]

As the comparison suggests, *sukha* in this context is not something which comes and goes in a moment, or which touches one superficially. On the contrary it is an experience of so enthralling and overwhelming a character that the meditator is occupied and absorbed, even immersed, in it, at times for days on end, to the exclusion of all other interests.

Non-Buddhist mystics who reach this stage, especially those belonging to schools which, like those of the Vedānta, define Reality in terms of bliss (*ānanda*), are prone to imagine that such an attainment is sufficient evidence of their having realized God, or Brahman, or whatever for them constitutes the ultimate goal of life. To the Buddhist, however, the experience of meditative bliss is only a milestone on the way, and even while most deeply immersed in it he is careful to cultivate an attitude of detachment towards it and to avoid the mistake of settling down in it as though it was a permanent and final achievement. The Scriptures more than once represent the Buddha as saying with reference to his own early practice of the *dhyānas*,

> Yet the happiness which in that way arose in me, could not obsess my mind.[55]

At the same time neither the Buddha nor his followers have ever tended to underestimate the role of happiness in the spiritual life. In a passage of striking force and beauty Lama Anagarika Govinda writes:

> Out of the 121 classes of consciousness which are discussed in [Theravādin] Buddhist psychology, sixty-three are accompanied by joy and only three are painful, while the remaining fifty-five classes are indifferent. A stronger refutation of pessimism than this statement is hardly possible. How deluded is man, that he mainly dwells in those three painful states of consciousness, though there are overwhelmingly more possibilities of happiness! But what a perspective this knowledge opens to those who strive earnestly, what an incentive even to the weak! The more man progresses, the more radiant and joyful will be his consciousness. Happiness, indeed, may be called a characteristic of progress. In the course of its development it becomes more and more sublime, until it grows into that serenity which radiates from the face of the Enlightened One with that subtle smile in which wisdom, compassion, and all-embracing love are mingled.[56]

What the Buddhist tradition in all its branches is concerned to emphasize is that however natural, healthy, and intense the experience of meditative bliss may be, the meditator must be careful not to allow it to overpower his mindfulness in such a way that the path to further progress is barred. The immediate nature of that progress is indicated by a number of scriptural aphorisms, such as 'The mind of the happy one becomes concentrated'.[57] Thus in causal association with *sukha* arises

(7) *Samādhi* or 'concentration'. Like that of several other terms in the series, the meaning of *samādhi* tends to vary according to context. At its simplest it is mere one-pointedness of mind, or concentrated attention on a single object. Such one-pointedness may be associated with a morally healthy or unhealthy, or with a neutral, consciousness. The minds of the fornicator and the murderer are certainly concentrated on their respective objects, but being concentrated through lust in the one case and hatred in the other their concentration is said to be unhealthy. *Samādhi* is therefore properly not one-pointedness of mind in general but healthy one-pointedness, *kauśalya-ekagrata-citta*, (Pāli *kuśala-ekaggata-citta*).

In connection with the systematic cultivation of this *nidāna* through the practice of definite spiritual exercises three degrees of depth and intensity of *samādhi* are distinguished: preparatory concentration – when the mind is fixed on the gross external object pertaining to the particular practice adopted, say on the process of respiration, an image of a Buddha or bodhisattva, or the sound of a mantra audibly repeated; intermediate concentration – when the mind is fixed on the subtle and frequently luminous counterpart that arises when the gross object has been attended to for a sufficient length of time; and full concentration – which is attained when the mind is absorbed in the subtle counterpart to such an extent that it becomes as it were one with it and no longer experiences it as something objective and external. Full concentration corresponds to *dhyāna* (Pāli *jhāna*). This in turn consists of eight degrees, four belonging to the 'form' (*rūpa*) and four to the 'formless' (*arūpa*) plane, each degree more refined than the one preceding.

In the first *rūpa-dhyāna* is present a residue of mental activity, besides the experience of *pīti* and *sukha*; in the second, mental activity subsides entirely, and *pīti* and *sukha* alone remain associated with *samādhi*; in the third *dhyāna* even *pīti*, comparatively the grosser factor, disappears; and in the fourth, *sukha* is replaced by *upekṣā*. Despite the drily analytical manner in which some of the older texts tabulate these experiences one is not to suppose that the mental content can really be thus split up into various component factors which literally appear or disappear as concentration deepens. What the series of *rūpa-dhyānas* in fact represents is the progressive unification of consciousness, especially of its cognitive and affective aspects, on the basis of a stability which the unification itself progressively strengthens and makes more profound.

The four *arūpa-dhyānas* appear not to carry this process of unification any further but to render the fully concentrated mind subtler and as it were more transparent, as well as simultaneously broader and more universal, by confronting it with ever sublimer cosmic objects. These *dhyānas* are: that of the sphere of infinite (space *ākāśānatyāyatana, Pāli ākāsānañcāyatana*), of infinite consciousness (*vijñānānantyāyatana*, Pāli *viññāṇañcāyatana*), of no-thing-ness (*ākiñcanyāyatana*, Pāli *ākiñcaññāyatana*), and of neither-perception-nor-non-perception (*naivasaṁjñānāsaṁjñāyatana*, Pāli *nevasaññānāsaññāyatana*). Some scholars are of opinion that the second set of four *dhyānas*, though known to the Buddha, was added to the first set so as to form a single continuous series only after his parinirvāṇa. Be that as it may, there is certainly a problem to be cleared up in connection with the Master's experience of the *dhyānas* the discussion of which will, even in the absence of a final solution, help to elucidate the true meaning of *samādhi* in the present context.

In the *Mahāsaccaka Sutta*, one of the great autobiographical discourses of the Pāli Canon, the Buddha describes to the Jain ascetic Saccaka, whom he addresses by his clan name, the course of fearful asceticism to which he had subjected himself prior to the attainment of Enlightenment. After relating how the attempt had failed he continued:

> This, Aggivessana, occurred to me: 'I know that while my father, the Śākyan, was ploughing, and I was sitting in the cool shade of a rose-apple tree, aloof from pleasures of the senses, aloof from unskilled states of mind, entering on the first meditation, which is accompanied by initial thought and discursive thought, is born of aloofness, and is rapturous and joyful, and while abiding therein, I thought: "Now could this be a way to awakening?" Then, following on my mindfulness, Aggivessana, there was the consciousness: This is itself the Way to awakening.'[58]

He then described how, after attaining the remaining three *rūpa-dhyānas*, he had developed the three superknowledges (*abhijñās*), eradicated the three biases (*āsravas*), and finally attained *sambodhi*. From the passage quoted it is evident that during the whole course of his 'noble quest', from the time of leaving his father's mansion to the time of abandoning the path of extreme asceticism, the Buddha had not experienced even the first of the *rūpa-dhyānas*. Yet earlier in the same discourse, as well as in the *Ariyapariyesana Sutta*, the Buddha relates his attainment of the spheres of 'no-thing-ness' and 'neither-perception-nor-non-perception', the last two *arūpa-dhyānas*, as already described (see p.15). If the two sets of *dhyānas* really constitute a single continuous series of meditative attainments how is it possible that the Buddha should have experienced the seventh and eighth members of the series before he had experienced the first? While the possibility that according to the Buddha himself the two sets of *dhyānas* are discontinuous and were arranged as a single series only later cannot be ruled out, there are other considerations relating to the true nature of *samādhi* which may help explain the discrepancy.

The distinguishing feature of the Buddha's boyhood experience of *samādhi* is its spontaneity; it came of itself, naturally and without effort. His later experience of the *dhyānas*, including that of the spheres of no-thing-ness and neither-perception-nor-non-perception, on the contrary seem to have been achieved at the cost of great exertion, as a result of a stupendous exercise of will-power involving the conscious and deliberate forcing of all his energies into a single narrow channel. What the sudden flashing of his boyhood experience into his mind probably conveyed to the Buddha was that the Way consisted not in achieving with grim determination goals fixed for itself by the conscious mind without reference to the total psyche but in the harmonious unfoldment, in and through mindfulness, of one's deepest potentialities. The way to Enlightenment was a middle way between making no effort at all and intellectually directed effort. In other words the Buddha discovered that the attainment of *samyak-samādhi*, the final stage of the Eightfold Path, as distinguished from the forcible fixation of the mind on any object however healthy or for however long a time, involves not merely the exercise of the understanding and the will but the transformation and integration of the total psyche in all its sublimest heights and most abysmal depths.

For this reason the practice of *samādhi* can never be reduced to the practice of a certain series of concentration-exercises or to a special technique, much less still to a matter of professional expertise. It was their awareness of this danger which prompted the Sōtō branch of the Zen School to insist that one does not sit to meditate: one sits to sit. Not all schools of meditation, not even all Buddhist schools, have succeeded in steering so clear of the danger. Hindu yoga is exclusively a system of techniques; however efficacious as a means of physical and mental hygiene, it therefore possesses by itself no spiritual value. The so-called New Burmese Method of Satipaṭṭhāna, with its system of grades, examinations, certificates, and titles, even apart from the other objections that have been urged against it, would seem open, in the case of some at least of its exponents, to similar criticism.

Yet one need not go to the extreme of denying that techniques have any place at all in the practice of meditation, thus avoiding the Scylla of technism only at the cost of falling a prey to the Charybdis of quietism. As the whole progressive sequence of causally associated factors leading up to *samādhi*, the present factor, itself serves to illustrate, the following of the spiritual path is from stage to stage less a matter of egoistically willed achievement as of a growth, in and through awareness, of the total psyche. As Tagore says,

> No hurried path of success, forcibly cut by the greed of result, can be the true path.[59]

Energetic recourse to techniques of concentration by one who had not cultivated the preceding *nidānas* could result in complete frustration or produce, if apparently successful, either a morbid state of hypnotic fixation or a violent reaction from those parts of the psyche which had not co-operated in the attempt. In the opposite case, however, that of one who had cultivated the preceding *nidānas*, even the moderate practice of a concentration-technique would be sufficient to induce profound *samādhi*-experience. It might even be enough for him to see a beautiful flower, or to look at something bright and shining. For him who had cultivated the five previous *nidānas* to perfection the *samādhi*-experience would arise as soon as he seated himself and was mindful; he would not need to 'meditate'. This seems to have been the case, practically, of the Buddha.

Diseased or injured seed will produce only a deformed and stunted plant. Unless the preceding factor has been cultivated, if not to perfection, at least to an advanced degree, the factor which arises next in causal association with it will be only a caricature of what it ought to be. Though true of every factor, this is particularly true of *samādhi*. *Samādhi* is the last of the *laukika* (Pāli *lokiya*), or mundane, factors; the one immediately succeeding it will be the first of the *lokuttara* or transcendental factors which, as regress from them is impossible, constitute the Path to Enlightenment proper. Scriptural aphorism indicates this supremely important, indeed crucial, transition, in such words as 'The concentrated mind sees things as they really are.' But if the *samādhi* is not true *samādhi*, but a mere forcible fixation of attention disrupting one part of the psyche from the rest there will arise in causal association with it nothing but delusions; one may imagine one has realized what one has not: in the case of a Buddhist, he may mistake purely intellectual reminiscence of the Dharma for actual penetration of its import. In any case, instead of safely traversing the point where Wheel and Spiral intersect one will, unknowingly, become more deeply and inextricably involved in saṁsāra than ever. Only in causal association with true *samādhi* arises

(8) *Yathābhūtañāṇadassana* (Sanskrit *yathābhūtajñānadarśana*), 'Knowledge and Vision of Things As They Are' or 'According to Reality'. What needs above all to be emphasized in connection with this *nidāna*, with the arising of which we enter on the Transcendental Path, is the fact of its being essentially an experience. The preceding *nidānas* were, of course, also experiences, in their case experiences, in varying degrees, of psychic wholeness; but the knowledge and vision now attained differs from them in being also an experience of the ultimate meaning of things. As the terminal part of the compound suggests, far from resembling knowledge in the ordinary sense this experience is, rather, analogous to physical sight. The same comparison is implied in the word *vipaśyana* (Pāli *vipassanā*) or 'insight', which, in its more restricted sense, may be regarded as synonymous with the present *nidāna*. Both terms are moreover related in meaning to *prajñā* (Pāli *paññā*) or 'wisdom'; the difference being – though the usage is by no means rigid – that whereas they stand for the first intermittent flashings of insight *prajñā* represents its steady beam-like radiation: *bodhi* or *sambodhi* is the same faculty when it has succeeded in saturating the entire psychic contents and organizing them around itself in a harmonious system.

Apart from its intrinsic importance, the fact that *yathābhūtañāṇa-dassana* stands for a transcendental experience has been emphasized because the term itself and those which are approximately synonymous with it have been subject to so long a process of scholastic elaboration that it might otherwise be overlooked. Just as there is the danger of *samādhi* being confused with the practice of concentration-exercises, so this *nidāna* might be identified with an understanding of the complex conceptual formulations of it that have been worked out over the centuries from Kātyāyana to Vasubandhu, and from Buddhaghosa and Anuruddha to Ledi Sayadaw. This does not however constitute an objection to such an elaboration, which as a means of giving the widest intellectual expression to the transcendental content of the experience is on its own level a quite legitimate activity. Though a rare orchid cannot really be valued in terms of money, the fact that a florist prices it at so many pounds sterling may stimulate the insensitive into a vague awareness of its beauty.

Historically perhaps the earliest, and 'philosophically' the most important, is that formulation according to which *vipaśyana* or *prajñā* – they are hardly differentiated at this stage – consists in seeing the true nature of all conditioned things, that is, in seeing them as characterized by impermanence, pain, insubstantiality, and ugliness as already described in a previous chapter. Inasmuch as, according to the explicit teaching of the great Mahāyāna schools, the conditioned in its depth is non-different from the Unconditioned, insight into the one becomes eventually insight into the other. The fact of this ultimate non-duality finds expression in the correspondence which all schools of Buddhism, both Hīnayāna and Mahāyāna, acknowledge to exist between the three characteristics (or first three perversities) and the three *vimokṣas* (Pāli *vimokkhas*). The latter represent different approaches to, or dimensions of, Nirvāṇa, access to any of them being obtainable through the cultivation of insight into the corresponding characteristic. They will be discussed in the next chapter.

As already insisted, the present *nidāna* is of crucial importance in the series as it represents the point of transition from the mundane to the transcendental order of existence. One who reaches this stage, for whom through insight into the three characteristics there arises Knowledge and Vision of Things As They Are, ceases to be a *pṛthagjana* (Pāli *puthujjana*), or ordinary man, and becomes one of the Noble, an *ārya* (Pāli *ariya*). Insight being of varying degrees of profundity, the

Noble do not all belong to one grade of attainment but make up a spiritual, or rather a transcendental, hierarchy. This hierarchy constitutes the Ārya Sangha (see Chapter 15). At the bottom rung of the great ladder stands the *śrotopanna* (Pāli *sotāpanna*) or Stream-Winner who, as his designation suggests, having escaped from the vortex of saṁsāra joyously abandons himself to the irresistible sweep of the mighty current that will infallibly bear him one day to the infinite ocean of Nirvāṇa. From the point of view from which the two are seen as a duality, the nearer one approaches Nirvāṇa the further behind he leaves saṁsāra. Thus in causal association with *yathābhūtañāṇa-dassana* arises

(9) *Nibbidā* (Sanskrit *nirvid, nirveda*) or disgust. As this *nidāna,* like the four other members of the transcendental series, remains associated with the state of perfect psychic wholeness termed *samādhi,* it would be a mistake to regard it as being merely a movement of recoil or withdrawal from the imperfections of the world in the ordinary psychological sense as, in fact, its translation by such words as disgust, aversion, and repulsion tends to suggest. The latter type of reaction is, of course, a common enough phenomenon in both worldly and religious life, and in the latter sphere may sometimes play a quite legitimate preliminary role; but it must never be confused with *nibbidā,* which it resembles only analogically. Disgust and aversion are generally rooted in unhealthy mental attitudes. *Nibbidā,* however, springs from an insight which, though based on healthy mental factors, is itself neither healthy nor unhealthy, but transcendental. The way in which insight into the three characteristics of conditioned things results in a 'serene withdrawal' from them as we might paraphrase the term – though in ordinary parlance serenity excludes the idea of speed – is the main point of Buddhaghosa's apt illustration of the relation between these two experiences.

> A man thought to catch a fish, it seems, so he took a fishing net and cast it in the water. He put his hand into the mouth of the net under the water and seized a snake by the neck. He was glad, thinking 'I have caught a fish.' In the belief that he had caught a big fish, he lifted it up to see. When he had seen three marks [on its head] he perceived that it was a snake, and he was terrified. He saw danger, felt revulsion for what he had seen, and desired to be delivered from it. Contriving a means of deliverance, he unwrapped [the coils from]

> his arm, and when he had weakened the snake by swinging it two or three times round his head, he flung it away, crying 'Go, foul snake!'[60]

Quite apart from the fact that three more *nidānas* remain to be developed, withdrawal is far from being the last word even at this stage. Though the fact was made fully explicit only by the Mahāyāna, inasmuch as *sambodhi* is not in the ultimate sense a personal acquisition, however much the structure of language may compel us to speak of it as such, concern for the temporal and spiritual welfare of others cannot be entirely excluded at any stage of the Path. Withdrawal must therefore be conjoined with compassion (*karuṇā*). In the beautiful words of Tsongkhapa:

> But since that withdrawal, too, unless controlled
> By a pure 'mind-generation' does not become the cause
> Of unsurpassed Enlightenment's consummate felicity,
> Intelligent ones should generate the excellent bodhi-mind.[61]

This bodhicitta or Will to Supreme Enlightenment not for one's own sake only but for the benefit of all sentient beings arises out of the conjunction of the present movement of serene withdrawal from the conditioned, viewed as impermanent, painful, and insubstantial, with the paradoxical feeling of compassion for sentient beings who, from the previous stage onwards, have been recognized as in reality no-beings. According to a popular Far Eastern exegesis the Buddha is called Tathāgata because he 'thus goes' (*tathā-gata*) out of the world through wisdom and 'thus comes' (*tathā-āgata*) back into it through compassion.

Nibbidā, therefore, at its own level of attainment, is to be confused no more with spiritual individualism and escapism than with a mere psychological reaction. This clarification will help us avoid an analogous misunderstanding of the next *nidāna*, to which attention must now be directed. In causal association with *nibbidā* arises

(10) *Virāga* (Sanskrit *vairāgya*) or 'dispassion'. Having recognized the true nature of conditioned things and finally 'withdrawn' from them the mind has now reached a stage where they are no more able to disturb or move it than the soft clouds nestling on the lower slopes of the Himalayas have the power to shake to its foundations the loftiest peak. This is the mental state of unruffled tranquillity which Buddhist art strives to depict in its vision of the majestically calm figure of the

Buddha seated, with eyes half closed, beneath the bodhi tree, while Māra's three daughters exhibit their charms, and the demon armies brandish their weapons, in vain. It is the attainment hymned in the eleventh verse of the *Maṅgala Sutta* as the culmination of all temporal and spiritual weal:

> He whose mind does not shake
> When touched by the [eight] worldly conditions,
> Being sorrowless, stainless and secure –
> This is the greatest blessing.

Despite the poverty of our vocabulary, which forces us to apply analogically to transcendental realizations terms derived from mundane experiences, the exalted state here described is much more than an ethical state of impassibility, like the Stoic apatheia, or a merely psychological condition of equanimity. To an even greater extent than its predecessor *virāga* is essentially the consequence of a profound 'metaphysical' cognition. This cognition, penetrating from the emptiness of the conditioned to the emptiness of the Unconditioned, comes to rest in the realization that all *dharmas* whatsoever, conditioned and unconditioned, are equally *śūnyatā* and that they are, therefore, in respect of their emptiness, identical. At the level of Buddhahood this type of realization is known as *samatā-jñāna*, the wisdom of sameness or equality, and is symbolized by the Buddha Ratnasambhava. The conditioned having been seen as in reality unconditionally identical with the Unconditioned there can be no question of any real movement from the one to the other. It is the absence of movement in this sense, and for this reason, that constitutes *virāga*. In causal association with *virāga* there arises, as the penultimate stage of the Path,

(11) *Vimutti* (Sanskrit *vimukti*) or liberation. This is often popularly interpreted in a dualistic sense simply as liberation from saṁsāra, and on its own level the interpretation is a perfectly valid one. But as we have already had occasion to point out, in order to be truly free one has to escape not only from bondage but from liberation, not only from saṁsāra into Nirvāṇa but from Nirvāṇa back into saṁsāra (see p.50). If one gets as it were 'stuck' in Nirvāṇa conceived as a totally distinct entity from saṁsāra, one is, indeed, in a sense free, but it is not the ultimate and absolute freedom, for in another sense one has only become subject to a still more subtle bondage. One can never be

really free so long as ideas, even the most highly refined and spiritualized, are treated as corresponding to ultimately real objects instead of as operative concepts.

Reference to the four degrees, or four successively more comprehensive dimensions, of *śūnyatā*, may help make the point clearer. (a) *Saṁskṛta-śūnyatā* or Emptiness of the Conditioned. Here one recognizes that being devoid of happiness, stability, and true being conditioned things are incapable of yielding any genuine or lasting satisfaction. (b) *Asaṁskṛta-śūnyatā* or Emptiness of the Unconditioned. The Unconditioned is seen as not only devoid of pain and the other characteristics of the conditioned but as being on the contrary a blissful, unchanging, and sovereign entity. These two degrees are represented by the Hīnayāna schools. (c) *Mahā-śūnyatā* or Great Emptiness. At this stage the concept of emptiness is recognized as devoid of ultimate significance. In reality there is no difference between the conditioned and the Unconditioned, an ordinary man and a Buddha. Consequently there is in the ultimate sense neither abandonment of saṁsāra nor attainment of Nirvāṇa. All concepts, even the most sacred, are merely words designating no separate real entities and possessing, therefore, no absolute significance. This degree corresponds to the general standpoint of the Mahāyāna, as exemplified in particular by the *Prajñāpāramitā* or 'Perfection of Wisdom' literature. (d) *Śūnyatā-śūnyatā* or 'Emptiness of Emptiness'. Here the concept of emptiness is itself rejected. As Vimalakīrti meant to convey, when he answered Mañjuśrī's question with a 'thunderous silence', in the ultimate sense nothing can be said. This degree is represented by the Vajrayāna which instead of trying to elaborate a systematic conceptual formulation of this degree concentrates all its energies on the task of actually realizing it in the present life. *Vimutti* corresponds to the third of the four degrees, Great Emptiness. Having transcended the relatively true, yet not absolutely false, distinction between saṁsāra and Nirvāṇa, it moves about as freely in the one as in the other. Hence this is also the stage of Absolute Compassion which, from the standpoint of the conditioned, appears to 'break through' from the Unconditioned in the form of the beneficent activity of Buddhas and bodhisattvas innumerable. However, the ultimate stage of the Path, though now in sight, has still not been reached. The pilgrim must press on to 'the endless end'. In causal association with *vimutti* arises

(12) *Āsavakkhayañāṇa* (Sanskrit *āsravakṣayajñāna*) or Knowledge of the Destruction of the Biases towards sensuous desire (*kāmāsava*), desire for continued existence (*bhavāsava*), and spiritual ignorance (*avijjāsava*). Despite the negative form of the first part of the compound it is far from representing a state of unrelieved annihilation: the emphasis is on the *knowledge* (*ñāṇa*) of the destruction of the *āsavas*. The correctness of this interpretation is sufficiently borne out by the number of times that, in what appear to be very early records, the Buddha's own attainment of *sambodhi* is spoken of in just these terms. Corresponding as it does to the fourth degree of *śūnyatā* in the absolute sense, nothing can be said about it. What little can usefully be said from the relative point of view belongs to the next chapter, when the truth behind the term will appear, not as the final member in the series of twelve positive *nidānas* which we have selected as the formulation that best exhibits the true nature of the Path, but independently, in its own right, as the Goal.

14

THE GOAL

MAN IS A CONSTANTLY changing stream of psychophysical energy capable of manifesting, under the laws of karma, as any form of sentient conditioned existence. His nature is therefore a no-nature. This no-nature is Buddha-nature. Such were the conclusions reached in the last chapter but one. Accordingly we may now assert that the goal of human life is to realize Nirvāṇa or *sambodhi*.

But what is Nirvāṇa? What is the nature of Enlightenment? Some there are who maintain that while the Buddha described the Path in copious detail he remained silent regarding the Goal. This is only partly correct. Though he strongly discouraged the very human tendency of indulging in speculations about Reality to the neglect of actually implementing the means to its attainment, his references to the Goal are for practical if not for philosophical purposes sufficiently explicit. At the same time it cannot be denied that in comparison to his long, systematic, and precise descriptions of the Path such references appear, for the most part, tantalizingly meagre and fragmentary.

As the centuries rolled by, it was inevitable that, with the constant growth and development of Buddhist thought, one reference to Nirvāṇa should be compared with another, and these correlated with yet others, until eventually as many of them as possible had been organized into a more or less systematic account of their great subject. Moreover, taking advantage of the immensely enhanced linguistic and other means of expression afforded them by a now highly developed tradition, some of the more gifted of the Buddha's followers began elaborating, out of their own spiritual experience, delineations of the Goal that were infinitely more rich, subtle, bold, grand, and complex than any before known. Though full documentation is impossible, most of these sources will be taken into consideration in the following short account.

In accordance with their natural phenomenology, descriptions of the Goal may be classified as negative, positive, paradoxical, and symbolic. Before proceeding to treat them in this order, however, we must introduce a formula which, since two of its terms belong to both the Path and the Goal, logically has a prior claim on our attention.

This is the formula of the three *vimokṣa-mukhas* (Pāli *vimokkha-mukhas*) or entrances to liberation. From a point of view somewhat deeper than that of their duality, conditioned and Unconditioned are not discrete but as it were continuous. Penetrating, through insight, into the painful, impermanent, and insubstantial nature of saṁsāra, one eventually catches sight of Nirvāṇa. Though the three characteristics are ultimately inseparable, one may begin by concentrating on any one of them. Fathoming the impermanence of conditioned things to its depth and emerging so to speak on the other side one sees the Unconditioned as the Imageless (*animitta*); penetrating their unsatisfactoriness, as the Unbiased (Sanskrit *apraṇihita*, Pāli *appaṇihita*); and plumbing their insubstantiality, as the Void (Sanskrit *śūnyatā*, Pāli *suññāta*). By *nimitta*, image or sign, is meant the whole structure of subjectively conditioned ideas and concepts which we first build up round a particular sensuous perception and then regard as constituting its true nature as the 'object' of that perception. Prominent among such concepts are 'being' and 'non-being'. Seeing conditioned things as impermanent does not mean seeing them first as actually existing and afterwards as no longer existing but rather in reducing them to an absolutely continuous flow, or pure 'becoming', in connection with which the terms 'being' and 'non-being' are meaningless. The Unconditioned is spoken of as imageless in the sense that it transcends all ideas and concepts whatsoever and in the ultimate sense can be spoken of neither as existent nor non-existent, nor yet as both, nor even as neither.

Perceiving conditioned things as *duḥkha* means realizing that even the best of them are incapable of giving full and permanent satisfaction to the human heart. In ordinary life, pleasure gives rise to greed (*lobha*), pain to hatred (*dveṣa*), neutral feeling to delusion (*moha*). Here, since the true nature of these experiences has been understood and there exists neither attraction nor aversion, nor even indifference in the worldly sense, no bias or tendency towards greed, hatred, or delusion obtains. Nirvāṇa is called the Unbiased because of its complete immunity from these three 'poisons'. The connection between the insubstantiality (*nairātmyatā*) of the conditioned and the emptiness (*śūnyatā*) of the Unconditioned has been explained already (see pp.81 *et seq*).

While the 'unbiased' and the 'empty' are reckoned as belonging to the Transcendental Path, as well as applying to Nirvāṇa, the 'imageless' *vimokṣa* is not so reckoned. This is because in the Abhidharma the Path is defined according to the nature of its objective reference. In the case of the other *vimokṣas* this is the Unconditioned; but the 'imageless', being occupied with actually opposing and destroying such concepts as eternalism (*śāśvatavāda*, Pāli *sassatavāda*) and nihilism (*ucchedavāda*), has for its objective reference these conceptual constructions. Hence it is not reckoned as included in the Transcendental Path. The drawing of this distinction raises a problem which, as Guenther points out, pursued to its logical consequences leads to the acceptance of the Madhyamaka view that the Path and the Goal cannot legitimately be separated.

> For when Nirvāṇa is śūnyatā and apraṇihita as is The Path, no logical reason exists to make a distinction between path and goal.[62]

The end is the extreme of means. In the same way, there is no absolute distinction between the conditioned and the Unconditioned.

Negatively speaking the Goal consists in the complete and permanent eradication of all unhealthy mental attitudes. To cover these there are several well-known formulas, such as the three 'poisons', the three 'biases' (*āsravas*), and the ten defilements (*kleśas*). When, for example, 'the wanderer who ate rose-apples' asked Śāriputra what Nirvāṇa was, the great disciple replied,

> Whatever … is the extinction of passion [*lobha*], of aversion [*dosa*], of confusion [*moha*], this is called nirvāṇa.[63]

In the formula of the Four Āryan Truths the third Truth, that of the cessation of pain (*duḥkha-nirodha*, Pāli *dukkha-nirodha*), is equivalent to Nirvāṇa. As we saw in connection with karma and the Wheel of Life, it is in dependence on our unhealthy, as well as on even our mundane healthy, volitions, that there takes place in any one of the five (or six) realms of conditioned existence a renewal of sentient being, popularly called rebirth. With the eradication of these attitudes or volitions, therefore, no further rebirth can occur. When its hub is smashed the wheel is no longer able to revolve. The oil in the lamp exhausted, the flame goes out. Hence the Goal also consists in the absolute cessation, so far as the individual sentient being is concerned, of the whole process of phenomenal existence. Nirvāṇa is whatever the world is not. Language having its origin in mundane experience, words are logically powerless to describe it except by negations. Typical of this approach is the famous passage in which the Buddha, solemnly addressing his disciples, declares:

> 'There is, monks, that plane where there is neither extension nor ... motion nor the plane of infinite ether ... nor that of neither-perception-nor-non-perception, neither this world nor another, neither the moon nor the sun. Here, monks, I say that there is no coming or going or remaining or deceasing or uprising, for this is itself without support, without continuance (in saṁsāra), without mental object – this is itself the end of suffering.
>
> 'There is, monks, an unborn, not become, not made, uncompounded, and were it not, monks, for this unborn, not become, not made, uncompounded, no escape could be shown here for what is born, has become, is made, is compounded. But because there is, monks, an unborn, not become, not made, uncompounded, therefore an escape can be shown for what is born, has become, is made, is compounded.'[64]

Some writers, stressing the introductory verb (*atthi*) with which each paragraph begins, classify this passage as a positive rather than as a negative description of the Goal. This is, we believe, an instance of the common error of reading metaphysical meanings into what are simply linguistic conventions. Nevertheless, taken even in this sense the quotation is not out of place, for it provides us with a means of transition to the second class of descriptions.

In the same way that negative descriptions of the Goal deny, so positive ones affirm, some aspect or feature of conditioned existence. They affirm it not in the ordinary manner, but eminently, or to a superlative degree of perfection impossible under mundane conditions. This is the well-known *via affirmativa* of mysticism as contrasted with the *via negativa*. Language arises out of man's experience of the mundane. Conditioned existence, in part the object and in part the subject of that experience, is reducible to the five *skandhas* or aggregates (see pp.89 *et seq*). Consequently the terms by means of which a positive description of the Goal is attempted must be derived ultimately from any one of these aggregates or from two or more of them in combination. Such descriptions are therefore necessarily in terms of form, feeling and emotion, knowledge, will, and consciousness. The first of these, being applied symbolically, belongs to the fourth category of descriptions of the Goal, and will be dealt with later. This leaves us with a fourfold classification of all positive descriptions.

In terms of feeling and emotion the Goal is bliss, peace, love, and compassion. Commenting on the fact that esoteric (i.e. Vajrayāna) Buddhism speaks of the ultimate realization as 'supreme bliss', Susuma Yamaguchi remarks that this 'sounds very sensual'.[65] Yet far from being peculiar to one school, descriptions of this type are a commonplace of Buddhist literature from the earliest period. '*Nibbāṇaṁ paramaṁ sukhaṁ*. Nirvāṇa is the supreme bliss,' says *Dhammapada*, verse 203, and one could hardly accuse the *Dhammapada* of displaying a tendency to sensuality. The scholastics, though, are always careful to point out that unlike its mundane counterpart nirvanic bliss arises not out of physical and mental contact but in the absence of any such contact. We have already seen that the Vajrayāna itself is not oblivious to such distinctions (see p.83).

As a feeling of peace, the Goal tends to be contrasted with the turmoil and 'unrest which men miscall delight' of worldly life. It is the state of *yogakkhema* (Sanskrit *yogakṣema*), defined in the Pali Text Society's dictionary as 'rest from work or exertion, or figuratively in scholastic interpretation "peace from bondage", i.e. perfect peace or "uttermost safety".' Like the term *samyak-sambodhi*, or complete perfect Enlightenment, with which it is ultimately synonymous, *yogakkhema* is often qualified by the prefix *anuttara*, unsurpassed or unexcelled. Being a state of utter peace the Goal is also one not only of complete harmony, balance, and equilibrium, but of absolute metaphysical axiality whereof the psychic condition of equanimity (*upekṣā*), the last of the four *brahma-vihāras*, constitutes but a faint mundane reflection. Nevertheless this state, though not one of 'life' as generally understood, is emphatically not inaction or death.

This aspect of the Goal as somehow involving a release of energy, an outflow, even as it were an overflow of itself, back on to the world, is covered when it is spoken of in terms of love (*maitrī*) and compassion (*karuṇā*). As the first and second *brahma-vihāras* these two terms cover not the ordinary feelings which go by these names, but levels of meditative consciousness representing certain non-hedonic emotional aspects of the state of perfect psychic wholeness or *samādhi*. The *brahma-vihāras*, however, are mundane, not transcendental. In order to distinguish the transcendental emotion of *karuṇā* (this term now being used exclusively) from its mundane analogue the former is usually spoken of as *mahākaruṇā*, 'great compassion'. Whereas ordinary compassion has for its object living beings conceived as separate real entities, and partially enlightened compassion their constituent psychophysical phenomena, Great Compassion has for its real object their ultimate voidness. So extraordinary was the importance of *karuṇā* in this sense felt to be that the Mahāyāna eventually recognized it as equal to and co-ordinate with the *mahāprajñā* or Great Wisdom. Speaking of this virtue, which must never be confused with mere sentimental pity, the *Amitāyur-dhyāna Sūtra*, or 'Meditation on the Buddha of Infinite Life', declares with reference to those who have practised the various exercises described therein:

> Since they have meditated on Buddha's body, they will also see Buddha's mind. It is great compassion that is called Buddha's mind.[66]

The *Nirvāṇa Sūtra* says:

> Great compassion and a great pitying heart is called Buddha-nature. Compassion is Tathāgata; Tathāgata is Compassion.[67]

In the *Dharmasaṅgīti Sūtra*, quoted by Śāntideva in his *Śikṣā-sammuccaya*, the bodhisattva Avalokiteśvara, himself the embodiment of compassion, is represented as thus addressing the Enlightened Lord:

> The Bodhisattva, Blessed One, should not be taught too many things. One virtue should be fully mastered and learned by him, in which are included all the virtues of the Buddha. And what is that? It is great compassion.[68]

Despite the later development of this tendency to speak of the Goal not in terms of feeling and emotion only, but above all as compassion, this is for Indian Buddhism as a whole the exception rather than the rule. Descriptions in terms of knowledge are not only commoner but more characteristic. Indeed, notwithstanding the much greater prominence given to compassion in its Far Eastern developments, especially by the highly devotional Jōdō Shin Shū of Japan, Buddhism is generally recognized as a religion of knowledge. For the Goal as a state of transcendental cognition there is naturally, therefore, a plethora of practically synonymous terms. Of these *bodhi*, awakening (often prefixed by *sam-*, full or complete) is perhaps the best known, if only because therefrom derives one of the most ancient and popular appellatives of the Master, as well as the modern coinage under which his teaching is now most widely current. The traditional preeminence of this term is indicated by the fact that it forms part of a number of important doctrinal compounds. One self-dedicated to the attainment of Supreme Enlightenment for the benefit of all beings is known as a bodhisattva. The thought of, or aspiration to, that same Enlightenment is called the bodhicitta, by the arising of which an ordinary person is transformed into a bodhisattva much as a beggar, on finding a jewel in a dunghill, instantly becomes rich. *Anubodhi*, 'after-Enlightenment', is a state of attainment subsequent to though identical with that of the Buddha which the disciple gains by following his instructions. Mindfulness, investigation of the Doctrine, energy, rapture, serenity, concentration, and equanimity,[69] a well-known canonical series, are collectively termed the seven *bodhyaṅgas* (Pāli *bojjhaṅgas*), the 'factors', 'links', or 'limbs' of Enlightenment. Even more important is the list of thirty-seven items, distributed over seven sets of practices and qualities, which according to the *Mahāparinibbāna Sutta* the Buddha, three months before his great decease, reminded his disciples he had taught them.[70] These subsequently became known as the *bodhipakṣya-dharmas* (Pāli *bodhipakkhiya-dhammas*) or 'principles conducive to Enlightenment'.

Among the other terms for transcendental cognition are *vidyā* (Pāli *vijjā*), 'knowledge', as when the Buddha, in the canonical recital of his attributes, is styled *vijjā-caraṇa-sampaññā*, 'The One Fully Endowed with Knowledge and Practice'; *yathābhūtajñānadarśana*, 'Knowledge and Vision of Things As They Really Are', as in the eighth positive *nidāna*; *vipaśyana* (Pāli *vipassanā*) or insight; *prajñā* (Pāli *paññā*), most inadequately rendered as wisdom; *jñāna* (Pāli *ñāṇa*), also from the root *jñā* 'to know', and *ārya-jñāna*, cognition and noble cognition respectively; *samyak-dṛṣṭi* (Pāli *samma-diṭṭhi*) or Axial Vision, commonly translated by such feeble equivalents as 'right understanding' and 'perfect view'; and *dhīḥ* (Pāli *dhi*), knowledge, best known as the last syllable of the mantra of Mañjughoṣa, 'The Sweet-Voiced One', the bodhisattva who *par excellence* embodies transcendental wisdom.

Despite their varying shades of meaning, every one of these descriptions of the Goal in terms of knowledge fundamentally denotes a cognition of the ultimate reality of things, a realization of the true meaning of life, the directness and immediacy of which is hinted at by such of them as either wholly or in part compare it with the act of seeing. On the conceptual side, the content of this cognition, ineffable in itself, is conterminous with the whole Dharma, hence with the entire contents of this Part.

Bondage is essentially a state of impeded volition. Freedom is unimpeded volition. In terms of will, therefore, the Goal is a state of absolute freedom from all restrictions. As *vimutti* (Sanskrit *vimukti*), the eleventh positive *nidāna*, this aspect has already been covered. All that need be added is that the restrictions meant are those imposed not by external circumstances but by the unhealthy affectivity and 'primitive beliefs about reality' (*kleśāvaraṇa* and *jñeyāvaraṇa*) of our own minds. In a spiritual sense bondage is subjection to oneself. True freedom, therefore, consists in freedom from oneself.

Though the Goal has now been described positively in terms of emotion, knowledge, and will, the descriptions remain somehow inadequate. For as we know them, these faculties go to make up a concrete living person. Prescinded from him and as it were suspended in mid-air they are apt to seem unreal, and a description of the Goal in terms of such bloodless abstractions does not always carry conviction. The Mahāyāna therefore describes it not only in terms of emotion *et cetera* taken separately but also as an Absolute Person in whom wisdom, compassion, and power in the highest conceivable degree of purity and perfection are found inseparably united. From this point of view the Buddha himself is the Goal and the Goal is the Buddha. Here by the Buddha is meant not simply the historical Śākyamuni, but that Eternal Buddha who, in the fifteenth chapter of the *Saddhārma-puṇḍarīka Sūtra* (the sixteenth chapter of the Chinese translation) brings the whole discourse to a climax by revealing that his transcendental compassionate activity is unlimited by space and time and eternally embraces the whole universe. Concrete doctrinal expression to this sublime conception is given in the teaching of the trikāya, or 'triple body' of the Buddha, an outline of which was attempted in Chapter 5.

As an Absolute Person, the Goal now becomes more and more the object of worship and devotion. One cannot adore an abstraction. Except metaphorically, one cannot love wisdom and compassion. The object of love is invariably a person. Parallel with the tendency to describe the Goal doctrinally in terms of an eternally Enlightened Absolute person there naturally developed, therefore, a popular movement which Conze has named the Buddhism of Faith and Devotion. For the adherents of this movement, which attained its apogee in China and Japan, faith (*śraddhā*, Pāli *saddhā*) occupies the position traditionally assigned to wisdom.

Both the doctrinal tendency and the popular movement associated with it are sometimes objected to as aberrations. How is it possible to describe the Goal in terms of personality when the Buddhist tradition invariably speaks of it as involving the complete eradication of the false view that things and persons are in themselves ultimately real? Does it not amount, as some scholars have maintained, to the deification of the Buddha, to the surreptitious introduction into non-theistic Buddhism of the incongruous notion of a God? In reply to the first objection it may be pointed out that if descriptions of the Goal as the Absolute Person are inadmissible, so will be those in terms of emotion and knowledge. Thus all attempts at positive delineation would have to be abandoned. In point of fact, however, the Absolute Person is no more a person as we understand the word than wisdom and compassion are the intelligence and pity of our ordinary experience. As we made clear at the beginning, positive qualities are affirmed of the Goal eminently, or to a superlative degree. Moreover, after realizing the Goal the historical Śākyamuni himself did not cease to function recognizably as a person. Personality and the Goal are not, it would therefore seem, incompatible. In any case, the inadequacy of all positive descriptions being fully admitted, it is not a question of *defining* the Goal as *being*, in the ultimate sense, personal, but of describing it *as though* it was such for practical purposes. After all, personality, even of the 'normal' human type, is the highest category available to ordinary consciousness, and premature renunciation of the use of it might involve the risk of the Goal being conceived not as transcendent to personality so much as infra-personal. As for the charge of deification, no Buddhist text, of any school, attributes to the

Buddha the creation of the universe. God as Creator the Buddha therefore most certainly is not, either in the Hīnayāna or the Mahāyāna. Murti, however, in a penetrating discussion of 'Absolute and Tathāgata', has not hesitated to assert:

> Buddha is Bhagavān, God, endowed as he is with power and perfection. He possesses, in entirety, all power, splendour, fame, wealth, knowledge, and act.[71]

Though not overlooking the difference between the two in respect of their cosmic functions, as God he therefore speaks of the Tathāgata throughout the chapter. The difficulty is at bottom one of definition. A Christian missionary, finding no word for God in the Thai language, is said to have coined a neologism meaning 'the-Buddha-who-created-the-universe'. The Buddha of the Mahāyāna might be described as the God who did not create the universe. Whether the latter term will be able to bear so profound a modification of its traditional meaning cannot now be predicted.

The description of the Goal in positive terms as consciousness, the fifth *skandha*, seems to have been a tradition from early times. A few scattered references are found even in the Pāli *Nikāyas*. In the *Kevaddha Sutta*, for example, a monk asks what that place is where distinctions such as water and earth, fire and air, disappear absolutely. Correcting and expanding his question, the Buddha in part replies:

> It is consciousness [which is] invisible, infinite, radiant on all sides (*viññāṇam anidassanaṁ anantaṁ sabbato pahaṁ*).[72]

Elsewhere he is represented as declaring:

> This consciousness (*citta*) is radiant, but it is defiled by adventitious defilements.[73]

Whether all such descriptions refer to Nirvāṇa or to a state somewhat short of it is a moot point. According to Buddhaghosa's commentary the infinite radiant consciousness of the first quotation is identical with Nirvāṇa.[74] About the *citta* of the second quotation we cannot be so sure. In the absence of clear contextual indication, uncertainty is created with regard to the correct meaning of this and the few other similar passages by the fact that throughout the *Nikāyas citta* and *viññāṇa* denote empirical mind, or mundane consciousness: their use in a higher, transcendental sense would be in any case exceptional for this literature.

Despite these difficulties, it is clear that there existed in Buddhism from the beginning a definite, though undeveloped, tradition of idealism. This tradition eventually found vigorous expression in a group of idealist sūtras in which the Goal was the realization, by the bodhisattva, of the truth that the three worlds were 'Mind-Only' (*citta-mātra*). From this point of view Nirvāṇa became the state of absolutely pure, blissful, and radiant consciousness. This state was sharply distinguished from the *paramātman* or 'Supreme Self' of certain non-Buddhist schools. Whereas the latter was static, the former was dynamic. Being dynamic it was void (*śūnya*). The fact that in order to prevent serious misunderstanding it is necessary to speak of Absolute Mind as empty shows that for Buddhism idealism cannot be the last word. In view of its close connection with meditation, however, it remains even at the penultimate stage of the Path an indispensable stepping-stone.

The paradox is a figure of speech widely current in mystical literature. In this context it may be defined as the attempt to describe an ineffable state or experience by the forcible juxtaposition of contradictory attributes. Thus for Dionysius the Deity is 'a deep but dazzling darkness'; Jesus declares that we must lose our life in order to find it; Kabir urges us to listen to 'the unstruck sound'. Despite its universal currency in this semi-poetic form, deliberate and systematic recourse to paradox as the best means of describing the spiritual life in all its aspects and at every stage is a development that tends to come late in the evolution of spiritual traditions, if at all. It flourishes as 'the chrysanthemum of Autumn' rather than as 'the orchid of Spring'. Early Buddhist literature seems entirely innocent of this sophistication. Positive and negative descriptions of the Goal, as well as of the successive steps of the Path, are the rule; paradoxical ones not even the exception. But with passage of time, as one generation of teachers succeeded another, the categories of Buddhist thought tended to become fixed and rigid, description hardened into definition, while teachings that had originally been suggestive rather than definitive were interpreted with ever-increasing literal-mindedness. This naturally led to the movement of reaction, and of restatement of fundamentals, known to us as the Mahāyāna.

The literary spearhead of the movement was the continually-expanding *Prajñāpāramitā* or 'Perfection of Wisdom' corpus. Herein the fact that in emptiness the logical principle of contradiction is abrogated is explicitly affirmed: A is A because it is not-A. Out of this affirmation arises the need for having exclusive recourse to paradox, as the one type of description compatible with a logic of contradiction. In terms of paradox, therefore, the *Prajñāpāramitā* describes not only all possible objects of cognition but also the time-honoured categories of Buddhist thought. The *dharmas*, in the Abhidharma sense of ultimate elements of existence, are non-*dharmas*; therefore they are *dharmas*. In reality there are no sentient beings to be delivered; therefore the bodhisattva should vow to deliver them. One should abide in a state of non-abiding. That which is supported has no support. Nirvāṇa should be attained by means of a non-attainment.

Besides serving to counteract the Hīnayāna tendency to think of the Goal as actually existing 'out there' with a real path leading up to it as though to the door of a house, this devastatingly radical procedure created a new awareness of the fact that Reality was in truth ineffable, that all attempts to divide and classify it were futile, and that in the end the only way of reaching the Goal was by realizing that there was in the ultimate sense no Goal to be reached. Though enjoying a considerable vogue wherever the *Prajñāpāramitā* literature circulated, the method of description by paradox did not come fully into its own, perhaps, until the rise of the Ch'an or Dhyāna School in China and its continuation in Japan as Zen. Brought very much down to earth, it lived on in the *kung an* (Chinese) or *kōan* (Japanese).

For descriptions of the fourth class symbolical is perhaps not the best word. Poetical might have been better. Though resembling the paradox in being a figurative rather than a scientific statement of truth, it differs from it by speaking the language not of abstractions but of concrete images. Twentieth-century work in psychology, especially that of Jung and his disciples, has helped to rehabilitate the image as an independent vehicle of psychological and spiritual truth, and no more than the 'legends' of the Buddha's life need we dismiss as worthless the symbolical descriptions of the Goal found in Buddhist literature. Pāli texts speak in symbolical terms of the Goal only by way of an occasional simile or metaphor: Nirvāṇa is the Cool Cave, the Island in the Floods, the Further Shore, the Holy City.

The Sanskrit scriptures are more expansive. Whole sūtras, such as the Larger and Smaller *Sukhāvatī-vyūha* or 'Array of the Happy Land', are taken up by lengthy and elaborate accounts of the glories and beauties of a realm which, though apparently a 'heaven' located within the phenomenal universe, is really the transcendental state of Nirvāṇa as expressed not abstractly but in terms of a harmonious disposition of images aglow with supernatural life and movement. Though music and perfumes are not absent, the impression is predominantly one of light and colour. Against a background of radiance millions of rays and beams spring up, intersect, and weave themselves into incredibly beautiful patterns. Rainbows appear and disappear. There is a shining forth as of silver and gold and everything flashes as though with strings and nets of multicoloured gems. Flowers fall like rain. At the centre of this blaze of splendour, its focal point and its crown, sits as Lord of the Happy Land the Buddha of the Mahāyāna, the rays converging into a canopy above his head, the flowers at his feet, and his unnumbered auditors ranged in attitudes of expectancy and devotion on all sides.

A more formal and geometrically organized version of this exalted scene, which is the usual setting for the revelation of a Mahāyāna sūtra, is found in the mandala, a definition of which was given on page 88. What Lama Anagarika Govinda writes of the latter is relevant to the whole question of description in terms of images:

> In order to understand the qualities of sunlight or the nature of the sun, we have to separate its rays in the spectrum. Likewise, if we want to understand the nature of an Enlightened One or of the consciousness of Enlightenment, we have to spread out before our inner eye the various qualities of such a state. Because an unenlightened being cannot grasp an Enlightened mind in its totality, but only in separate aspects, which – according to the plane on which they are experienced and the range of their manifold relations and mental associations – lead to an ever wider and deeper understanding.[75]

While negative descriptions of absolute whiteness tell us it is not black, positive ones that it is like milk or snow only whiter, and paradoxical ones that it is in reality a non-whiteness, symbolical or poetical descriptions exhibit before us all the magic colours of the rainbow. Vajrayāna tradition in fact speaks of Reality in terms of divine images appearing and disappearing in the Void like rainbows in a clear blue sky or like reflections coming and going in a spotless mirror. As the *Prajñāpāramitā-hṛdaya Sūtra* or 'Heart of the Perfection of Wisdom' reminds us:

> Form is not separate from voidness; voidness is not separate from form.[76]

Open though it may be to popular misunderstanding, the symbolical description of the Goal in terms of concrete sensuous images at least possesses the merit of protecting us against the more insidious error of thinking of it in merely abstract terms as a featureless and inert Absolute.

Part Three

THE SANGHA

15

THE ASSEMBLY OF THE NOBLE

WITHOUT A CENTRE, a radius, and a circumference a circle cannot exist. Of the circle of Buddhism the Buddha is the radiant centre, the Dharma, as the shortest distance from potential to actual Enlightenment, the radius, and the Sangha the perfect unbroken circumference. Each of these terms is multidimensional, possessing sphere within sphere of spiritual significance which no one rendition can exhaust. The Buddha is, simultaneously, a unique historical figure, the supreme object of the religious consciousness, and Reality itself; his Dharma is the sum total of conceptual formulations of the Teaching as well as the spiritual principle which both transcends all formulations and, running at the same time through every one of them, communicates to them vitality and meaning. Even so does the Sangha, literally 'assembly', meet not at one level of existence only but at several. The term stands, according to context, for a spiritual élite, an ecclesiastical corporation, and the whole community of the faithful, monk and lay, as well as covering various intermediate shades of significance. Of the three principal meanings, that of the spiritual élite is the primary one; all the rest are secondary. Whether one is in spiritual relation with the Buddha, through the Dharma, and therefore whether one is truly a segment of the circumference of the circle, is determined not by the assumption of external differentiae, nor by verbal professions, but by whether one actually practises the Dharma or not.

In a well-known episode the Buddha declares that he who walked step by step behind the Master, holding fast to the hem of his robe, but who did not follow his instructions, was far from him. But one who, on the contrary, though living a thousand miles away, yet realized the import of the Teaching, dwelt in his very presence. The true criterion of the relation between the Buddha and his followers is not physical, not spatio-temporal, but spiritual. Whether now or in what we call, from the historical point of view, his 'own' times, or whether in the future even, we are nearest to him when we most perfectly follow his example. The Sangha is primarily the community of those who, by virtue of their immediate or remote approximation to Enlightenment, stand in spiritual relation to the Buddha and dwell spiritually in his presence. It is the community of those who, through their relationship with him, are also all spiritually related to one another. The Sangha is the Buddha's spiritual family. In the *Nikāyas* he is indeed represented as telling his disciples:

> Ye are mine own true sons, born of my mouth; heirs of the Dhamma, not heirs of worldly things.

Centuries later the same theme finds beautiful expression as a trinity consisting of the Buddha as Father, the Dharma as Mother, and the Sangha as Son.

As the spiritual élite the Sangha is known as the Ārya Sangha or 'Assembly of the Noble', the word *ārya* here connoting an aristocracy not of race but of transcendental attainment. As an ecclesiastical corporation it is known as the bhikṣu-sangha or 'Assembly of Monks', and as the whole community of the faithful as the mahā-sangha or 'Great Assembly' and the *caturvarga* or 'Four Classes'. Like many other doctrinal categories, the term 'Ārya Sangha' underwent a certain narrowing at the hands of the Hīnayānists and had to be reinterpreted by the Mahāyanists who, while not rejecting the earlier formulations, did their best to incorporate them within the broader framework of their own ampler version of the Buddha's teaching. Though precise demarcation is impossible, the earlier and the later interpretations are best dealt with separately.

Intelligent sentient beings are either *āryas* or *anāryas*. In the Scriptures the latter are generally referred to as *pṛthagjanas* (Pāli *puthujjanas*) or average men. As they outnumber the *āryas* by many millions to one the term *bahujana* or 'many-folk' may also be applied to them. An average man is one who, dominated by the delusion of 'I' and 'mine', identifies himself with, or imagines he possesses, form, feeling, conception, volition, and consciousness. He is the fool (*bāla*) described in the *Dhammapada* verse 62:

> 'Sons are mine, wealth is mine,' thus the fool torments [himself].
> Indeed, he does not belong to himself. Whence sons? Whence wealth?

Not knowing the true Dharma, he develops attachments to things which should be avoided, thereby creating and strengthening the biases towards thirst for sensuous experience, prolonged mundane existence, and spiritual ignorance. Hence he continues to revolve with the Wheel of Life, occupying now one and now another of its segments.

Not only most men, but most gods too, are *pṛthagjanas*. For this reason the Buddhist expects no spiritual help or guidance from them. In Tibet they are known as the Gods of the Round. The exceptions are those who, either during the Buddha's earthly lifetime or later, had an opportunity of hearing the Teaching and developing transcendental insight. These together with the bodhisattvas, whom they resemble in certain respects, make up the Deities of the Path, and from them inspiration and spiritual guidance can be received.

Āryas are in the first place of two kinds: Arhants and *śrotopannas* (Pāli *sotāpannas*). An Arhant is literally a 'Worthy One', the term being (according to the Pali Text Society's dictionary) 'before Buddhism used as honorific title of high officials like the English "His Worship"; at the rise of Buddhism applied popularly to all ascetics.' It is interpreted scholastically as meaning one who, by virtue of his supreme attainment, is worthy of the respectful offerings of the whole world. There are several stock descriptions of such beings. In the Pāli scriptures they are frequently represented as declaring, upon attainment:

> Destroyed is (re-)birth; lived is the higher life; done is what had to be done; after this present life there is [for me] no beyond.

The Large *Prajñāpāramitā Sūtra*, probably following Sarvāstivādin sources, exclaims of a gathering of them:

> Their outflows dried up, undefiled, fully controlled, quite freed in their hearts, well freed and wise, thoroughbreds, great Serpents, their work done, their task accomplished, their burden laid down, their own weal accomplished, with the fetters that bound them to

> becoming extinguished, their hearts well freed by right understanding, in perfect control of their whole minds.[77]

In later Hīnayāna, as well as earlier Mahāyāna literature, the Arhant is represented as having gained Nirvāṇa for himself alone; in the latter he therefore stands for spiritual individualism.

A *śrotopanna* or 'Stream-Entrant' occupies a position midway between the average man and the Arhant, at the point of intersection between the vicious circle of mundane existence and the spirals of the Transcendental Path. Having died to the grosser aspects of worldly life he is now reborn into the spiritual family of the Buddha. He is no longer liable to be reborn in the three lowest spheres of sentient existence, that is to say the world of animals, of revenants, or of tormented spirits. Henceforward, he is incapable of relapse; though further progress may be delayed, the attainment of Nirvāṇa within not more than seven human or heavenly births is assured. At its own much higher level Entering the Stream corresponds to the psychological phenomenon of religious conversion. It marks not only the beginning of the end of mundane existence, but a transvaluation of values more radical than any envisaged by Nietzsche. Consequently the texts are loud in its praises. Says the *Dhammapada* verse 178:

> Better is the fruit of Entering the Stream than sole sovereignty over the earth, than going to heaven, than rule supreme over the entire universe.

This decisive and far-reaching reorientation, this spiritual revolution, takes place upon the initial flashing forth of transcendental insight into the true nature of existence, upon the first overwhelming glimpse of Nirvāṇa. Thus it coincides with the eighth positive *nidāna*, that of Knowledge and Vision of Things As They Are, as well as with Axial Vision (*samyak-dṛṣṭi*), the first step of the transcendental – as distinct from the mundane – Eightfold Path. For this reason the Path of Stream Entry (*śrotāpatti-mārga*) is also known as the Path of Seeing (*darśana-mārga*).

But tremendous though the impact of this experience is – for it represents the first triumphant irruption of the transcendental order into a particular psychophysical continuum – and shaking though it does the individuality almost to its foundations, the irruption is not a taking of complete possession, the shaking not a demolition of the entire superstructure. To accomplish this is the work of the stage intermediate between that of the Stream-Entrant and the Arhant which, on account of the extreme difficulty with which it is traversed, is divided, as will be seen below, into various sub-stages. It is known as the Path of Practice or Path of Development (*bhāvanā-mārga*). What is developed is of course the whole individuality, not merely in its sublimest heights, as in the Path of Seeing, but also in its murkiest depths. The term is perhaps best translated as Path of Transformation. Since *bhāvanā* is widely used in the sense of meditation there is the implication that the transformation is to be effected principally by this means. It coincides with the last four positive *nidānas* and with the transcendental Eightfold Path from Axial Emotion (*samyak-saṅkalpa*), the second member, to Axial Absorption (*samyak-samādhi*), the eighth – the latter here representing not merely 'right concentration', as in the mundane Eightfold Path, but the state of purity and pellucidity consequent upon the complete saturation of the entire psychic contents with the light of transcendental realization.

The *bhāvanā-mārga* is subdivided into the stages of the *sakṛdāgāmin* (Pāli *sakadāgāmin*), or 'Once-Returner', the *anāgāmin* or 'Non-Returner', and the Arhant. By including the Stream-Entrant, and combining this subdivision with other principles of classification – such as temperament, the number of fetters destroyed, and the number of rebirths remaining to be undergone – the Hīnayāna arrived at a total of seven, or eight, or nine *ārya-pudgalas* (Pāli *ariya-puggalas*) or Holy Persons who, from different points of view, collectively make up the Ārya Sangha or Assembly of the Noble.

The seven Holy Persons are:

(1 and 2) The *śraddhānusārin* or 'Faith-Follower' and the *dharmanusārin* or 'Doctrine-Follower'. This distinction calls attention to the vital role temperament plays in the religious life. According to some authorities differences of temperament exist even in the Buddhas, who respectively exhibit a predominance of knowledge, or love, or activity. This would seem to indicate that such differences are innate, hence not to be ignored by any truly practical scheme of spiritual self-culture. The Faith-Follower, as the name itself indicates, is one of predominantly devotional temperament. Emotions of love, worship, admiration, and surrender are apt to well up in him uncontrollably, and he is highly susceptible to suggestions of religious exaltation in the surrounding atmosphere. In the spiritual life of such a person the

guru occupies an absolutely central place. Scriptures and studies count for nothing. Drawn only by the grace of the guru, and solely out of faith in him, a person of this type takes up the systematic practice of mindfulness, or any other spiritual exercise, without developing at the same time, or even caring to develop, an intellectual appreciation of the Doctrine. Provided the guru in whom he has taken refuge is himself Enlightened, a Faith-Follower will make good progress; otherwise he may become emotionally unbalanced, or a fanatic, or even a religious hysteric.

The Doctrine-Follower typifies the predominantly intellectual approach. He takes up the practice of the whole body of spiritual exercises after an extensive and painstaking course of scriptural study. Relying on the guru much less than the Faith-Follower does, or even not at all, he abides by the Buddha's dying injunction that his disciples should be 'islands unto themselves, refuges unto themselves', and makes his own understanding of the sacred tradition his guide to the attainment of Nirvāṇa. Though in no danger of emotional extravagance, the Doctrine-Follower, unless upheld by an exceptionally strong desire for Enlightenment, may sink into sterile scholasticism or even scepticism; misled by his learning, he may also be tempted to deviate from the norm of doctrinal orthodoxy. A Doctrine-Follower who succeeds in avoiding the pitfalls peculiar to his type, however, is capable of making to the elucidation and development of the Doctrine contributions of profound and far-reaching significance.

According to some sources not all *śraddhānusārins* and *dharmanusārins* are members of the Ārya Sangha, but only those who have attained to the Path of Stream Entry (*śrotāpatti-mārga*). The discrepancy is due to the fact that between the average man and the Stream-Entrant there is the 'lightning-like transitional stage'[78] of the *gotrabhū*, literally 'one who has entered the lineage [of the *āryas*]'. A *gotrabhū* in this sense (there are higher senses) is sometimes reckoned as an *ārya*, sometimes as an *anārya*. It seems agreed, though, that whether *āryas* or not, all such *gotrabhūs* are either Faith-Followers or Doctrine-Followers.

Such differences of religious temperament are well known to all students of comparative religion. In Hinduism a distinction is made between the *bhakta* or devotee, who follows the Path of Devotion (*bhakti-mārga*), and the *jñānin* or knower, who follows the Path of Knowledge (*jñāna-mārga*). A similar difference can be traced between the intellectual mysticism of Eckhart and the devotional mysticism of St Teresa of Avila – to take no more extreme examples. In Theravādin terminology the *śraddhānusārin* is said to follow the Way of Contemplative Insight (*vipassanā-dhura*) and the *dharmanusārin* the Way of Study (*ganthadhura*). Drawing on the Tibetan tradition it may be said that Milarepa provides a good example of the first, Tsongkhapa of the second. Types in whom devotion and understanding are almost, if not quite, perfectly balanced do of course exist; but when present at the beginning difference of temperament may persist, as we shall see, up to the very farthest reaches of the Transcendental Path.

(3 and 4) The *śraddhādhimukta* (Pāli *saddhāvimutta*) or 'Faith-Liberated One' and the *dṛṣṭiprapta* (Pāli *diṭṭhippatta*) or 'Vision-Attained One'. These are respectively the designations of the Faith-Follower at all the remaining stages of the Transcendental Path and of the Doctrine-Follower at all of them save the last one.

(5) The *kāyasākṣin* (Pāli *kāyasakkhī*) or 'Body-Witness'. This would seem to be the name of an independent type of Holy Person distinct from both the Faith-Follower and the Doctrine-Follower, though more closely allied to the latter, for according to the texts such a one receives the same designation at all stages of his career. It corresponds to what may be called the psychic type. The Body-Witness is the yogin *par excellence*. All the sources, canonical and extra-canonical, Theravādin and Sarvāstivādin, speak of him as practising a set of concentrations known as the eight *vimokṣas* (Pāli *vimokkhas*) or 'releases' from thought-constructions. As one has not met, nor even heard of, anyone with a personal experience of these states, the elucidation of the cryptic formulas with which the Scriptures are content to describe them is a matter of some difficulty. Nalinaksha Dutt, following the *Abhidharmakośa-vyākhyā*, says of the first four:

> In the first Release, a meditator introspects his own body, its colour and contents as also those of others and realises only that the colour and other characteristics of his own body is undesirable (*aśubha*) and substanceless (*suññā*). He controls his visual perception and therefore he does not perceive the colour of his body and regards it as unattractive (*amanojṇam*). In the second Release, the meditator thinks no longer of his own body but his attention is still diverted to others' body and its characteristics, internal and external, which he then tries to regard as undesirable (*aśubha*) and substanceless (*suññā*). In the

> third Release, the meditator derives a feeling of satisfaction, which pervades his whole body on account of his success in removing his mental obsessions caused by his previous notions about his own and other's body. In the fourth Release, the meditator frees his mind from the notion of material objects (*rūpa*) and their repercussive nature (*paṭigha*) and dismisses from his mind the sense of distinction, which exists among beings and objects, and regards the world as just infinite space free from all obstructions.[79]

The remaining four *vimokṣas* are identical with the four formless *dhyānas* (see p.102). The Body-Witness is so designated because he not only experiences personally (*kāyika*) ever higher levels of concentration, but with the detachment of a mere observer (*sākṣin*) realizes their true nature. Though perhaps extinct as an independent practice, the eight *vimokṣas* would seem to have been incorporated into the Vajrayāna tradition; the Thai *sammā-arahaṁ* method of meditation may also owe something to their influence.

According to the canonical definitions of these terms the Faith-Follower is one who, at the beginning of his spiritual career, being filled with resolution, considers the aggregates as impermanent (*anitya*); similarly, the Doctrine-Follower, filled with wisdom, considers them as insubstantial (*anātman*). The Body-Witness is one who, filled with tranquillity, considers them as painful (*duḥkha*). By making the painfulness, rather than the impermanence, of conditioned things his object, a Faith-Follower who has attained the Path of Stream Entry (*śrotāpatti-mārga*) may as it were change his type and become a Body-Witness.

(6 and 7) *Prajñāvimukta* (Pāli *paññāvimutta*) or 'Wisdom-Liberated One' and *ubhayatobhāgavimukta* (Pāli *ubhatobhāgavimutta*) or 'Doubly-Liberated One'. Both these types are Arhants. The distinction between them is based not on any difference in the actual content of their realization but in the mode of its attainment. A Doctrine-Follower on becoming an Arhant is known as a Wisdom-Liberated One, while the Faith-Follower and the Body-Witness alike receive the designation of Doubly-Liberated One. Despite the misunderstandings at present current in some parts of the Buddhist world, the former does not attain Arhantship by means of wisdom (*prajñā*) alone; for to the development of wisdom itself, in the sense of transcendental insight into the true nature of existence, concentration (*samādhi*) is

accessory. In the spiritual life of the Doctrine-Follower, the one does not exclude, but only predominates over, the other. Speaking in terms of the eight *dhyānas*, it is therefore said that such a one attains Nirvāṇa by means of wisdom having experienced the four lower, but not the four higher, of these superconscious states. Similarly the predominantly devotional and contemplative career of the other types does not altogether exclude wisdom. Nirvāṇa is simultaneously a state of perfect knowledge and absolute mental purity. What the distinction between the two types of Arhant on the whole means is that whereas one type perfects first wisdom and then concentration, the other proceeds in the reverse order. The traditional Theravādin distinction between *cetovimutti*, emancipation of mind, and *paññāvimutti*, emancipation of wisdom, refers not so much to two mutually exclusive attainments as to this difference of procedure. Consequently the Buddha is time and again represented in the Scriptures as saying that 'a monk, after destroying the biases, himself realizes, in this life, through his higher attainments, emancipation of both mind and wisdom.'

Nevertheless, the fact that perfect knowledge necessarily involves absolute mental purity, but not *vice versa*, is explicitly recognized at least by the Sarvāstivādins. Consequently they recognize what is termed *samayavimukti*, temporary emancipation, that is to say the possibility, in the case of an Arhant who had been a Faith-Follower, of a fall from Arhantship if after perfecting concentration he did not make a special effort to perfect wisdom.[80] Though the subject has been much debated,[81] whether in the interval between perfecting concentration and perfecting wisdom one can properly be called an Arhant, or not – which is all the controversy really amounts to – would seem to be largely a matter of definition.

The eight Holy Persons are:

(1 and 2) The Stream-Entrant counted twice over, as two persons, in respect of his attainment of the Path of Stream Entry (*śrotāpatti-mārga*) and of the Fruit of that path (*śrotāpatti-phala*). By *mārga*, according to the Abhidharma, is meant – both here and in the case of the remaining Holy Persons – the moment of entering upon one or another of the stages of the Transcendental Path, while by *phala* is meant those moments of consciousness which follow immediately after the moment of entry and which may, under certain conditions, go on repeating themselves an indefinite number of times. Thus the former

represents the actual process of breaking through from the mundane into the transcendental, and the latter the continuing resultant state of having broken through. At what level the breakthrough takes place depends on how many of the *daśa-saṁyojana* or 'ten fetters' of mundane existence one is able to break.

In the case of the Stream-Entrant, besides being endowed with unshakeable faith in the Three Jewels, perfect observance of the Five Precepts, and other spiritual qualities, he is required, in order to reach his own stage of the Transcendental Path, to break the first, second, and third of them. These are *satkāyadṛṣṭi* (Pāli *sakkāya-diṭṭhi*) or 'personality-view', *vicikitsā* (Pāli *vicikicchā*) or doubt, and *śīlavrata-parāmarśa* (Pāli *sīlabbata-parāmāsa*) or 'dependence on moral codes and religious observances'. All of them represent various aspects not of greed or aversion but of spiritual blindness or ignorance. This is because the Path of Stream Entry is also the Path of Seeing, the attainment of which depends less on the eradication of unhealthy emotions than on the removal of the intellectual obstacles to clear vision. Together they embody the irreducible minimum of wrong ideology of which an average man must rid himself before he can become one of the Noble.

Personality-view is of two kinds: one posits the survival, after death, of a separate, immortal, unchanging soul or self (*ātman*) eternally distinct from the body; the other, identifying the personality either with the body or the body plus the mind, maintains that at death it perishes. The first is a form of *śāśvatavāda* (Pāli *sassatavāda*) or eternalism, the second of *ucchedavāda* or annihilationism. The next fetter, only most approximately rendered as doubt and scepticism, represents not that honest doubt in which, so the poet assures us, 'there lives more faith than half the creeds', but rather a culpable state of uncertainty and indecision; a reluctance, even a refusal, finally to make up one's mind about the Buddha, Dharma, and Sangha and *commit* oneself – in the Existentialist sense – wholeheartedly to the logical consequences of having taken refuge in them.

Dependence on moral codes and religious observances, the third fetter, is often mistranslated and misunderstood. Protestantizing English writers of the nineteenth century, with the great Ritualist controversy fresh in mind, understood it as belief in the efficacy of rites and ceremonies. *Śīla*, however, means behaviour, especially ethical behaviour; *vrata* covers the sacrificial and other observances of the Vedic tradition as well as the more eccentric types of ascetic practice. What this fetter in fact consists of is the wrong belief that any external observance, whether one's own or another's on one's behalf, is in and by itself sufficient for, or even conducive to, the attainment of salvation. Not by *śīla*, or even by *samādhi*, can the Transcendental Path be gained, but only by *prajñā* based upon *śīla* and *samādhi*.

Ritual, in the sense of symbolical or spiritually significant acts, far from being condemned in Buddhism in fact forms part of the heritage of all schools, not excluding even the Theravāda. In the Vajrayāna especially it plays an important part. Ceremonies of course are inseparable from organized religious life and though its estimate of their value may be a comparatively low one Buddhism no more excludes them on principle than does any other religion.

(3 and 4) The *sakṛdāgāmin* (Pāli *sakadāgāmin*) or 'Once-Returner'. Whereas the Stream-Entrant is sure to attain Nirvāṇa in not more than seven human and heavenly births, the second type of Holy Person, as his name reveals, will attain it after returning once more only to the world of men. Having broken already the first three fetters, he achieves the Path of Once-Return (*sakṛdagāma-mārga*) by weakening the fourth and fifth. These are *kāma-rāga* or sensuous craving and *vyāpāda* or aversion. The fact that at this stage these fetters are merely weakened, not broken, reminds us that we have now left the Path of Seeing and arrived at the Path of Transformation. Guenther's remarks on the importance of the distinction are worth quoting in this connection:

> It shows that it is a fairly simple task to get rid of intellectual fetters. It is easy to accept the findings of science, to use modern examples, to discard the 'ghost-in-a-machine' theory of the relation between body and soul, to attend to a problem seriously instead of talking hazily about it and in order to conceal one's ignorance about it, resorting to sophistry and misapplied scepticism, to discard mere ritualism because in all honesty in most cases it has turned into a meaningless formalism; but it is a gigantic task to tame or to sublimate our deep-rooted emotions. I may believe anything about myself, whether it makes sense or not, but anything that attempts to encroach upon my precious ego will be met with undisguised hostility. Emotions are not sublimated by recognizing the validity of a proposition or by seeing things by themselves, but only by paying the closest attention

> to that which is the nature of any living process, by working hard on ourselves. Hence the emotions are refined by the path of practice (*bhāvanāmārga*). When, therefore, the texts speak of three paths that have to be walked to the end, viz. the Second, Third and Fourth Path, they imply the difficulty of refining our emotional nature.[82]

(5 and 6) The *anāgāmin* or Non-Returner. In his case sensuous craving and aversion are not merely weakened but wholly eradicated. Thus up to and including this stage of the Transcendental Path five fetters in all have been broken. These are the five lower fetters, so called because they bind one to repeated birth in the world of sensuous experience (*kāma-loka*), the lowest of the three into which conditioned existence is stratified. Only five fetters now remain. These are known as the five higher fetters, as through them one is bound to continued existence in the world of pure form (*rūpa-loka*) and the formless world (*arūpa-loka*). Not having broken them the Non-Returner, though exempt from human birth, on death passes to the *śuddhāvāsa* (Pāli *suddhāvāsa*) or Pure Abodes, a group of celestial sub-planes located at the summit of the world of pure form. They are five in number: the worlds known respectively as the *avṛhā* (Pāli *avihā*) or Not-Great, the *atapā* (Pāli *atappā*) or Unscorched, the *sudṛśā* (Pāli *sudassā*) or Clearly-Visible, the *sudarśanā* (Pāli *sudassī*) or Clear-Visioned, and the *akaniṣṭhā* (Pāli *akaniṭṭhā*), Greatest or Highest. From one or another of these sub-planes the Non-Returner, now a divine being, traverses the remaining stages of the Transcendental Path and attains Nirvāṇa. According to whether this takes place within the first or second half of the celestial life-term, with or without exertion, or after he has been in each of the Pure Abodes successively, five sub-types of Non-Returner are distinguished. By enumerating the *anāgāmin* as one of the eight Holy Persons and describing him as above, the Hīnayāna bears witness to the fact that the possibility of post-mortem emancipation has been recognized in Buddhism from the earliest times. One has no reason to feel astonished, therefore, if later on similar ideas crop up, albeit within a modified doctrinal framework, in the Nyingmapa and the Jōdō Shin Shū traditions.

(7 and 8) The Arhant (Pāli *arahant*) or Worthy One. As this type of Holy Person has been discussed already we now need concern ourselves only with the fetters he must break in order to achieve his exalted station. The five higher fetters are: *rūpa-raga* and *arūpa-raga*,

or craving for existence in the world of pure form and in the formless world, *māna* or conceit, *auddhatya* (Pāli *uddhacca*), restlessness, and *avidyā* (Pāli *avijjā*) or lack of a clear understanding of Reality. From the point of view whence they appear as a duality – a duality that for the Hīnayāna is final – mundane and transcendental experience, Nirvāṇa and saṁsāra, are sharply distinguished. The true, the ultimate goal of the spiritual life is not any state of conditioned existence, however sublime, but solely the Unconditioned. However subtle, however 'spiritualized' it may be, the craving for personal immortality, for eternal life in heaven, leads not to emancipation but only to continued rebirth. Here, as invariably in the spiritual life, the good is the enemy of the best. That which for the average man would be an achievement the Noble regard as a failure. Broadly speaking, the first and second of the higher fetters stand for the danger of theism.

By the third fetter is signified not conceit in the ordinary worldly sense, but its spiritual counterpart. The average man is dominated by the awareness of 'I' and 'mine' in its grossest form. But subtler forms persist and linger on up to the very threshold of Enlightenment. The Stream-Entrant is subtly aware of himself as such; this awareness vanishes upon his becoming a Once-Returner. At each stage of the Transcendental Path there is a conceit which can be eradicated only by the attainment of the next succeeding stage. *Māna* is the subtlest conceit of all, that of the Non-Returner, which is destroyed only in the Arhant. According to the Mahāyāna, however, because he strives only for his own individual emancipation there is present in the Arhant himself a still more subtle self-awareness which he must overcome by having recourse to the highest stage of all, that of the bodhisattva who aspires to Perfect Buddhahood for the sake of all sentient beings. *Auddhatya* is far from being restlessness in the ordinary physical or mental sense; it is not even the much subtler psychic instability which may occur at the various levels of concentration. Rather it is the last, faintest tremor or vibration of consciousness between the most rarefied heights of the conditioned, on the one hand, and the Unconditioned, on the other, before it achieves that state of immovable tranquillity, of transcendental axiality, whereof *upekṣā* or ordinary meditative equanimity is a remote mundane analogue. Similarly *avidyā*, the fifth of the higher fetters, is the last faintest shadow of non-understanding of Reality to disappear when in the fullness of its undimmed glory Nirvāṇa dawns at last in one indistinguishable blaze of light.

Finally, the nine Holy Persons are the seven Holy Persons plus:

(8) The *pratyekabuddha* (Pāli *paccekabuddha*) or 'Solitary', 'Independent', or 'Private' Buddha. What type of spiritual ideal this personage was originally intended to stand for is still a mystery. Traditionally he occupies a position intermediate between the Arhant and the Perfect Buddha. Whereas an Arhant neither himself discovers the Path nor, after reaching the Goal, declares it to others, and the Perfect Buddha discovers, realizes, and reveals it by his own efforts, the Solitary Buddha, though able to discover the Path independently, fails to reveal and teach it to the world. If wisdom and compassion are really co-ordinate, a defect in the latter – and failure to preach argues such a defect – surely implies a corresponding defect in the former. Theravādin sources indeed seem to suggest as much. The *Puggala-Paññātti* or 'Designation of Human Types', probably the first Abhidharma work to be compiled by this school, defining the Private Buddha says:

> Here a certain person who, in regard to doctrines he has not heard of before, himself thoroughly understands the truths but attains neither the omniscience nor the mastery over the fruition thereof.[83]

Even this, however, does not altogether suffice to explain the enigmatic silence of the Solitary Buddha. Leaving aside the case of the Arhants, whom the Buddha himself exhorted to go about preaching the Dharma out of compassion (see p.17), even *āryas* of lesser attainments feel impelled to share the fruit of their experiences with others. For the Mahāyāna tradition the Pratyekabuddha, like the Arhant, represents spiritual selfishness. This may not be the whole story. Some Theosophists assert that his function in the spiritual world is not pedagogic but administrative. The entire subject awaits further investigation.

(9) The *samyak-sambuddha* (Pāli *sammā-sambuddha*), the Fully or Perfectly Enlightened One. This foremost of all Holy Persons has already been systematically dealt with in Part One. With the exception of Chapter 5, therefore, on the trikāya – a doctrine not accepted by the Hīnayānists, though the germs of it are discernible in their canons – whatever was said there should be understood as being repeated here. The sole difference is that we are now concerned, not merely

with the historical Śākyamuni, but with the particular type of Holy Person which he alone has exemplified in historical times.

Of the sets of seven, eight, or nine Holy Persons constituting the Ārya Sangha the second came to be regarded by the Hīnayāna as the definitive one. This is significant, for with its formalistic pattern of four main types, each subdivided according to Path and Fruit, its enumeration of the fetters broken at each stage, and the number of rebirths remaining, this was the most unimaginative, schematic, and rigid of them all. References to the more complex and spiritually vital sets of seven and nine do, indeed, occur from time to time in scholastic literature, but they are rarely if ever met with in modern manuals and never made the basis of popular expositions of the subject. Such a whittling down of the Assembly of the Noble is symptomatic of the general movement, not merely of conservatism, but of contraction, rigidity, and, eventually, of progressive spiritual petrifaction which set in within a century or two of the Buddha's parinirvāṇa. In particular it is symptomatic of the stunting of spiritual ideals that then took place. According to the Hīnayāna one should aim not at Perfect Buddhahood but at Arhantship, or emancipation for oneself alone. In the light of such a development as this its marked preference for the set of eight Holy Persons becomes intelligible, for by diverting attention from the set of nine, ending with the Perfect Buddha, it is able virtually to exclude the latter from the Ārya Sangha, thus implying that for the whole body of the faithful there is no higher goal than Arhantship. The exclusion of the Buddha automatically leads to the exclusion of the bodhisattva, who, according to the majority of Hīnayāna schools, is simply the Śākyamuni in his pre-Enlightenment days, and not, as maintained by the Mahāyāna, a universally valid ideal.

This lowering of spiritual standards was paralleled by movements of contraction in other fields. Though their own scriptures contained evidence to the contrary, the Hīnayāna schools tended more and more to regard the higher spiritual attainments as prerogatives of the monk. Thus the Ārya Sangha became in effect a subdivision of the bhikṣu-sangha or Monastic Order. For the laity it was sufficient to make offerings to the monks and on the strength of the merit thus accumulated to aspire to a happy heavenly birth. 'Keeping up the faith of the laity' in this sense is still a major preoccupation of the Sangha in Theravādin lands. Since the quantity of merit accruing from an offering depends on the virtue of the recipient, and since the appearance of virtue is more easily achieved than the reality, the growth of ethical formalism, and eventually of conscious or unconscious hypocrisy, is inevitably encouraged. Moreover, the absence of a more inspiring ideal soon affected the Hīnayāna monks themselves, and after the rise of the Mahāyāna such religious activity as there was among them increasingly tended to take the form of scholasticism in the sense of a purely formal elaboration of existing doctrinal patterns. The Sarvāstivādins succeeded in counting 147,825 kinds of Faith-Followers and 29,565 kinds of Doctrine-Followers.[84] The Uttarapāthakas, alone even among the Hīnayāna schools, distinguished themselves by eliminating compassion from their conception of Buddhahood.[85] Fortunately, long before these extreme developments took place the Mahāyāna had already outlined its own revivified and greatly enlarged conception of the Buddha's spiritual family.

16

THE GLORIOUS COMPANY OF BODHISATTVAS

THE BUDDHA OF the Mahāyāna is not merely a historical figure but the embodiment of the highest and most universal ideal of spiritual life. Consequently the Mahāyāna conception of his spiritual family is universal too. Essentially it comprises all those who, moved by the sufferings of others, dedicate themselves to the attainment of the highest spiritual good not for the sake of their own salvation only but in order that they may be able to benefit all sentient beings. A great soul of this type is technically called a bodhisattva and the spiritual community to which he belongs is known as the bodhisattva-sangha. It is to the flower of this 'ocean-wide' assembly that the Buddha, in his *sambhogakāya*, principally addresses the teachings recorded in the Mahāyāna sūtras. Many of these sūtras open with a vivid description of the vast and brilliant concourse then in attendance upon him, the description being idealized and emotionally heightened in such a way as to raise the mind to an exalted spiritual plane and prepare it for the apocalyptic revelations that are to follow. Thus after describing 1,250 Arhants in the terms already quoted (see p.131), and noticing 500 liberated nuns, laymen, and laywomen, the 'Large Perfection of Wisdom' speaks of

> hundreds of thousands of niyutas of kotis of Bodhisattvas – (1) all of whom had acquired the Dhāraṇīs; (2) dwellers in emptiness, their sphere in the signless, who had not fashioned any desire for the future; (3) who had acquired sameness and patience; (4) who had

> acquired the Dhāraṇī of non-attachment; (5) who had imperishable superknowledges; (6) were of acceptable speech; (7) not tricksters; (8) not chatterers, (9) with thoughts that had left behind all desire for reputation and gain, (10) disinterested demonstrators of the spiritual dharma; (11) ready to accept deep dharmas without reserve; (12) who had obtained the grounds of self-confidence; (13) had transcended Māra's deeds, (14) were free from obstacles caused by their (past) deeds; (15) and skilful in expounding the analysis of investigations into dharma; (16) who had formed their vows incalculable aeons ago; (17) who address others with smiling countenances; (18) without a frown on their faces; (19) skilful in songs, chants and benedictions; (20) with thoughts free from sluggishness; (21) with their flashes of ideas uninterrupted; (22) endowed with self-confidence when engaged in overpowering endless assemblies; (23) skilled in going forth during endless kotis of aeons; (24) resolutely intent on dharmas which they held to be like an illusion, a mirage, a reflection of the moon in water, a dream, an echo, an apparition, an image in the mirror, a magical creation; (25) skilful in understanding the destiny of beings, their subtle thoughts, their conduct and intentions; (26) with unobstructed thoughts; (27) endowed with extreme patience; (28) skilful in teaching others how to penetrate to the true character of reality; (29) acquiring through their vows and their setting-out the endless harmonies of all the Buddha-fields; (30) always face to face with the concentrated recollection of the Buddhas of countless world systems; (31) skilful in soliciting innumerable Buddhas; (32) skilful in appeasing the various views, biases, prepossessions, and defilements; (33) and in producing a hundred thousand concentrations and in playing with them.[86]

Some of the more distinguished bodhisattvas, ending with Maitreya, are then enumerated.

Iconographically the 1,250 Arhants are depicted as elderly shaven-headed monks clad in yellow robes, each holding a begging-bowl or a staff; they stand stiffly, with compressed lips, and their attitude seems not altogether free from strain. The bodhisattvas, by way of contrast, are all beautiful young princes. Gem-studded tiaras sparkle on their brows, while their nobly proportioned limbs are clad in light diaphanous garments of coloured silk. They wear gold bracelets and strings of jewels, and round their necks hang garlands of fragrant flowers. Their expression is smiling, their poses graceful and easy. These splendours do not indicate that the bodhisattvas are laymen; they symbolize their status as heirs of the Buddha, the King of the Dharma, and the untold spiritual riches to which they will one day succeed when, in the final stages of their career, they are themselves consecrated to Buddhahood. Despite the difference between their respective ideals, it is noteworthy that the Mahāyāna does not exclude the Arhants from membership of the Buddha's spiritual family. In the second chapter of the *Saddhārma-puṇḍarīka Sūtra*, or 'White Lotus of the Good Law', some members of the assembly, who apparently believe themselves to be Arhants, are so scandalized by the Buddha's announcement that they have something further to learn that they stage a walkout by way of protest – an episode that is not without its humbler parallels in the Buddhist world today.

As in the case of their Hīnayāna brethren, those making up the Glorious Company of Bodhisattvas are not all equal in attainment but distributed into a spiritual hierarchy consisting of various grades: some stand nearer to the throne of the Buddha, others further away. An account of this hierarchy, in brief but luminous outline, as well as of the various types of bodhisattva, is essential for a full understanding of the present subject. At the same time, here much more than when dealing with the Assembly of the Noble, must we be on our guard against the ever-recurrent danger of treating what is above all an ideal – according to the Mahāyāna the supreme ideal – of spiritual life, in so drily analytical a fashion, subdividing stages of progress and cataloguing their respective attributes, that the ideal as such is lost sight of. The anatomist may know every bone, and be able to trace every vein and sinew, of a dead human body, but he does not thereby know the living spirit of man. A mere enumeration of virtues and stages will never reveal to us the secret of bodhisattvahood. Such a warning is all the more necessary because much of the enormous quantity of canonical and commentarial literature dealing with the subject contains a strongly analytical element. In a truly Mahāyāna environment this is no disadvantage, for the living spiritual tradition, continued down to the present day by those who exemplify the bodhisattva ideal in their own persons, is powerful enough to correct the doctrinal tradition and prevent it from degenerating into scholasticism. But in the case of a purely theoretical account such as the present one awareness of the existence of such a possibility is not out of place. Before describing the different degrees and types of bodhisattva let us therefore contemplate the bodhisattva ideal itself in all its grandeur so that some reflection of the unique spiritual glory thereof may irradiate the details that follow.

The best picture of the bodhisattva is of course given in the Mahāyāna sūtras. Answering its own question as to how 'a son or daughter of good family' first aspires to become a bodhisattva, the *Aṣṭasāhasrikā* or *Perfection of Wisdom* 'in 8,000 Lines' says:

> He becomes endowed with that kind of wise insight which allows him to see all beings as on the way to their slaughter. Great compassion on that occasion takes hold of him. He surveys countless beings with his heavenly eye, and what he sees fills him with great agitation: so many carry the burden of a karma which leads to immediate retribution in the hells, others have acquired unfortunate rebirths (which keep them away from the Buddha and his teachings), others are doomed to be killed, or they are enveloped in the net of false views, or fail to find the path, while others who had gained a fortunate rebirth have lost it again. And he attends to them with the thought that: 'I shall become a saviour to all those beings, I shall release them from all their sufferings!'[87]

Despite the emphasis on compassion the bodhisattva is no mere sentimentalist. Nor, for all his tenderness, is he an effeminate weakling. He is the Great Hero, the embodiment not only of wisdom and compassion, but also of *vīrya* or vigour, a word which like the etymologically equivalent 'virility' signifies both energy and masculine potency. This aspect of the bodhisattva's personality is prominent in the well-known Ahicchatra image of Maitreya, with its powerful torso, massive yet graceful limbs, and clinging nether garment that covers without concealing his evident masculinity. The right hand is raised palm facing outwards and fingers slightly curved in the symbolical gesture of bestowing fearlessness (*abhaya-mudrā*).[88] Literary expression to the conception of the bodhisattva as Great Hero is given in another chapter of the sūtra already quoted.

> Suppose [says the Lord to Subhūti] that there were a most excellent hero, very vigorous, of high social position, handsome, attractive and most fair to behold, of many virtues, in possession of all the finest

> virtues, of those virtues which spring from the very height of sovereignty, morality, learning, renunciation and so on.

A whole catalogue of virtues and accomplishments then follows. After demanding of Subhūti whether such a person would not feel 'ever-increasing joy and zest' and receiving a reply in the affirmative, the Lord continues:

> Now suppose, further, that this person, so greatly accomplished, should have taken his family with him on a journey, his mother and father, his sons and daughters. By some circumstance they find themselves in a great, wild forest. The foolish ones among them would feel fright, terror and hair-raising fear. He, however, would fearlessly say to his family: 'Do not be afraid! I shall soon take you safely and securely out of this terrible and frightening forest. I shall soon set you free!' If then more and more hostile and inimical forces should rise up against him in that forest, would this heroic man decide to abandon his family, and to take himself alone out of that terrible and frightening forest – he who is not one to draw back, who is endowed with all the force of firmness and vigour, who is wise, exceedingly tender and compassionate, courageous and a master of many resources?
>
> Subhūti: No, O Lord. For that person, who does not abandon his family, has at his disposal powerful resources, both within and without.... He is competent to deal with the situation, and is able, unhurt and uninjured, soon to take out of that forest both his family and himself, and securely and safely they will reach a village, city or market town.
>
> The Lord: Just so, Subhūti, is it with a bodhisattva who is full of pity and concerned with the welfare of all beings, who dwells in friendliness, compassion, sympathetic joy and impartiality.[89]

These two quotations depict the bodhisattva from without, as he appears to others. Is it not possible to have a glimpse of his mind? Śāntideva, who was himself a bodhisattva, quotes from the *Vajradhvaja* or 'Diamond Banner' *Sūtra* a passage wherein the Great Being resolves and reflects as follows:

> I take upon myself the burden of all suffering, I am resolved to do so, I will endure it. I do not turn or run away, do not tremble, am not terrified, nor afraid, do not turn back or despond.

> And why? At all costs I must bear the burden of all beings. In that I do not follow my own inclinations. I have made the vow to save all beings. All beings I must set free. The whole world of living beings I must rescue, from the terrors of birth, of old age, of sickness, of death and rebirth, of all kinds of moral offence, of all states of woe, of the whole cycle of birth-and-death, of the jungle of false views, of the loss of wholesome dharmas, of the concomitants of ignorance – from all these terrors I must rescue all beings.... I walk so that the kingdom of unsurpassed cognition is built up for all beings. My endeavours do not merely aim at my own deliverance. For with the help of the boat of the thought of all-knowledge, I must rescue all these beings from the stream of Saṁsāra, which is so difficult to cross, I must pull them back from the great precipice, I must free them from all calamities, I must ferry them across the stream of Saṁsāra. I myself must grapple with the whole mass of suffering of all beings. To the limit of my endurance I will experience in all the states of woe, found in any world system, all the abodes of suffering. And I must not cheat all beings out of my store of merit. I am resolved to abide in each single state of woe for numberless aeons; and so I will help all beings to freedom, in all the states of woe that may be found in any world system whatsoever.
>
> And why? Because it is surely better that I alone should be in pain than that all these beings should fall into the states of woe. There I must give myself away as a pawn through which the whole world is redeemed from the terrors of the hells, of animal birth, of the world of Yama, and with this my own body I must experience, for the sake of all beings, the whole mass of all painful feelings. And on behalf of all beings I give surety for all beings, and in doing so I speak truthfully, am trustworthy, and do not go back on my word. I must not abandon all beings.
>
> And why? There has arisen in me the will to win all-knowledge, with all beings for its object, that is to say, for the purpose of setting free the entire world of beings.[90]

Even more fervent are Śāntideva's own outpourings in the *Bodhicaryāvatāra* or 'Introduction to the Way of Enlightenment'; but they are well known and need not be quoted here. What needs to be borne in mind is that the spirit of unprecedented altruism breathed by all these passages is the outcome not simply of mundane pity, nor even of spiritual compassion alone, but of compassion conjoined with wisdom. Self and non-self are equally real empirically and equally unreal metaphysically. To dedicate oneself to the salvation of others with the conviction that there in reality exist others who need saving is as much a source of bondage as to devote oneself to the task of one's own liberation under the impression that one has a real self to be liberated. The bodhisattva lives simultaneously in two worlds, the world of appearances and the world of reality, saṁsāra and Nirvāṇa, wisdom and compassion, though not because he commutes back and forth between them, but because of his realization that in the absolute sense they are not two. This dual – even paradoxical and contradictory – attitude of the bodhisattva, as it must seem from the standpoint of the rational mind, is the subject of endless repetition in the 'Perfection of Wisdom' literature. Thus at the very outset of the *Vajracchedikā* or 'Diamond-Cutter' *Sūtra* the Lord declares:

> Here, Subhūti, someone who has set out in the vehicle of a Bodhisattva should produce a thought in this manner: 'As many beings as there are in the universe of beings, comprehended under the term "beings" – egg-born, born from a womb, moisture-born, or miraculously born; with or without form; with perception, without perception, and with neither perception nor non-perception – as far as any conceivable form of beings is conceived: all these I must lead to Nirvāṇa, into that Realm of Nirvāṇa which leaves nothing behind. And yet, although innumerable beings have thus been led to Nirvāṇa, no being at all has been led to Nirvāṇa.' And why? If in a Bodhisattva the notion of 'being' should take place, he could not be called a 'Bodhi-being'. And why? He is not to be called a Bodhi-being, in whom the notion of a self or of a being should take place, or the notion of a living soul or of a person.[91]

Unless we keep steadily in view the transcendental insight and experience against which the glorious figure of the bodhisattva stands as against a background of gold, the exalted ideal that he embodies will inevitably degenerate into one of secular humanitarianism devoid of all higher spiritual content and value.

In the career of the bodhisattva, as he progresses from stage to stage of attainment, there occur three events of outstanding importance: the generation of the Will to Enlightenment (*bodhicitta-utpāda*), the becoming irreversible from Perfect Buddhahood, and the realization of the Three Bodies. The second is analogous to Stream Entry, the third to Arhantship. The first has no parallel, unless it be the taking of the Three Jewels (in the Hīnayāna sense) as one's sole refuge and undertaking to observe the Five Fundamental Precepts of ethical behaviour.

In preferring to render bodhicitta as the Will to rather than as the Thought of Enlightenment, we emphasize its essentially dynamic character. Though a cognitive element is not excluded, it is definitely a conative and emotional experience rather than an intellectual one. Suzuki in fact enthusiastically contends that *citta* in this context means desire and that the sense of *bodhicitta-utpāda* is really 'cherishing the desire for Enlightenment':

> It is a sort of conversion, the turning towards Enlightenment of the mind which was formerly engaged in something worldly, or the awakening of a new spiritual aspiration which has been dormant, or a new orientation of one's mental activities in a way hitherto undreamed of, or the finding of a new centre of energy which opens up an entirely fresh spiritual vista.[92]

Such being the case it is evident that the bodhicitta comes into being only after considerable preparation has been made. One must possess a stock of merit, be of good conduct, have equipped oneself with virtues, have respectfully served the Buddhas, have accomplished works of purity, enjoy the ministrations of spiritual friends, be thoroughly cleansed in heart, possess a firmly secured broadmindedness, have established a deep sincere faith and, above all, one's heart must be full of compassion.[93] Other lists of factors, all of which must be present before the desire for Enlightenment can arise, are also given.[94] Some of these obviously refer to external, others to internal, conditions. In keeping with the more social character of the Mahāyāna, the importance of the spiritual friend (*kalyāṇa-mitra*) is everywhere insisted upon. As the bodhisattva Mañjuśrī exhorts the youth Sudhana in the *Gaṇḍavyūha* or 'Flower-Array' *Sūtra*,

> If thou wishest to attain the knowledge which is possessed by the All-knowing One, be ever assiduous to get associated with good friends.[95]

So vital does Gampopa consider the part played in the life of the would-be bodhisattva by the meeting with such persons that he devotes to this topic the whole of the third chapter of *The Jewel Ornament of Liberation*. One of the canonical definitions of the *kalyāṇa-mitra* quoted by him reads:

> A Bodhisattva is known as a spiritual friend perfect in every way if he is endowed with eight qualities: (1) to possess a Bodhisattva's discipline in ethics and manners, (2) to be well versed in the Bodhisattvapiṭaka, (3) fully to comprehend the ultimately real, (4) to be full of compassion and love, (5) to possess the four intrepidities, (6) to have patience, (7) to have an indefatigable mind and (8) to use the right words.[96]

The essence of this and two other definitions Gampopa understands as being well versed in the message of the Mahāyāna and following the precepts of a bodhisattva.[97]

In reality the factors necessary for the production of the Will to Enlightenment consist of two quite distinct, even as it might seem at first sight contrary, series, which meet for the first time when that production takes place. The first series represents simple longing for the Unconditioned. In other words it stands for the religious impulse as understood by the Hīnayāna and, in forms of varying purity, by all the more highly-developed religions. It is the urge to get out, to escape, to withdraw; to find in the stillness of the Eternal that peace and rest one can never enjoy on earth. The second series represents a movement in the opposite direction. Living beings suffer. How can one forsake them? In the course of hundreds of thousands, even millions, of human births, has not every man and woman alive been at some time or other one's own father, one's own mother? The bonds of solidarity with all that breathe, with all that suffer, are surely too strong to be broken. In the being of the would-be bodhisattva both these tendencies struggle for fulfilment. As now one, now the other becomes uppermost, he is torn between the rival claims of Nirvāṇa and the world, self-realization and social service, the cloister and the hearth. Unless he is more richly endowed than the average, and unless he meets spiritual friends, he may break down under the strain and eventually try to solve the problem by suppressing one tendency and devoting himself exclusively to the cultivation of the other. Should this happen, he may well achieve success in whichever line he pursues; but he will not have exhausted the highest potentialities of human nature. The Mahāyāna advises the simultaneous cultivation of both tendencies. If this is done the would-be bodhisattva will ultimately reach a point of tension at which his dualistic notions snap and the two 'contradictory' tendencies coalesce to produce 'not a third note but a star'. This star is the bodhicitta. In it the tendency towards Nirvāṇa is represented by the wisdom-component, the tendency towards living beings by the compassion-component, the one being distinguishable but no longer separable from the other.

The bodhicitta is of two kinds, the absolute (*paramārtha*) and the relative (*samvṛtti*). Gampopa, following the *Sandhinirmocana Sūtra*, most beautifully describes the former.

> It is Śūnyatā endowed with the essence of Compassion, radiant, unshakable and impossible to formulate by concepts or speech.[98]

The latter, with which we are at present more concerned, is twofold, consisting of simple aspiration (*bodhipranidhicitta*) and actual 'establishment' or practice (*bodhiprasthānacitta*). Shorn of doctrinal elaborations, the first of these consists in desiring single-mindedly, wholeheartedly, and from the very depths of one's being, to attain Supreme Enlightenment for the benefit of all. Any intense desire tends to express itself spontaneously in verbal form as a definite resolution. In the case of the *pranidhicitta* this is technically known as the *praṇidhāna*, or vow, *mahāpraṇidhāna*, or great vow, and *pūrvapraṇidhāna*, or original vow, which every bodhisattva makes at the outset of his career. There are many versions of the vow, some of them being associated with the name of a particular bodhisattva. One of the shortest and best known is that which, according to Suzuki, is chanted in all Zen monasteries after a service, lecture, meal, or reading from the Scriptures:

> However innumerable beings are, I vow to save them;
> However inexhaustible the passions are, I vow to extinguish them;
> However immeasurable the Dharmas are, I vow to master them;
> However incomparable the Buddha-truth is, I vow to attain it.[99]

Other versions are much longer, consisting of a great number of clauses wherein the full implications of the vow are set forth in such detail as to provide almost a complete picture of the Mahāyāna religious ideal. In the *Sukhāvati-vyūha* or 'Array of the Happy Land' *Sūtra*, Dharmākara the bodhisattva, who after his Enlightenment became known as the Buddha Amitābha, is described as making a series of (according to the Chinese translation) forty-eight vows, of which the eighteenth – known as 'The King of the Vows' – is regarded by the Jōdō Shin Shū of Japan as constituting one of the main foundations of their faith.

> When I have obtained Buddhahood [resolves Dharmākara] if those beings who are in the ten quarters should believe in me with serene thoughts, and should wish to be born in my (Buddha-) country, and should have, say, ten times thought of me (or repeated my name) – if they should not be born there, may I not obtain the perfect knowledge; – barring only those beings who have committed the five deadly sins, and who have spoken evil of the good Law.[100]

However long or however short the bodhisattva's vow may be, he makes it publicly in the presence of a Buddha who thereupon predicts his attainment of Enlightenment after such-and-such number of aeons have passed and tells him the name by which, as a Buddha, he will then be known, together with the name of his Buddha-field. The inner meaning of these details is not difficult to interpret. The presence of the Buddha symbolizes the great truth that Enlightenment is a permanent possibility in the universe and the prediction (*vyākaraṇa*) the fact that its having been attained already by one human being guarantees its attainment by another possessing the same qualifications.

While the *pranidhicitta* is compared to the decision to walk, the *prasthānacitta* is said to resemble the actual process of walking. It embodies all the practices whereby a bodhisattva gradually becomes a Buddha. Prominent among these are the *pāramitās* or 'perfections', a set of six transcendental virtues associated especially with the bodhisattva ideal. They are *dāna* or giving, which is threefold, in respect of material things, education and culture, and spiritual knowledge; *śīla* or morality; *kṣānti* or patient acceptance, whether of abuse, physical suffering, or the more paradoxical and profound teachings of the Mahāyāna; *vīrya* or exertion, mental, physical, and spiritual, for the benefit of all beings; *dhyāna* or absorption in states of superconsciousness without allowing them to become the basis for future celestial rebirth; and *prajñā*, or wisdom, in the distinctively Mahāyāna sense of insight into the emptiness of persons and things and an understanding of the fundamental non-duality, in the absolute sense, of saṁsāra and Nirvāṇa. Strictly speaking *prajñā* is the sole *pāramitā*, for only in association with it are the other *pāramitās* reckoned as such. When cultivated for the sake of mundane benefits, including rebirth in heaven, or in order to gain individual emancipation, they may be very great and noble qualities but they are not *pāramitās*. A *pāramitā*, in fact, is essentially any virtue practised by the bodhisattva in association with *prajñā* in order to gain Supreme Enlightenment for the benefit of all beings. Four more *pāramitās* were subsequently added to the original list of six: *upāya-kauśalya*, or skilful means; *praṇidhāna* or vow; *bala* or power, and *jñāna* or knowledge. The first of these is equivalent to compassion as spontaneously expressing itself in innumerable ways and means of leading sentient beings on the Path of Deliverance. The reappearance of *praṇidhāna* reminds us that the bodhicitta is not a phenomenon which arises once at the beginning of a bodhisattva's career and then subsides: like a tiny spark that develops from a flame into a world-engulfing conflagration it grows as he progresses. At his present level of attainment (for as we shall see later the *pāramitās* are correlated with a series of stages of spiritual progress known as the *bhūmis*) that which was once a simple aspiration has become a cosmic force showering grace and blessing on all within the sphere of its influence. *Bala* or power, the third of the additional *pāramitās*, represents this force raised to the highest possible degree and universalized. *Jñāna* or knowledge stands for the subtlest type of *prajñā*, that which sees not only the non-duality of the conditioned and the Unconditioned but also that this non-duality does not stand in the way of the one being the spontaneous outpouring of the other.

With the arising of the relative twofold bodhicitta one passes beyond the stage of an ordinary being (says the *Gaṇḍavyūha Sūtra*), enters into the rank of bodhisattvahood, is born into the family of the Tathāgatas, is irreproachable and faultless in his (Buddha-) family honour, stands away from all worldly courses, enters into a superworldly life, is established in things belonging to bodhisattvahood, abides in the abode of the bodhisattva, is impartially ushered into the Tathāgata-groups of the past, present, and future, and is ultimately destined for Supreme Enlightenment.[101] It is natural, therefore, that the Mahāyāna should attach great importance to this experience and be loud in its praises. Maitreya tells the youth Sudhana:

The Bodhicitta is like a seed because from it grows all the truths of Buddhism. It is like a farm because here are produced all things of purity for the world.

The Bodhicitta is like the earth because all the worlds are supported by it. It is like water because all the dirt of the passions is thereby cleansed. It is like the wind because it blows all over the world with nothing obstructing its course. It is like fire because it consumes all the fuel of bad logic.

The Bodhicitta is like the sun because it leaves nothing unenlightened on earth. It is like the moon because it fills to perfection all things of purity. It is like a lamp because it brings things out in the light. It is like an eye because it perceives where the road is even and where it is uneven.

The Bodhicitta is like a highway because it leads one to the city of knowledge. It is like a sacred ford because it keeps away all that is not proper. It is like a carriage because it carries all the Bodhisattvas. It is like a door because it opens to all the doings of the Bodhisattva.

The Bodhicitta is like a mansion because it is the retreat where Samādhi and meditation are practised. It is like a park because it is where the enjoyment of truth (*dharmarati*) is experienced. It is like a dwelling-house because it is where all the world is comfortably sheltered. It is like a refuge because it gives a salutary abode to all beings. It is like an asylum because it is where all the Bodhisattvas walk.

The Bodhicitta is like a father because it protects all the Bodhisattvas. It is like a mother because it brings up all the Bodhisattvas. It is like a nurse because it takes care of all the Bodhisattvas. It is like a good friend because it gives good advice to all the Bodhisattvas. It is like a king because it overpowers the minds of all the Śrāvakas and the Pratyekabuddhas. It is like a great sovereign because it fulfils all the excellent vows.

The Bodhicitta is like a great ocean because it harbours all the gems of virtues. It is like Mount Sumeru because it towers impartially above all things. It is like Mount Cakravada because it supports all the world. It is like Mount Himalaya because it produces all sorts of knowledge-herbs. It is like Mount Gandhamādana because it harbours all kinds of virtue-fragrance. It is like space because it infinitely spreads out the merit of goodness....[102]

And so on for scores of pages.

The next great event that occurs in the bodhisattva's career is the attainment of what is technically called *avaivartika* or 'irreversibility'. On his first setting out he may not have realized fully how long and difficult would be the path to Supreme Buddhahood. For some time after the bodhicitta has arisen, therefore, the possibility exists that as the magnitude of the task he has undertaken gradually dawns on him the bodhisattva may become depressed, dispirited, and afraid, so that, overwhelmed by a sense of his own inadequacy, he may even decide to renounce his aim and fall back to the comparatively short and easy path of the Arhant or the Private Buddha. Only when he is so far advanced on the Path to Supreme Buddhahood that such a possibility no longer exists is he said to be irreversible. According to some sources, this takes place when he fully realizes the meaning of wisdom in the Mahāyāna sense, that is, when he knows that Nirvāṇa and saṁsāra are equally void and that between them there is as it were nothing to choose. For one bent on Arhantship saṁsāra is a positive process of origination, Nirvāṇa the negative counter-process of cessation, each process being different from the other and both real. As soon as the bodhisattva realizes that these two terms are discriminations of the mind, and that there is in the highest sense no difference between them, abandonment of the former in order to achieve the latter for him ceases to be even a possibility. Like a traveller on whom it dawns that what he took for a city is a mirage, so that he feels no further inclination to go there, the irreversible bodhisattva cannot be tempted by the Nirvāṇa of the Hīnayāna because for him it does not exist. Such a bodhisattva has reached a very lofty state. He is no longer an individual in the ordinary sense. Consequently it is very difficult to describe him, or to explain at length in what his irreversibility consists. The seventeenth and (in part) twentieth chapter of the *Aṣṭasāhasrikā* do, however, enumerate some of the attributes, tokens, and signs by which an irreversible bodhisattva can be recognized. In any case, the question of recognition is one which concerns only those who are not of this category, for one of the tokens is that to the irreversible bodhisattva himself it does not occur to ask whether he is irreversible or not.[103]

As listed in this sūtra, the attributes are very miscellaneous in character, ranging from the profound to the trivial. Haribhadra, the author of the *Abhisamayālaṅkāra*, does his best to schematize them by distributing them among various stages of progress.[104] Many are simply moral qualities of the true monk, and have no doctrinal or higher spiritual significance; others make more explicit one or another aspect of the bodhisattva ideal itself. Only a few are really relevant and striking. Thus when at the beginning of the seventeenth chapter the subject is first raised, and Subhūti asks what are the attributes, tokens, and signs of an irreversible bodhisattva, and how he can be known as such, the Lord replies:

> The level of the common people, the level of the Disciples, the level of the Pratyekabuddhas, the level of the Buddhas – they are all called the 'Level of Suchness'. With the thought that all these are, through Suchness, not two, not divided, not discriminated, undiscriminate, he enters on this Suchness, this nature of Dharma. After he has stood firmly in Suchness, he neither imagines nor discriminates it. In that sense does he enter into it. When he has thus entered on it, even when he has gone away from the assembly where he has heard about Suchness, he does not hesitate, does not become perplexed, does not doubt, and he is not stupefied by the thought (concerning form, etc.) that 'it is not thus'. On the contrary, he firmly believes that 'it is just this, just Suchness,' and like that he plunges into it.[105]

Suchness is a more 'positive' synonym for the Void. The irreversible bodhisattva realizes that in the absolute sense there is no difference between the Path of Arhantship and the Path of Bodhisattvahood. On the relative plane this realization finds expression in the teaching that it is possible for an Arhant who has become aware of the limitations of his attainment to develop the bodhicitta and traverse the remaining stages up to Perfect Buddhahood. In other words the irreversible bodhisattva is not attached to his own *yāna* as to an independent reality: he knows that, as the *Saddhārma-puṇḍarīka Sūtra* teaches in the Parable of the Burning House, the distinction of paths is due to differences of individual temperament and ability, and that the *yānas* of the disciple, the Pratyekabuddha, and the bodhisattva all ultimately converge into the Buddhayāna. Further tokens are that he does not pander to *śramaṇas* and *brāhmaṇas* of other schools and pays no homage to strange gods. He is not liable to be reborn as a result of karma on the planes of the animals, the revenants, and the tormented spirits, nor as a woman, though in pursuit of his mission he may, out of compassion, voluntarily assume any of these forms. Probably by way of checking any tendency to antinomianism, always a danger in India, the immaculate purity of his moral conduct is strongly insisted upon, and he is described as being ever mindful and vigilant. Formidable temptations may assail him. A monk may tell the bodhisattva:

> What you have heard just now, that is not the word of the Buddha. It is poetry, the work of poets. But what I here teach to you, that is the teaching of the Buddha, that is the word of the Buddha.[106]

Similarly he may be urged to put an end to all suffering in this very life, or it may be suggested that since even those who have been following the Path of Bodhisattvahood for aeons have not yet reached full Enlightenment his own case is hopeless. Such temptations are all the work of Māra, the Evil One. If a bodhisattva succeeds in overcoming them it is yet another sign of irreversibility. The twentieth chapter confines its attention to three signs, all of great interest. Suppose one bodhisattva is asked by another who wants to win full Enlightenment what kind of aspiration one should form in one's mind. If he speaks merely about Nirvāṇa, without including in his reply any reference to compassion, he is not irreversible. But if on the other hand, whether he has heard of the Perfection of Wisdom teachings or not, he hits upon the correct answer, then he is to be known as an irreversible bodhisattva. Another mark of irreversibility relates to dream experiences. A bodhisattva may, for instance, behold in his dreams that all *dharmas* are like a dream, yet not realize the experience regarding it as final; he may see himself as a Buddha, surrounded by monks and bodhisattvas, and preaching the Doctrine; or, again, he may have the experience of remaining quite unafraid even when his head is about to be struck off. Such experiences indicate that in the case of the irreversible bodhisattva the bodhisattva ideal has sunk so deep as to influence and transform even his unconscious mind. The last mark concerns irreversibility and the magical power of veracity. As for Indian thought in general, it is axiomatic for Buddhism that truthfulness is a power capable of producing tangible results. A bodhisattva may, therefore, make a solemn asseveration of his irreversibility and on the strength thereof conjure a ghost to depart from a person of whom it had taken possession. Should the ghost depart, it could be inferred that the bodhisattva was irreversible.[107] The twenty-first chapter, however, hastens to add that the ghost might be driven out by Māra in order to make the bodhisattva think himself irreversible when in fact he was not. This possibility introduces a whole new series of temptations not directly connected with the topic of irreversibility.

About the bodhisattva's third and crowning experience, the transmutation of his body, speech, and mind into the Triple Body of Perfect Enlightenment, even less can be said than about his attainment of irreversibility, for the further he progresses along his chosen path the less accessible he becomes even to the most highly refined categories of human thought. The sūtras themselves prefer to depict this experience symbolically in terms of a solemn ceremony of consecration (*abhiṣeka*, literally 'sprinkling'), or coronation as it would be in the West, at which, in the same way that the heir to an Indian throne was formally invested with the royal dignity, an assembly of all the Buddhas raised the bodhisattva to the rank of a Fully Enlightened One and endowed him with all the powers of his new position. The literal enactment of this ceremony between an enlightened human guru and his disciple came later on to occupy a place of central importance in the Vajrayāna tradition. Historically speaking, the bodhisattva's Enlightenment occurs under conditions much the same as those obtaining in the case of Gautama the Buddha, within the period of whose dispensation we still live. As for the content of the experience, and the nature of the Goal realized therein, all that has been said before on these topics in this book is no less relevant to the present context. One additional word only need be said. Though what are termed the 'early' Mahāyāna sūtras, including the bulk of the *Prajñāpāramitā* corpus, do not teach explicitly in so many words the doctrine of the Three Bodies (*trikāya*), the later and more fully developed tradition is positive that on his consecration to Buddhahood the bodhisattva obtains not only the *dharmakāya*, but also the *sambhogakāya* and *nirmāṇakāya*, and that through the perfect instrumentality of these two bodies, the first of which is in a sense common to all Buddhas, he continues for endless time and throughout boundless space his work of universal salvation.

The arising of the bodhicitta, the attainment of irreversibility, and consecration, as well as other lesser experiences, are strung out like landmarks along a series of stages of progress generally known as *bhūmis* (literally 'grounds'). Different canonical sources give of these stages descriptions which do not tally in all particulars, not even with regard to the total number of them or their respective names.

Eventually, however, the enormously detailed and systematic account given in the *Daśabhūmika Sūtra* won acceptance as the standard one. As the name of this sūtra reveals, it reckons the *bhūmis* as ten in number. Their names are the Joyful (*pramuditā*), the Immaculate (*vimalā*), the Illuminating or Radiant (*prabhākarī*), the Blazing (*arciṣmatī*), the Very Difficult to Conquer (*sudurjayā*), the Face-to-Face (*abhimukhī*), the Far-Going (*dūraṅgamā*), the Immovable (*acalā*), Good Thoughts (*sādhumatī*), and the Cloud of the Doctrine (*dharmameghā*). Most of these terms are obviously symbolic and poetic rather than scientific. This reminds us of the fact that divisions and subdivisions are not to be taken too literally, and that essentially the Bodhisattva Path is not an affair of steps and stages but of continuous progressive growth in wisdom and compassion. Nevertheless, a special feature of the *Daśabhūmika Sūtra* is that it distributes among the ten *bhūmis* all the more important doctrinal categories and spiritual practices of Buddhism. Thus in the third *bhūmi* the bodhisattva cultivates the four *brahma-vihāras*, in the fifth he understands the Four Noble Truths. Perhaps the most valuable instance of this procedure, which constitutes the *Sūtra* a veritable encyclopedia of Buddhism, is that which correlates the ten *pāramitās* or transcendental virtues with the ten *bhūmis*, the practice of giving predominating in the first *bhūmi*, that of morality in the second, and so on. Why a teaching should be assigned to one stage rather than to another is not always clear, however. Moreover, every one of the stages is packed so full of doctrines and practices, and they are all highly praised in such identical terms, that a number of them are in danger of losing their individuality. Yet despite the presence of all these trees, the wood is not quite lost to sight. Thanks to the ten *pāramitās*, and to the placing of the three crucial experiences of his career, which provide the most important points of reference, the outlines of the bodhisattva's progress stand out with sufficient sharpness. With the arising of the bodhicitta he enters upon the first *bhūmi*, where he makes his great vow and receives his prediction. Having stood face to face with the common reality of Nirvāṇa and saṁsāra in the sixth, and reached the seventh by going far from the possibility of gaining Arhantship, he attains the immovable state of irreversibility in the eighth *bhūmi*. In the tenth *bhūmi* he receives his consecration.

Taking these three great events, and the stages in which they occur, as lines of demarcation, we find that as regards their degree of attainment bodhisattvas may be classified as belonging to four groups. First there is the novice bodhisattva, or aspirant to bodhisattvahood, who accepts intellectually the bodhisattva ideal, and does his best to live up to it, while at the same time making efforts for the generation of the bodhicitta. He may or may not have received the formal bodhisattva initiation described in the following chapter. To this group belong the vast majority of professing Mahāyāna Buddhists, whether monks, nuns, or lay devotees. The second group consists of all who have attained any of the first six *bhūmis*, and who may, therefore, be called bodhisattvas of the Path. In this group are also included the so-called Hīnayāna bodhisattvas, from the Stream-Entrant up to the Arhant, for if they so desire these can, according to the most liberal Mahāyāna teaching on the subject, at any time renounce the idea of individual emancipation and follow instead the bodhisattva ideal. Because of its correspondence with this group the Assembly of the Noble is regarded as comprised in the Glorious Company of Bodhisattvas. The third group is made up of the irreversible bodhisattvas, who are the bodhisattvas *par excellence*. They have already been separately dealt with. The fourth and highest group is that of the bodhisattvas of the *dharmakāya*. This includes those who, after Perfect Enlightenment, retain their bodhisattva form, as well as all who are the direct emanations of the *dharmakāya* and have no human history. Between such bodhisattvas and the Buddhas there is no real difference. Broadly speaking, the former embody the static, the latter the dynamic aspect of the *dharmakāya*.

So far we have dealt with the bodhisattvas collectively. Individual bodhisattvas are, however, well known in the Mahāyāna, thousands of them being in fact mentioned in the Scriptures by name. The greatest, who are comparatively few in number, occupy in the religious life of the Mahāyāna a place not second to that of the historical founder of Buddhism himself, being regarded as supreme objects of devotion and sources of the highest spiritual inspiration, illumination, and guidance. Uninformed or unsympathetic writers on Buddhism often refer to them as gods, a misleading usage which, for those belonging to a different religious *milieu*, at once equates the worship of bodhisattvas with polytheism, and reduces Buddhism to the level of a pagan cult.

The most popular bodhisattvas constitute two well-known groups, one consisting of five and the other of eight members. The five dhyāni-bodhisattvas (as they have been styled by Western writers) are associated with the five so-called dhyāni-Buddhas, iconographically as their attendants, but in reality as their dynamic counterparts or emanations. The relation is also envisaged as one of spiritual sonship. Thus Samantabhadra is associated with Vairocana, Vajrapāṇi with Akṣobhya, Ratnapāṇi with Ratnasambhava, Avalokiteśvara with Amitābha, and Viśvapāṇi with Amoghasiddhi. Together with their respective *ḍākinīs* or *prajñās*, or Feminine Counterparts, and a host of minor emanations, these make up the Five Spiritual Families (*pañca-kula*), on the complex symbolism of which is based much Vajrayāna practice, especially in the realms of art and meditation, and to one or another of which, by reason of individual temperament and line of spiritual practice, every follower of the Vajrayāna is normally affiliated. The Eight bodhisattvas are Samantabhadra, Vajrapāṇi, Avalokiteśvara, Mañjuśrī, Maitreya, Ākāśagarbha, Kṣitigarbha, and Sarvanivaraṇaviṣkambhin. Two more, Mahāsthāmaprāpta and Trailokyavijaya, are sometimes added, raising the number to ten. Some writers make a sharp distinction between the two groups, designating the latter as that of the human, and the former that of the divine bodhisattvas; but though a difference undoubtedly exists, the fact that several bodhisattvas belong to both groups shows it is not an absolute one.

After making deductions on account of the three duplicated names, we are left with a total of twelve bodhisattvas, some better known than others. The best known, whether in China, Japan, or Tibet, are Mañjuśrī, Avalokiteśvara, Vajrapāṇi, Maitreya, Samantabhadra, Mahāsthāmaprāpta, and Kṣitigarbha. For the devotee, each of these great beings possesses a distinctive spiritual personality, and is as much a reality to him as Christ and the saints to a devout Christian, or the deified heroes Rāma and Kṛṣṇa to a pious Hindu.

This is especially true of the first three, who as a triad are worshipped throughout Tibet and Nepal as the Three Family Protectors (Tibetan *rig-sum-gon-po*), the families being those of their respective Buddhas – Vairocana, Amitābha, and Akṣobhya – who form the original nucleus out of which was developed the well-known scheme of five 'dhyāni' Buddhas. Since there is a correspondence between the transcendental axiality of Buddhahood and the mundane axiality of the human state, it is natural that the three chief bodhisattvas, as embodiments of main aspects of the *dharmakāya*, should correspond to the three principal functions of the mind. Thus Mañjuśrī represents wisdom, or transmuted intellect, Avalokiteśvara compassion, or purified emotion, and Vajrapāṇi power, or sublimated volition. This distribution of attributes is the principal factor determining the characters and types of spiritual activity of these great beings.

Mañjuśrī-Kumarabhuta, 'Gently Auspicious One, Who Became a Prince', is known by many other names and titles. He is Mañjughoṣa, 'Gentle-Voiced One', Mañjunātha, 'Gentle Saviour', and Vagīśvara, 'Lord of Speech'. In China he is known by the transliteration Man-chu-shi-li, as well as by the epithet Wên-shu, 'He of the Five [Mountain] Peaks' (a misunderstanding of Pañcaśikha, 'He of the Five [Hair-]Crests'). The Buddhists of Tibet, translating 'Gentle-Voiced One' into their own tongue, call him Jambeyang; those of Japan simply Monju. His appearance in the oldest Mahāyāna literature testifies to his pre-eminence from an early date. Besides being the main object of minor works devoted specially to his cult, he plays a leading role in the *Saddhārma-puṇḍarīka* and figures prominently in the *Prajñāpāramitā*. In the *Vimalakīrti-nirdeśa*, or 'Exposition of Vimalakīrti', he alone among the bodhisattvas ventures to call on that formidable old debater. As Mahāmati, 'The Greatly Intelligent One', he is the principal interlocutor of the *Laṅkāvatāra*; in the *Gaṇḍavyūha* he ranks as one of the two leaders of the 500 bodhisattvas of that sūtra, as well as first teacher of the youth Sudhana, whom he instructs and sends forth on his long quest; and he is honourably mentioned in the Smaller *Sukhāvatī-vyūha*. His place in Vajrayāna literature is no less distinguished, for he gives his name to the *Mañjuśrī-mūla-kalpa*, or 'Basic Rite', 'a voluminous text which represents the transitional stage from sūtra to tantra'.[108] Iconographically he is depicted in a bewildering variety of forms: Bhattacharyya lists thirteen principal ones according to Indian tradition.[109] Usually, however, he manifests as a beautiful youth, sixteen years old, golden in hue, richly clad in the silks and ornaments of a bodhisattva, and wearing at the parting of his hair and over his ears three blue lotuses. His special emblems are the lotus, book, and flaming sword; his animal, the lion. One of his most popular forms is Arapacana, so called from the first five letters of the mystic alphabet, as whom he sits cross-legged on a moon-mat and lotus brandishing the fiery Sword of Knowledge above his head with the right hand, while with the left he presses to his heart the Book, understood to represent the *Prajñāpāramitā*, the scripture of wisdom *par excellence*, with which he is specially associated. As the patron of arts and sciences, inspirer of literature, and supreme master of sacred eloquence, he is invoked, worshipped, and meditated upon, and his mantra repeated, particularly for a retentive memory, knowledge of the Scriptures, understanding of the Doctrine, and power of exposition. With what attitude his devotees approach him is best illustrated by the following *stuti* or Hymn of Praise, wherein the author, *siddhācarya* Vajrayudha, lauds by turns his mind, composed of wisdom and compassion, his speech, and his body.

> To thee, whose understanding, purifying like a cloud-free sun the two obscurations (*āvaraṇa*), and very clear,
> Sees all matters whatsoever (as they are), wherefore thou dost hold the volume (of *Prajñāpāramitā*) to thy heart;
> [To thee who] in kindness, as though to an only son, to living beings – covered as they are in the prison of temporal existence
> With the darkness of *avidyā* and afflicted by *duḥkha* – [dost utter] Thy Speech, with a sixty-(four-)fold voice,
> Resounding loud as thunder, waking the sleep of the *kleśas*, unfastening the iron fetters of karma,
> Dispersing the darkness of ignorance, and [who,] cutting off every sprout of *duḥkha*, [dost] grasp the sword:
> To the body of the chief among Jinas and their sons, his body-of-virtues perfected,
> Pure from the start and arrived at the end of the ten *bhūmis*,
> Adorned with the ten tens of ornaments and twelve, dispersing the darkness of our mind – to [thee] Mañjughoṣa we bow.

The meaning of the name Avalokiteśvara has been the subject of much scholarly debate. Iśvara indisputably means Lord. According to whether it is understood as a passive or as an active participle Avalokita may mean either one who is gazed at or one who gazes. In the latter case the name would mean, being interpreted, the Lord who looks down in pity on the miseries of the world, a popular etymology. Sometimes the last part of Avalokiteśvara is identified not with *iśvara* but with *svara*, meaning sound. The usual Chinese translation is based on this interpretation. Whatever its dictionary meaning, the sacred name undoubtedly combines, most appropriately, the ideas of spiritual sovereignty and compassion. Among the hundreds of other names of this bodhisattva are Padmapāṇi, or 'Lotus-in-hand',

Lokanātha, 'Saviour of the World', and Mahākārunika, 'Greatly Compassionate One'. In Tibet he is known as Chenrezi, 'He Who Sees With Bright Eyes', in China (where he underwent transformation into a female bodhisattva) as Kuan-yin or Kuan-shih-yin, 'Regarder of the Cries of the World', and in Japan as Kwannon. As simply Nātha, the saviour, he continues to be worshipped in Theravādin Sri Lanka, having temples and servitors of his own at Kandy and elsewhere. Literary references to Avalokiteśvara are fewer than to Mañjuśrī. The *Mahāvastu*, which belongs to the third century BCE, contains two *Avalokita Sūtras*, but these consist mainly of accounts of Gautama Buddha's Enlightenment, and have nothing to do with the bodhisattva. He is mentioned in the Larger *Sukhāvatī-vyūha*, and in the *Amitāyur-dhyāna*, where as an attendant of the Buddha of Infinite Life he is described in the tenth series of sixteen meditations on the glories of the Happy Land. Though having no special connection with the *Prajñāpāramitā*, he appears at the opening of the famous 'Heart Sūtra', the contents of which are presented as a revelation of his spiritual experience as he courses in transcendental wisdom. The main canonical sources of his cult are the *Saddhārma-puṇḍarīka* and the *Kāraṇḍa-vyūha Sūtra*. In the twenty-fourth chapter of the former (the twenty-fifth of the Chinese translation) – which often circulates as an independent work and may have been composed separately and afterwards inserted into the sūtra – he appears as Samantamukha, 'The One Facing Everywhere', and is praised for the benefits he confers on all his worshippers. This chapter also contains the bodhisattva Akṣayamati's 'Hymn to Avalokiteśvara', one of the jewels of Mahāyāna literature. The *Kāraṇḍa-vyūha*, reputedly the first Buddhist text translated into Tibetan, is a composite work displaying marked Hindu features that departs so far from doctrinal orthodoxy as to describe, among the exploits of the bodhisattva, how he created the world in the time of Vipaśvin Buddha, producing the sun and moon from his eyes and the gods of Hinduism from different parts of his body. It also relates how Avalokiteśvara obtained the great six-syllabled mantra *oṁ mani padme hūm*, perhaps the most famous of all Buddhist invocations. Both these sūtras reflect the Mahāyāna conviction that the bodhisattva is concerned with the temporal as well as the spiritual welfare of his devotees. According to the *Saddhārma-puṇḍarīka* Avalokiteśvara delivers those who call on his name from such dangers as fire, flood, shipwreck, execution by the sword, attacks of wicked demons, imprisonment, and robbery. Those possessed by craving, hatred, and delusion have only to remember and revere him and they will be set free. A woman who desires a child should pray to him. Endowed as he is with such amiable qualities it is small wonder that his cult should have flourished above that of any other bodhisattva. As depicted in art his figure is hardly less attractive than that of the Buddha. Iconographically speaking he possesses at least fifteen major forms,[110] but one of the best known, even as it is among the most beautiful, is that of a slenderly built young prince in a high jewelled headdress who, with body gracefully bent, stands bearing a lotus in his left hand and making the gesture of bestowing alms with the right, while his beautiful face is alive with tenderness and compassion. More bizarre, though equally expressive, is the form in which he appears with eleven heads and a thousand arms, signifying the omnipresence and omnipotence of his compassion. In the palm of each hand is an eye, suggesting that even in its remotest operations compassion is never divorced from wisdom. His universality does not however exclude a specific cosmic function. As the spiritual son of Amitābha, of whom Gautama is the earthly reflex, he is responsible for the spiritual evolution of the human race during the interregnum between the withdrawal of the last human Buddha and the advent of the next.

Vajrapāṇi, or 'The Thunderbolt-Handed One', despite his enormous popularity throughout Tibet, Mongolia, and China, figures hardly at all in the great canonical texts of the Mahāyāna. As from his name one might expect, his distinctive emblem is the *vajra*, originally meaning thunderbolt, and sculptures and paintings invariably depict him with it. Sometimes it rests at shoulder level upon an open lotus, the stalk of which he holds; or he may press it against his chest with his right hand, or balance it upon its point on his palm. Indeed, the bodhisattva's later rise to fame may be due partly to his association with this emblem, which after its transformation into the chief symbol for wisdom and the Void, gave its name to the Vajrayāna. As befits his position as the embodiment of transcendental power, Vajrapāṇi, unlike Mañjuśrī and Avalokiteśvara, is venerated less under his peaceful (*śānta*) than his wrathful (*krodha*) aspect as destroyer of the darkness of spiritual ignorance. In Tibet, where he is known as Dorje-lek-pa and Chagna Dorje, both of which translate the Indian name, he is depicted in religious art with tremendous zest. There are many forms, but he is usually dark blue in colour, with a stout body, protuberant belly, and thick, short limbs. His heads, which may be one or many, are crowned with skulls, and his facial expression is one of terrific anger. He may be naked save for ornaments of human bone, or draped in a tiger-skin. According to the number of his arms, he carries the *vajra*, a snake, a small drum, a chopper, and a human skull filled with blood, while the disengaged hands assume various *mudrās*. Generally he moves to the right, one foot uplifted to trample upon prostrate figures representing the forces of mundane existence. Around him swirls an aureole of flames. For those brought up in, or familiar with, the Tibetan tradition, the contemplation of this awe-inspiring figure is productive of heroic emotions of fearlessness and an intense spiritual exaltation.

Like other great bodhisattvas the Three Family Protectors project or emanate from themselves various other bodhisattvas who thereafter assume an independent or quasi-independent existence. No hard and fast line of demarcation can however be drawn between their forms and their emanations, the difference being one of degree rather than of kind. A bodhisattva's emanations, which may themselves be polymorphous, are often of that wrathful type, the most important representatives of which are known as *dharmāpalas*, or 'defenders of the faith', it being their duty to guard the Doctrine against all hostile forces. Thus Mañjuśrī emanates Yamāntaka, 'The Destroyer of Death', who in his black naked form as Vajrabhairava, 'The Fearful Thunderbolt', with nine heads, the centre one that of a bull, and thirty-four arms, two of which clasp his feminine counterpart, is the tutelary deity of the Gelugpas. Avalokiteśvara emanates Padmanarteśvara, 'The Lotus Lord of Dance'. He is generally represented in a dancing attitude, with one head and eighteen hands, all of which hold double lotuses, and he is the Tutelary Deity of the Nyingmapas. The most attractive emanation is undoubtedly the female bodhisattva Tārā, meaning both 'Saviouress' and 'Star', who appears in a multiplicity of peaceful and wrathful forms. A beautiful legend tells how she was born from the tears of Avalokiteśvara as he wept over the miseries of the world. As such she embodies the very quintessence of compassion. Her two best-known forms are the White Tārā and the Green Tārā. As the former she holds a white lotus, as the latter a blue lotus. Both depict her as a benign and beautiful woman, neither young nor old, wearing the customary silks and jewels of a bodhisattva. Besides being worshipped throughout Tibet and Mongolia, where she is known as Jetsun Dolma, 'The Faithful Dolma', she is adored in Nepal and in parts of China, and has even managed to survive under her own and other names in Hindu India. On account of her maternal qualities she is related to her devotees in a particularly affectionate and intimate manner.

Maitreya (Pāli Metteyya), 'The Friendly One', also known as Ajita, 'The Unconquered', is without question the most prominent of the remaining bodhisattvas. As the one destined to become the next human Buddha, he enjoys the unique distinction of being the only bodhisattva recognized throughout the entire Buddhist world, in Theravādin as well as in Mahāyāna lands, for which reason it has been suggested that his worship might constitute a means of unification among Buddhists. Though his name occurs only once in the *Nikāyas*, when the Buddha prophesies his advent,[111] he is frequently alluded to in Pāli exegetical literature: Buddhaghosa concludes the *Visuddhimagga* (according to the Sinhalese texts) with a fervent poetical aspiration to attain Arhantship in his presence. He is also mentioned in the earlier Sanskrit and Mixed Sanskrit works such as the *Lalitavistara*, the *Divyāvadāna*, and the *Mahāvastu*. In the *Saddhārma-puṇḍarīka* he plays a prominent part, but still is subordinate to Mañjuśrī, who acts as his instructor. Minor works such as the *Maitreya-vyākaraṇa* or 'Prediction Concerning Maitreya' relate in detail the circumstances of his coming. Strictly speaking, he is at present a bodhisattva of the ninth *bhūmi*, but tradition often speaks of him, by anticipation, as a Buddha, and as such he is frequently depicted in art. Of brilliant golden hue, he bears for emblems the wheel, the *stūpa*, and the sacred vase (*kalasa*). The last of these, now closed, contains ambrosia, representing the Truth with which he will one day besprinkle mankind. Both as Buddha and as bodhisattva he often sits not in the more usual cross-legged posture, but as though upon a chair, in European fashion, thus indicating his readiness to descend from the Tuṣita Heaven, where he now resides, to the Earth, in order to fulfil his original vow by traversing the tenth and last *bhūmi* and gaining Supreme Buddhahood for the benefit of all. Various attempts have been made by non-Buddhists to identify Maitreya with their own spiritual heroes. Christian missionaries, in an attempt to undermine the loyalties of the faithful, have been known to argue that the Buddha's predictions about Maitreya really refer to Christ. J. Krishnamurti has been similarly acclaimed. For the Buddhist world, however, the messianic hopes which centre on the person of Maitreya are as yet unfulfilled. According to widespread beliefs, his advent will be preceded by the reappearance of Nāgārjuna and other ancient sages, and by the unification of the whole world under the rule of a righteous Buddhist king. Meanwhile, throughout Central Asia and the Himālayan borderlands, where his cult is strongest, the presence of numerous gigantic images, mountain rocks carved with the imploring inscription 'Come, Maitreya, come!' and even the horse-races held in his honour during the Tibetan New Year, testify to the faith with which his devotees expect and the fervour with which they seek to hasten his coming.

Samantabhadra, 'The All-Good', and Mahāsthāmaprāpta, 'Attained to Great Strength', are both mentioned the *Saddhārma-puṇḍarīka*, the twenty-eighth chapter (of the Chinese version) being dedicated to the one and the twentieth to the other. Together with Mañjuśrī, Samantabhadra figures prominently in the *Gaṇḍavyūha,* which according to Suzuki is 'in a sense the history of the inner religious consciousness of Samantabhadra',[112] while Mahāsthāmaprāpta is described at length in the *Amitāyur-dhyāna,* together with Avalokiteśvara, as attending upon the Buddha of Infinite Light and Life in the Happy Land. As embodiments respectively of compassion and of power they resemble and in a way duplicate Avalokiteśvara and Vajrapāṇi; but by virtue of his association with an outstandingly popular group of sūtras Mahāsthāmaprāpta was able largely to supersede Vajrapāṇi throughout the Far East. In Indian iconography they are depicted in the same princely form as other bodhisattvas: Samantabhadra, white in colour, bears on a lotus his family emblem, the wheel; Mahāsthāmaprāpta is white or yellow and holds either a bunch of six full-blown lotuses or a sword. In China and Japan, where his cult flourished and he became more recognizably an individual, Samantabhadra (Chinese: P'u-hsien, Japanese: Fugen) is green in colour and rides a white elephant. He is depicted thus when, in a popular group known as the Śākya Trinity, he and Mañjuśrī, who rides a lion, appear on either side of a larger central figure of the Buddha.

Kṣitigarbha or 'Earth-Womb' also is more popular in the Far East than he ever was in India. From a bare mention in the roll of the Eight Bodhisattvas he has risen, in China and Japan, to a popularity second only to that of Avalokiteśvara. The reasons for this development are obscure, though it is clear it began in Turkestan. As his name suggests, Kṣitigarbha is connected with the depths. Like all bodhisattvas, he aspires to deliver sentient beings wandering astray in the five (or six) paths of mundane existence; but he specializes, as it were, in delivering them from hell. This expresses exoterically an extremely profound and esoteric aspect of the bodhisattva's compassionate activity: he takes upon himself the fearful task not merely of plumbing the depths of existence, and bringing relief and consolation to those in torment, but of personally transforming and uplifting the vast inchoate mass of fear, hatred, and despair swarming and pullulating in the pitch darkness of the Abyss. He is that loving condescension of the highest to the lowest which, abandoning its own bright seats, does not shrink from working under conditions the most difficult and appalling – amidst scenes of horror, madness, and desolation – at the seemingly hopeless task of reclaiming what is irrecoverably lost. Kṣitigarbha is the principle of spiritual sublimation in its most radical aspect, powerful enough to transform not merely hell into heaven but the foulest dregs of saṁsāra, even, into the pure radiance of Nirvāṇa. He is the supreme embodiment of spiritual optimism, the extremest development of Mahāyāna universalism, which wills that not so much as a grain of dust should be left outside the scheme of salvation. This seems to have been imperfectly understood in the Far East. In China, where he was known as Ti-tsang (Japanese: Jizō), he became 'not so much a Saviour [from hell] as the kindly superintendent of a prison who preaches to the inmates and willingly procures their release'.[113] In Japan he underwent changes even more surprising. As his popularity grew, besides greatly expanding the scope of his bodhisattva activities, he became not only a sort of god of the roads, and the special protector of children, but also the patron saint of warriors. Indian iconography generally depicts him as yellow or green in colour, showing the *bhūmisparśa* or 'earth-touching' gesture with his right hand and bearing in his left a lotus with the *kalpa-vṛkṣa* or wish-fulfilling tree. Chinese and Japanese art represent him in monastic dress grasping the *khakkhara* or ringed staff of the Sarvāstivādin monk with his right hand and holding in his left the *cintāmaṇi*, or wish-granting gem, which is properly the emblem of his celestial counterpart Ākāśagarbha.

Though the majority of them are human, in the sense of having once lived on the earth as men, the bodhisattvas described above are hardly historical figures in the scientific sense: their reality is not of the mundane but primarily of the spiritual order. The Mahāyāna does however recognize another important type of bodhisattva who is both human and historical. This category consists of the most outstanding of those spiritual heroes who, as inspirers of movements and founders of schools, have been makers of Buddhist history and moulders of Buddhist thought and who, by example and precept, have in times of stagnation and decay given a fresh impetus to the practice and dissemination of the Doctrine. Prominent among them towers the mighty figure of Nāgārjuna, founder of the Madhyamaka School, whose vindication of the *Prajñāpāramitā* teaching and dialectical demonstration of the futility of all one-sided views stands as a watershed separating the Hīnayāna and the Mahāyāna. Numerous other names, the brightest in Buddhist history, could be mentioned. They would include dauntless pilgrims like Hsüan-tsang who, in quest of the Dharma, traversed waterless deserts and pathless jungles; scholars like Kumārajīva whose lives were devoted to translating the Scriptures; saintly ascetics such as Milarepa who, in forest or in mountain cave, passed their days deep in *samādhi*; zealous reformers of the type of Tsongkhapa who 'waged contention with their time's decay'; and lastly, royal supporters like Shōtoku Taishi under whose patronage the Buddha's precepts were translated into principles of national life. Many of these were undoubtedly bodhisattvas of the Path; a few, irreversible bodhisattvas. Among the greatest of the last, again, some are traditionally revered not as men become bodhisattvas but as bodhisattvas become men. Such are Tsongkhapa, the father of the Gelugpa School, who on account of his wisdom and kindred virtues is regarded as a manifestation of Mañjuśrī, and a number of other personages prominent in the history of Tibetan Buddhism. Such also, if we can take his word for it, is Nichiren, founder of the most militant Japanese sect, who identified himself with the bodhisattva Visiṣtacaritra of the *Saddhārma-puṇḍarīka*. Some bodhisattvas, indeed, are for all practical purposes identical with their manifestations. The so-called 'Laughing Buddha', for example, is Maitreya in the form of a medieval Chinese monk.

Bodhisattvas may also appear not only singly, as one more or less well-known historical figure, but as a recognizably continuous series of personalities dedicated to Enlightenment for the good of all throughout a succession of human lives. In Tibet and the adjoining regions, from Ladakh to Mongolia, where Tibetan spiritual traditions prevail, bodhisattvas of this type are known as *tulkus*. Uninformed Western writers generally refer to them as incarnate lamas and living Buddhas. *Tulku* in Tibetan corresponds to the Sanskrit *nirmāṇakāya* or 'created body' – *kāya* here standing not for 'body' as opposed to 'mind' but for the whole psychophysical aggregate – a term which also designates the third of the Three Bodies of the Buddha. More elaborate classifications are possible, but broadly speaking *tulkus* are of two kinds. There is the series that starts from a historical figure such as Sarahapada or Tāranātha, and the series that starts from a great bodhisattva such as Avalokiteśvara or Mañjuśrī. In the first case the succeeding human personality does not arise in dependence on the preceding one by virtue of the law of karma, but is voluntarily created by it out of compassion as a means of carrying on its mission. Here, as elsewhere in the Doctrine, though concessions may sometimes be made to conventional modes of speech, there is no question of the 'reincarnation' of an unchanging ego-entity. As was shown in Part Two, the law of conditioned co-production is universal, comprising both the Round and the Path. In terms of this law one might say of this kind of *tulku* that he arises in dependence on the wisdom, compassion, and vow of a deceased human bodhisattva. Thus the series to which he belongs is a horizontal one. In the case of the second kind of *tulku* we are concerned with the direct emanation or manifestation – the word *avatāra* or 'descent' can also be used – of a non-human bodhisattva. Hence the series to which this kind belongs, though apparently horizontal, is in reality vertical, the human personalities of which it consists being not so much a series of 'rebirths' as a succession of descents from a common transcendental source. As the *nirmāṇakāyas* of an irreversible bodhisattva or a bodhisattva of the Path possess, once emanated, a spiritual life of their own, the possibility of an initial vertical descent followed by a horizontal series of 'rebirths' cannot be ruled out. In neither case, though, does there ever occur a descent of divine soul into human body, such as the expression 'Incarnate Lama' implies; for according to the Mahāyāna the difference between mind and matter is not absolute: each *nirmāṇakāya* is projected as an indivisible psychophysical whole. The best known example of this kind of *tulku* is, of course, the series consisting of the four religious kings of Tibet and the line of Dalai Lamas, the present one being the fourteenth, all of whom are regarded as manifestations of Avalokiteśvara. Altogether, including those of both human and of non-human origin, there are – or were – distributed throughout Tibet and its cultural-religious dependencies about a thousand *tulkus*. The way in which they are discovered and identified has often been described. An interesting and authentic account of the present supreme spiritual head and temporal ruler of Tibet is given by Lobsang Phuntsok Lhalungpa, and the sequence of events described by him is typical of the discovery of most *tulkus*.[114]

Numerous other types of bodhisattva might also be mentioned, for as the reality of Supreme Enlightenment transcends space and time the possibilities of compassionate activity are infinite. This is not the place to discuss the significance of the fact that bodhisattvas may be either male or female, professed *réligieux* or lay devotees. Notice ought however to be taken before we conclude of the fact that in modern times liberal Mahāyanists, especially those of Japan, have begun to wonder whether the spiritual masters of other religions whose teachings in some points coincide with the Buddha's might not be bodhisattvas. The names of Lao-tse, Christ, Eckhart, St John of the Cross, and Guru Nanak have been proposed in this connection. Some advocates of universalism go indeed so far as to contend that all benefactors of humanity, including poets, artists, scientists, statesmen, philanthropists, and social reformers are as much bodhisattvas as those engaged in specifically religious activities. To interpret the ideal as liberally as this might be to obscure its real meaning. In any case, a distinction would have to be drawn between those who on account of their altruistic and dedicated lives approximate to the conduct expected of a human bodhisattva and those who are manifestations of one or another of the great bodhisattvas for the fulfilment of a specific purpose. Evidence would moreover be required in any given case, whether of the one kind or the other, that the career of the alleged bodhisattva was motivated by compassion, that he actually worked for the good of others, that the means adopted by him were in accordance with the ends proposed, and that he was free from wrong views. Such as pass these tests are the most distant members of the Buddha's spiritual family, the outermost of those vast concentric circles of compassionate activity whereof the Glorious Company of Bodhisattvas is the radiant nucleus and the Buddha himself the dazzling heart and centre.

17

THE MONASTIC ORDER

CORRESPONDING TO, and in the best periods largely coinciding with, the Sangha as a spiritual élite, is the Sangha as a community of men and women treading the Path and striving to realize the Goal by following either the Arhant or the bodhisattva ideal. As in one form or another is the case in most organized religions, this community consists of two kinds of members: those whose experience of the Path is sufficient to modify the course of their lives without radically changing it and those who, to adopt the language of William James's definition of the religious man, though not necessarily having the most 'religious experience' make their experiences their *centre of gravity*. While for the first kind religion is only one among a multiplicity of interests, for the second it is the supreme, even the sole, interest to which all others must be subordinated and, if necessary, sacrificed. Thus Buddhism as an institutional religion comprises both a larger body of lay followers known as *upāsakas* (fem. *upāsikās*), whose practice of the Dharma is occasional and partial, and a very much smaller body of bhikṣus (fem. *bhikṣuṇīs*) who dedicate to its realization their whole life and the sum total of their energies. The latter form the bhikṣu-sangha, the order of monks, or the Monastic Order, which is the primary ecclesiastical sense in which the word 'sangha' is now used.

This Order did not come into existence all at once. Like other living things, whether organisms, empires, or ideas, it has in the course of its history passed through various stages of development. This fact, obvious though it is from a careful study of the records, is generally ignored by writers on Buddhism. Some, indeed, would have us believe that the Sangha sprang fully formed from the brain of the Buddha even as Pallas Athene leapt complete with shield and spear from the forehead of Zeus. Did it not command wide acceptance, a view so astonishingly naïve would not be worth mentioning. In reality the Sangha passed, during the first few generations of its existence, through three well-marked stages of development, each with certain distinctive features.

(1) According to the 'legend' of the Four Sights (see p.29), and as other canonical sources abundantly testify, the Buddha – or the bodhisattva, as he then was – decided to seek a solution to the problem of suffering by adopting the life of the *parivrājaka* (Pāli *paribbājaka*) or one who had 'gone forth' (the literal meaning of the word) from life at home to be a homeless wanderer. Whether, as Sukumar Dutt suggests, and as seems probable, the *parivrājakas* were originally the north-east Indian counterparts of the *brāhmaṇas* of the Āryan society to the north-west,[115] does not concern us. It is sufficient that the Buddha, both before and after his Enlightenment, was a *parivrājaka*, and that nearly all his closest associates were either recruited from this class or joined it in order to be with him and follow his teaching. Like Mahāvīra, the restorer of Jainism, and other teachers whose names are preserved in early Buddhist literature, the Buddha appeared to the general public of his times as the founder and head of one of the various sodalities into which the *parivrājaka* community was divided. Like other heads of sodalities, moreover, he professed and taught a special Dharma, and it was this, rather than their mode of life, which distinguished him and his adherents from the rest.

At this stage of its development the Sangha was therefore simply that section of the *parivrājaka* community which acknowledged the Buddha as master and accepted his doctrine. As yet there was no question of any code of 'monastic' discipline peculiar to the followers of the Buddha. The term *vinaya* – later appropriated as the collective designation of the monastic regula – which appears frequently in the well-known compound *dharma-vinaya*, bore at this time the more general import of the way of life conducive to the realization of the Master's teaching. The Buddha and his homeless disciples observed the unwritten traditional code of the *parivrājakas* and acted according to what public opinion considered proper in those who had 'gone forth'. They, too, spent the greater part of the year roaming from place to place, lived on alms, and abstained from sexual intercourse, from theft, from the taking of life, and from making false claims to supernormal attainments (the four *pārājikas* or 'defeats' of the later Monastic Code). Except during the three months of the rains, when they took shelter in a hut or cave, they too were without fixed abode. Like the members of other sects, they held a fortnightly congregational service, known as the *poṣadha* (Vedic *upavastha*, Pāli *uposatha*), on the full-moon and new-moon days, at which they recited a *prātimokṣa* (Pāli *pāṭimokkha*) or verse summary of the special Dharma to which they adhered. One such *prātimokṣa* has been preserved in the *Dhammapada*, verses 184–6, as well as in the *Mahāpadāna Suttanta* of the *Dīgha-Nikāya*; the latter attests its extreme antiquity by attributing it not to Gotama Buddha, but to Vipassin, one of his remote 'legendary' predecessors. According to the *Dhammapada*, which reverses the order of the first and second stanzas, it runs:

> Abstention from all evil,
> Cultivation of the wholesome,
> Purification of the heart:
> This is the Message of the Buddhas.
>
> Forbearance is the highest ascetic practice;
> 'Nirvāṇa is supreme,' say the Buddhas.
> He is not a 'gone forth' one who harms another;
> He is not a recluse (*samaṇa*) who molests another.
>
> Not to speak ill, not to injure,
> To observe the *pāṭimokkha*,
> To be moderate in eating,
> To live alone in a secluded abode,
> To devote oneself to meditation:
> This is the Message of the Buddhas.

In the Buddha's day it was the Dharma as embodied in such stanzas as these, and *not* a code of rules, that constituted the bond of union (probably the original meaning of *prātimokṣa*) between his followers. Similarly, the rite of *upasampadā* meant at that time not initiation into a Monastic Order fully equipped with rules and regulations but simply the formal recognition of the Buddha as teacher and the 'acceptance' (the literal meaning of the word) of his teaching. At first, this was considered as taking place when the Buddha uttered the words 'Come, bhikṣu'. Later on, applications for admission having greatly increased, he permitted the senior disciples to receive candidates on his behalf by causing them to repeat the formula of taking refuge in the Buddha, the Dharma, and the Sangha. The body of adherents which thus grew up around him and often accompanied him as he walked from place to place was known as the Bhikṣu-Sangha of the Four Quarters. An invaluable glimpse of the Sangha at this stage of its existence, termed by G.F. Allen 'The Pristine, Ascetic Stage',[116] is provided by the oldest portions of the *Sutta-Nipāta*, especially the *Aṭṭhaka-* and *Pārāyana-vaggas*, and by the *Bhikkhu-vagga* of the *Dhammapada*.

(2) After the parinirvāṇa of the Buddha his disciples found themselves confronted by a number of problems, not the least of them being that of the preservation of the Dharma-vinaya. For some, perhaps most, the proper fulfilment of this great responsibility involved not only creating from their individual recollections of what the Buddha had said and done a common stock of oral tradition but also adopting a code of discipline the observance of which might further differentiate them from the rest of the *parivrājaka* community. The drawing up of the rudiments of such a code was perhaps the principal item on the agenda of the First Council, which the Pāli canonical texts describe as a *Vinaya-saṅgīti*.[117] Ancient *parivrājaka* conventions which had received the stamp of the Buddha's approval, directives which he had himself issued from time to time, either on his own initiative or in response to public opinion, together with – in all likelihood – a few regulations thought necessary by the Council itself, were collected and classified. The resultant body of rules, which was made binding on every individual bhikṣu, eventually became fixed at 550 items. Since it was recited at the fortnightly congregational meetings, displacing the original Dharma-stanzas, it gradually took over the designation *prātimokṣa*. In other words, during the second stage of its existence the Sangha besides continuing to possess a spiritual bond of union in the Dharma in addition acquired an external bond of union in the form of the Monastic Code.

This development had far-reaching consequences. From being socially indistinguishable from the other *parivrājaka* groups the Sangha became an independent ecclesiastical corporation recognizable as such to the general public. *Upasampadā* was no longer a simple acceptance of the Buddha and his teaching; it became the ceremony of ordination into a Monastic Order. From a common declaration of faith the *poṣadha* was transformed into a service of confession of individual failures to observe the Code. The difference between monk and layman was accentuated, being no longer merely that between those who had left and those who had not left home but between the ordained, who observed the Code, and the unordained, who did not. Yet though much was altered, much remained the same. The bhikṣus were still largely eremitical, still lived on alms, and still remained in one spot during the rains.

(3) The third stage of development arose out of a change more radical than any that had previously taken place. During the Buddha's lifetime, even, parks and gardens had been donated to the Sangha with provision for accommodation during the rains. These were certainly not monasteries in the modern sense, and whether in art or in literature, or merely in one's own imagination, it is a grave anachronism to depict Anāthapiṇḍada or Bimbisāra as putting up large and complex structures of brick and stone. Scattered up and down the donated area, known as the *āvāsa*, were a number of lodgings or *vihāras* in the form of wattle-and-daub huts such as can be seen all over India even today. A bhikṣu had the right of occupying one of these lodgings during the rains. When the rains were over he continued his wanderings. Later on it became possible to reserve the lodging one had just vacated and thus to spend a number of rainy seasons consecutively in one *vihāra*, as the Buddha himself had done at Śrāvastī.

In the stage of development that had now been reached the Sangha took the revolutionary step of abandoning the *parivrājaka* tradition of a wandering life in favour of permanent residence at an *āvāsa*. The reasons for this transition from the eremitic to the coenobitic type of religious life are obscure; they are probably bound up with the growth of the Monastic Code and with the need for collating the floating mass of oral tradition existing in the memories of hundreds of reciters. Be the reasons for it what they may, the change modified the constitution of the Sangha to an unprecedented degree. The Sangha of the Four Quarters was replaced, for all practical purposes, by the local Sangha resident at a particular *āvāsa*. As the *prātimokṣa*, or Monastic Code, was unable to cover all the exigencies of the more complex type of communal life that now rapidly developed it was in practice supplemented and to some extent superseded by the *Skandhakas* (Pāli *Khandhakas*) or *The Chapters*, a series of elaborate treatises on such subjects as medicine, robes, ordination, and schism. This led to another change in the *poṣadha*; from a confessional it became a liturgical service at which the *prātimokṣa* was solemnly recited not, as before, in order that erring monks might confess and atone for their transgressions, but simply as a formal expression of the unity and solidarity of the local, coenobitical, Sangha. Similarly *upasampadā* now meant ordination not so much into the Sangha of the Four Quarters governed by the *prātimokṣa* as into the resident Sangha of a particular *āvāsa* living in accordance with what, by yet another appropriation of an ancient term, came to be known as the *Vinaya*. Moreover, as it settled down in the *āvāsas*, the Sangha naturally became more accessible to the laity. Donations therefore poured in and endowments multiplied. Eventually, though some remained faithful to the old tradition, it was no longer necessary for the monks to go out and beg their food from door to door.

Exactly how long it took for the characteristic features of each of these stages to emerge is not clear. The Sangha of the third stage, which was responsible for compiling the extant biographical-cum-disciplinary traditions into a Vinaya Piṭaka (or Piṭakas: there were several versions), being anxious to father its distinctive innovations upon the Master himself, telescoped them into a period coeval with that of his pastoral activity and manufactured, as part of his biography, incidents and episodes out of which they were supposed to have arisen. These legends (in the sense of fictions), which were incorporated into the Vinaya Piṭaka, cannot stand up to critical examination. The entire process of development from primitive eremitical to sophisticated coenobitical 'monasticism' must in fact have taken at least a century, so that we may safely conclude that probably by the time of the Second Council, the Council of Vaiśālī, and certainly that of Aśoka's accession to the throne of Magadha, it was complete. Whether earlier by a few decades or later, though, the fact that such a process had taken place does not mean, nor in the history of Buddhism ever meant, that a later stage of development supplanted, in the sense of ousting and wholly superseding, an earlier one. As with the Doctrine, so with the Discipline (in the widest sense of the term Vinaya), development almost invariably took place by way of a process of gradual accretion and elaboration rather than by one of summary rejection and reform. The second stage of the process overlaid, without being able entirely to conceal, the first, and was in its turn overlaid but not concealed by the third. Thus from the beginning of the third period the individual bhikṣu, or member of the Sangha, grew up under the influence of, and was confronted by, three different, not to say contradictory, ideals of 'monastic' life. He was simultaneously exhorted to 'wander alone, even as the horn of the rhinoceros is single',[118] the refrain of an early ballad, without caring for rules and regulations;[119] to observe scrupulously the 150 clauses of the individualistic Monastic Code; and to participate in, even identify himself with, the complex corporate life of a permanently resident monastic community.

These discrepancies did not escape the notice of the Indo-Bactrian king Milinda, or Menander, who, with a critical acumen quite modern, quoted verses pertaining respectively to the earlier eremitical and the later coenobitical stage and propounded the obvious contrast of ideals to Nāgasena as his forty-first dilemma.[120] In the life of the Sangha their conflicting demands naturally generated a certain amount of tension. However, as it was believed that the Buddha himself had, at different periods, sanctioned both ideals, the latter admittedly by way of concession to the weaker brethren, the tension between them never became a disruptive influence. The doctrine of concessions finds classic expression in that part of the *upasampadā* ceremony where, having been exhorted to subsist on alms, wear robes made from cast-off rags, live at the foot of a tree, and use cow's urine for medicine (the four *nissayas* or 'supports'), the newly ordained bhikṣu was informed that accepting invitations from the laity, wearing robes offered by them, dwelling in *vihāras*, and having recourse to ordinary medical treatment, were also permissible.[121] This in effect meant that he was free to follow the eremitical or the coenobitical ideal, or a compromise between the two, according to his individual temperament and convictions. Nevertheless, owing not only to human weakness but to the necessity of preserving and transmitting enormous bodies of traditionary lore, as well as to the fact that much of this was compiled and edited under coenobitical auspices, it was the coenobitical type of monasticism that triumphed. In its fully developed form it eventually reached its apogee in such great institutions as the Mahāvihāra, Nālandā, and Drepung, and even today constitutes, in most parts of the Buddhist world, the normal working basis, though not necessarily the sole theoretic ideal, of the Monastic Order.

Before describing the life of a bhikṣu under the dominant coenobitical system we shall have to guard against a possible grave misunderstanding. We have already seen that the whole course of development of the Sangha, with its three clearly marked stages, was probably complete by the time of the Second Council, the Council of Vaiśālī. Now it was in connection with this Council, held 100 or 110 years after the parinirvāṇa, that there occurred the first great schism in the Sangha, that between the conservative minority known as the Sthaviravādins, and the progressive majority, known as the Mahāsāṁghikas. This means that the development of coenobitical monasticism preceded the rise of the Mahāyāna, which as a distinct historical movement originated among the Mahāsāṁghikas. The point is important and significant because, in recent times, certain uninformed followers of the Theravāda (an offshoot of the original Sthaviravāda) have accused the Mahāyanists of having no Vinaya, no *upasampadā* lineage, and therefore no bhikṣus or bhikṣuṇīs and no real Monastic Order. In the case of the Chinese, Tibetan, Korean, and Vietnamese adherents of the Mahāyāna the accusation is completely unfounded. Far from rejecting any of them, the Mahāyāna took up and incorporated in its own movement the whole stock of primitive traditions, including the Monastic Code and *upasampadā* lineage as transmitted by the Mahāsāṁghika, the Sarvāstivāda, and other early schools. For historical reasons there have survived in the Buddhist world only two of the ancient traditions of coenobitical monasticism, the Theravāda and the Sarvāstivāda. The former is transmitted with Pāli for its literary medium in the Theravādin countries of South-east Asia; the latter, the medium of which was originally Sanskrit, in China, Japan, Tibet, Korea, and Vietnam and other parts of the 'Mahāyāna' world in the languages of those countries. Despite minor discrepancies between these two great traditions in regard to both material included and the manner of its arrangement, there can be no doubt that their respective versions of the Monastic Code and *The Chapters*, at least, represent different recensions of one and the same basic material.[122] Both the Theravādin monks of Sri Lanka, and the 'Mahāyāna' (strictly Sarvāstivādin) monks of Tibet, for example, are the true lineal descendants of the original coenobitical Monastic

Order which came into existence during the third stage of development of the early Sangha.

As it has the same spiritual orientation, and is based upon what are, substantially, the same Vinaya traditions, the pattern of monasticism naturally varies little from one part of the Buddhist world to another. This fact makes possible an account of the monastic life which, ignoring variations due to differences of national culture, directs attention to its main features.

The bhikṣu's life begins with ordination. This is of two kinds, known respectively as *pravrajyā* and *upasampadā*. The former, which may be taken as soon as one is old enough to earn a living by scaring crows, that is to say, at any time after the age of seven or eight, consists in shaving hair and beard, donning the saffron robes, and taking from an *upādhyāya* (Pāli *upajjhāya*) or preceptor the Three Refuges (*tri-śarana*): in the Buddha, the Dharma, and the Sangha, and the Ten Precepts (*daśa-śikṣāpada*): to abstain from injury to living beings, from taking what has not been given, from unchastity, from wrong speech, from intoxicating drinks and drugs (the Five Precepts of the upāsaka, except that unchastity here replaces sexual misconduct), from untimely meals, from dance, song, music, and unseemly shows, from the use of garlands, perfumes, unguents, and things that tend to beautify and adorn the person, from lofty and luxurious seats, and from handling gold and silver. The latter may be conferred on any virile male human being who has attained the age of twenty (reckoning from conception, not birth), whose begging-bowl and three monastic robes are complete, who has obtained the permission of his parents, if living, and who moreover is free from serious disease, from civil obligations, and from various other disqualifications. Unlike its orthodox Hindu counterparts, known as *saṇnyāsa*, which traditionally is open only to those who are brahmins by birth, the *upasampadā* is given without any restriction of caste, nationality, race, or social position – an attitude of typical Buddhist universality to which the practice of the Siyama Nikāya of Sri Lanka constitutes a unique and most regrettable exception.

The actual ordination is effected by means of what is known as a *saṅgha-karma* (Pāli *-kamma*) or corporate official act of the Sangha consisting, in this case, in the unanimous passing of a formal resolution (*jñāpti*, Pāli *ñatti*) by the entire Sangha resident at a particular *āvāsa*, and assembled for the purpose, the number of such bhikṣus being not less than five (ten in the 'Middle Country'), all of whom must be exempt from certain technical disabilities. Having been interrogated regarding his freedom from the disqualifications by one of the bhikṣus, known in the Sanskrit tradition as the *rahonusāsaka-bhikṣu* or privy admonisher (*not* 'monk who imparts the esoteric teaching'),[123] the candidate for ordination is brought within the circle of the Sangha where, after saluting the bhikṣus one by one in order of seniority, he petitions the Sangha for ordination with a certain elder, whom he names, and who, generally, is the seniormost bhikṣu present, as his preceptor (*upādhyāya*). Then, in the presence of the Sangha, he is formally interrogated regarding the disabilities by the *karmakaraka-bhikṣu* or 'master of ceremonies'. Finally the subject-matter of the proceedings, namely that the candidate, being a virile male and so on, desires ordination from the Sangha with the elder named as his preceptor, is embodied in a formal resolution (*jñāpti*), which, after being proposed to the assembly by the master of ceremonies, is repeated three times in the form of a declaration (*karmavacana*, Pāli *kammavacana*). If the bhikṣus remain silent the resolution is taken as passed, and the master of ceremonies announces that the *upasampadā* has been granted.

After the date and exact time of the candidate's formal admission to the Sangha have been ascertained, various monastic obligations are taught and explained. In particular he is informed of the four *niśrayas* (Pāli *nissayas*) or 'supports' and the various concessions allowed with regard to them (see p.182) and of the four *patanīya-dharmas* or things bringing about downfall. The latter are identical with the four *pārājikas* or 'defeats' (see p.178). The remaining sets of obligations need not be taught immediately after the formal ceremony. They comprise the four *śramaṇakāraka-dharmas*, or duties of an ascetic, the 150 prohibitions of the Monastic Code, and various duties which the newly ordained monk has to perform towards his *upādhyāya*. The first set embodies the principle of non-retaliation. Even when others revile, or become angry with, or beat, or upbraid him, the *śramaṇa* must refrain from acting in like manner. The 150 *śīlas* of the *prātimokṣa* or Monastic Code are divided according to the nature of the penalties incurred by their descending order, from the graver to the lighter offences. These all concern the conduct of the individual bhikṣu. A seventh category, which is binding upon the Sangha collectively, consists of rules for the settlement of internal disputes at an *āvāsa*.

According to the nature of the penalties involved the seven categories of offences are known as (1) *pārājika* or 'defeat', permanent expulsion from the Sangha without the possibility of readmission in the present lifetime; (2) *saṅghāvāśeṣa* (Pāli *sanghādisesa*) or temporary suspension from full membership of the Sangha; (3) *aniyata* or undetermined, an offence of one or another type having been committed or not committed according to circumstances; (4) *naiḥsargika-pātayantika* (Pāli *nissaggiya-pācittiya*) or forfeiture and expiation, when the possession of a prohibited article is acknowledged as a fault and the article surrendered; (5) *pātayantika* or *prayascittiya* (Pāli *pācittiya*) or expiation by simple acknowledgement; (6) *pratideśanīya* (Pāli *pāṭidesaniya*) or confession; and (7) *adhikaranasamatha* (Pāli *adhikaraṇasamatha*) or rules of procedure for the settlement of disputes within the Sangha. As might be anticipated, the four 'defeats' are identical in all Vinaya traditions. The seven categories are also common to the Theravāda and the various branches of the Sarvāstivāda. Excluding the *aniyata* and *adhikaranasamatha*, many differences do however exist with regard to the number of offences included in a category, the nature and wording of the offences, and the order of their arrangement.[124] The Sarvāstivāda, for instance, gives the number of the *pātayantika* rules as 90 whereas according to the Theravāda there are 92. Nevertheless such differences, though not to be overlooked, are so much less numerous and striking than the resemblances that the predominant impression remains one of uniformity. Nalinaksha Dutt, the editor of the Gilgit Manuscripts, indeed states categorically that 'substantially the Pāli and Sanskrit versions agree not only in the main contents but also in details and sometimes one version appears to be based on the other'.[125] It is curious, though, that while the Sarvāstivādins and their branch the Mūlasarvāstivādins both managed to preserve 150 *prātimokṣa* rules the Theravāda, while retaining the traditional number for the total, has actually transmitted 152 – a fact for which there appears to be no explanation. All Vinaya traditions also transmit, in addition to the Monastic Code proper, a list of *saikṣa* (Pāli *sekhiya*) rules which differ from the *prātimokṣa* in being binding on both bhikṣu and *śrāmaṇera*. As they are concerned with matters of etiquette, decorum, and good manners rather than with ethics or discipline, no penalties attach to their infringement. The Sarvāstivādins transmit 113 such rules, the Mūlasarvāstivādins 108, and the Theravādins 75. Adding the 150 prohibitions of the *prātimokṣa* (152 for the Theravāda) to their respective lists of *saikṣa* rules we arrive at the grand total of rules transmitted by each of these schools in their individual versions of the full Monastic Code for bhikṣus – namely 263, 258, and 227 respectively. Bhikṣuṇīs observe a much larger number of rules, 371 in the Mūlasarvāstivāda and 311 in the Theravāda. Except that there are no *aniyata* or undetermined rules these are distributed into the same categories as those governing the bhikṣu. The Theravādin bhikṣuṇī-lineage, though extinct in the Theravādin countries, is said to have survived in China.

The relation between the *upādhyāya* and his *saddhivihārika* or 'co-resident', as the newly ordained monk is called, is essentially that of father and son transposed to the spiritual plane. Besides learning from him, the *saddhivihārika* is expected to render the *upādhyāya* all manner of personal service, and upon each is incumbent for life the duty of nursing the other when sick. Without the permission of the *upādhyāya* the *saddhivihārika* may do nothing. This condition of spiritual tutelage is known as *niśraya* (Pāli *nissaya*), literally 'dependence' (on a teacher) and it lasts for a minimum of five, usually for ten, years, during which period the *saddhivihārika* resides permanently with the preceptor: a dull or undisciplined bhikṣu may be kept under such tutelage all his life. Probably because the seniormost elder of an *āvāsa* is often obliged to ordain more disciples than one person can train, an *ācārya* (Pāli *ācariya*) or instructor also is appointed. The relation between the *ācārya* and his *antevasika*, as the young monk is termed in relation to him, is identical with that between *upādhyāya* and *saddhivihārika*. Nevertheless the *upādhyāya* enjoys a certain precedence, for whenever all three happen to be together *niśraya* towards the *ācārya* automatically ceases. It is, though, the *ācārya* who, under the *upādhyāya*, is responsible for the day-to-day teaching and training of the newly ordained monk. Only those monks who are richly endowed with various ethical and spiritual qualities, and who have completed ten years in the Sangha, are considered fit to ordain and teach others. They should be deeply learned, with a natural understanding of educational psychology, and capable not only of instructing the disciple but skilled in resolving his doubts and dispelling the moods of depression to which he may be subject during the training. They must be able to nurse him should he fall ill. The relation between master and disciple is the axle upon which turns the entire monastic system. Some bhikṣus, out of devotion and a desire to learn, remain with their tutor for some years after the cessation of formal *niśraya* or even attend permanently upon him until his death.

In the early days of Buddhism, when the Dharma-Vinaya was transmitted orally, much time was spent in learning the words of the sacred tradition by heart and reciting them in unison. As it was of vast extent, and constantly expanding, the tradition soon transcended the powers of all save a few prodigies of mnemonic capacity. Specialization therefore became the rule; individual monk-reciters learned, and in turn passed on to their own disciples, not the whole Dharma-Vinaya as handed down at a particular *āvāsa* or group of *āvāsas* but only a section of it. Sūtrāntikas transmitted the sūtras, Vinayadharas the Vinaya, and so on. They also explained and commented upon what was transmitted, thus building up a secondary tradition of exegesis which could easily become confused with the primary one. This is particularly the case with the Abhidharma, which was elaborated out of the *mātṛkās* or 'matrices' transmitted by the Mātṛkadharas and finally came to be regarded, in some circles at least, as canonical. When the sacred tradition was committed to writing, probably in the fourth century after the parinirvāṇa, all this was changed. Though learning by heart continued to be a highly respectable occupation for a monk, and enjoyed great prestige long after its utility had been exhausted, the emphasis eventually shifted from reciting to reading: the oral became a literary tradition. At the same time the curriculum of monastic studies broadened. Time was devoted not only to the Scriptures, commentaries, and independent expository texts, but ancillary subjects such as grammar, rhetoric, and prosody. Quasi-religious subjects, ranging from ecclesiastical history to logic and dialectics, and from medicine to various branches of the fine and applied arts, were also introduced. Secular literature was cultivated and non-Buddhist religious and philosophical texts critically studied. Like their later European counterparts, the monasteries came to be not only centres of spiritual life and religious activity but repositories of all the learning and culture of the age. This naturally encouraged further specialization. Each *ācārya*, on the basis of a sound knowledge of the Scriptures, took up a single subject or group of subjects. Once this stage had been reached there was nothing left for the coenobitical monastic system to do but to evolve, out of the very perfection of its development, its own antithesis. The best *ācāryas* were not always available all under the same roof. In some parts of the Buddhist world, therefore, part of the novitiate became a kind of *Wanderjahr*, with the young monk begging his way from one monastic centre to another and sitting for a season at the feet now of one, now of another, great specialist in Buddhistic lore until his monastic education was complete. Hsüan-tsang's 'pilgrimage' to India partly conforms to this pattern, which in China itself seems to have been a popular one.

Every member of the Sangha possessed as such certain inherent rights. These the young monk learned to exercise not only by studying the Vinaya but by participating in the communal religious life of the *āvāsa* to which he belonged. For instance his personal property was limited to certain articles, known as the *aṣṭapariskāra* (Pāli *aṭṭha-parikkhāra*) or 'eight requisites': the three robes, the begging-bowl, a razor, a needle, the girdle, and a water-strainer. All other property, whether lands, buildings, or furniture, was vested in the Sangha; that is to say it belonged, even when nominally dedicated to the Bhikṣu-Sangha of the Four Quarters, to the monks resident at an *āvāsa* in their collective capacity. This property the individual bhikṣu was entitled to utilize. The most important right he possessed, however, was that of participating in all corporate official acts of the Sangha. Without his presence, or his formal consent to the proceedings if unable to attend, no such act was valid. As Sukumar Dutt insists,

> The right of direct participation in the Sanghakamma inheres in each duly qualified member of an āvāsa and is very jealously guarded.[126]

This right conferred upon the Sangha a strictly republican character. Though the minimum number of bhikṣus required for a particular type of corporate official act varied from four to twenty, an act would not be valid if carried out by them alone without the participation of all the other bhikṣus who, at the time, happened to be resident at the *āvāsa*. In other words, every assembly of the Sangha had to be complete in respect of the *āvāsa* concerned.

Among the more important corporate acts of the Sangha, apart from the *upasampadā*, were the *poṣadha*, the *varṣāvāsa*, the *pravāraṇā*, and the *kaṭhina*, all of which occurred, or recurred, at fixed points in the ecclesiastical year. In its original form, the *poṣadha* was a full-moon and new-moon day observance common to all the *parivrājaka* communities, its introduction into Buddhism being due to the suggestion of certain lay devotees. As an institution of coenobitic monasticism, it consisted in the solemn ceremonial recitation of the Monastic Code.

Sometimes the entire Code was recited, sometimes only the more serious offences. In either case, at this stage in the development of the Sangha, infringements were no longer confessed in the course of the actual recital; instead, the participating bhikṣus made mutual confession in pairs beforehand. This preliminary ceremony, known as *pariśuddhi*, purification, ultimately became as much a formality as the ceremony it preceded. The three remaining *saṅgha-karmas* occurred only once a year. In the rhythm of the old eremitic monastic life the *varṣāvāsa* (Pāli *vassāvāsa*) or 'rains residence' naturally occupied a place of the highest importance. But as the Sangha gradually settled down into permanent residence at the *āvāsas* that had served, in the earliest days of its existence, merely as temporary shelters from the torrential monsoon rains, the institution lost much of its original significance. For the majority of bhikṣus the only difference between this period and the remaining eight or nine months of the year was that during the one they might not and did not travel, while during the other they might but did not. Nevertheless, formal observance of the institution continued, and a monk's seniority was still reckoned according to the number of rains residences he had observed since ordination. Countries where there were no seasonal rains could not observe the rains residence even as a formality. In some parts of the Buddhist world, such as China, it therefore became a summer residence. Eventually the 'residence' developed into a kind of spiritual retreat, for the duration of which the monks observed the Vinaya more strictly than usual and devoted themselves to intensive study, teaching, and meditation. In this form the institution lives on in almost all Buddhist lands and possesses enormous value.

The *pravāraṇā* (Pāli *pavāranā*), which marked the conclusion of the *varṣāvāsa*, was generally held on the fourteenth or fifteenth day of Kartika (October-November), that is to say, on the full-moon day of that month or the day after. On this occasion the bhikṣus, having observed the rains residence together, assembled to give 'satisfaction' (the literal meaning of the term) to one another by inviting inquiry as to their conduct during this period, confessing their transgressions, and mutually asking forgiveness for any fault committed. The *kaṭhina* or 'difficult' ceremony was that of the distribution, among the monks who had completed the *varṣāvāsa*, of the robes or robe material offered on the occasion by the laity. It received its designation from the hardship originally suffered by the eremitic monks who, at the official conclusion of the residence – which did not always coincide with the end of the actual monsoon – had to resume their travels without sufficient protection from the weather. In addition to these the Sangha performed, as circumstances required, a variety of other acts. It might have to try a case of alleged breach of the Monastic Code and, if the accused was found guilty, impose on him the prescribed penalty; or appoint the various officers necessary for the running of a large coenobitic establishment; dedicate a building or part of a building for any special purpose, settle the boundary of an *āvāsa*, or determine the succession to the personal belongings of a deceased bhikṣu. In all these proceedings every monk of good standing had the right and the duty of full participation.

The practice of meditation also was not forgotten. In the earliest days of the Sangha, during the lifetime of the Buddha and immediately after, the best part of a monk's time was spent in this manner. Such portions of the Scriptures as reflect the life of this period describe how, having returned from the almsround and rested a while after eating, the monk passed the remainder of the day under a tree absorbed in *dhyāna*, sometimes practising until far into the night. According to the Tibetan version of the *Vinayavastu* of the Mūlasarvāstivādins the Buddha introduced the practice of meditation and the observance of the *poṣadha* simultaneously, which suggests a special connection between them.[127] The prologue to the Pāli *Sāmaññaphala Sutta*, *Digha-Nikāya* 2, relates that when, one beautiful full-moon night in autumn, Jīvaka the physician escorted Ajātasattu on a visit to the Blessed One, they found him and 1,200 disciples sitting together in absolute silence. On another *uposatha* day, when the monks had been meditating half the night, the Buddha held up the proceedings for several hours until an impure monk, who had failed to leave of his own accord, had been ejected by Moggallāna. Only when the assembly was pure did he allow the *pāṭimokkha* to be recited.[128] If it represents the general practice of the Sangha at that time, this incident shows the *poṣadha* observance originally consisted of two parts, group meditation and the recitation of the Dharma-stanzas. As the coenobitic system developed, however, the practice of meditation declined. The necessity of transmitting the Dharma-Vinaya took precedence, for the time being, over all other duties. *The Chapters*, in its several versions, draws a picture of monastic life devoted almost exclusively to study, recitation, and doctrinal discussion. The first part of the *poṣadha* observance, namely the group meditation, was abolished, possibly at the same time that the second part became a recitation of the Monastic Code. Hsüan-tsang, describing the glories of seventh-century Nālandā, has much to say about lectures, studies, and general academic routine; but he is strangely silent regarding meditation. We are not to infer, of course, that so vitally important a subject was ever totally neglected. Every monk certainly learned the theory of meditation and acquired the rudiments of the practice of one or another of the various methods in vogue. All the same, there prevailed from an early period the feeling that study and meditation were incompatible, and that one could be wholeheartedly prosecuted only at the expense of the other. Buddhaghosa, in the *Visuddhimagga*, says of books that 'for one who is constantly busy with recitations, etc.' they are an impediment to *samādhi*.[129] Having students to instruct is another impediment. The same author's enumeration of the eighteen faults of a monastery indeed suggests that the busy life of any large coenobitic establishment is in itself unfavourable to meditation.[130] A division of labour, as it were, therefore became the rule; one group of bhikṣus devoted itself to study, the other to meditation. In India the first group seems to have predominated, though the evidence on which an impression is based, being itself literary, is not really conclusive. In any case, a movement known as the Yogācāra, devoted – as its name suggests – to the practice of meditation, eventually sprang up and gained many adherents. China and Japan, and to a lesser extent Tibet, where the meditative tradition flourished in the form of independent schools, saw the rise of a new type of coenobitical monasticism, organized in accordance with the special requirements not of the life of study but the life of meditation. And all over the Buddhist world, in every age, a few meditating monks remained aloof from every form of organized monasticism, preferring to dwell alone, like their predecessors of old, in dense forests and remote mountain caves.

18

THE PLACE OF THE LAITY

WITH THE EXCEPTION of the eventful weeks succeeding the Enlightenment (see p.17), when Buddhahood made its first tremendous impact on mankind, only a small percentage of the faithful ever belonged to the spiritual élite, whether of *āryas* or bodhisattvas, or even to the Monastic Order. Everywhere and at all times the great majority were common people for whom the Dharma was an important but not the predominant interest of their lives. In the broadest sense of the term the Sangha therefore coincided with the entire Buddhist community, consisting of what became known as the *caturvarga* or 'four companies', namely bhikṣus, bhikṣuṇīs, upāsakas, and upāsikās. As such it was called the mahā-sangha or 'Great Assembly'.

During the lifetime of the Master relations between the eremitical monks who had 'gone forth' and the householders at whose doors they daily stood for alms, and in whose outhouses and gardens they lodged during the rains, were close and cordial, and a spirit of camaraderie prevailed. The latter could, if necessary, bring to the notice of the Master public complaints against the *parivrājakas*, and suggest changes in their mode of living. Such equalitarianism was natural. Their common devotion to the Buddha, and the extent to which his attainments transcended theirs, tended to reduce all distinctions among his followers, including that between monks and laymen, to a position of comparative insignificance. His impatience with the formalistic element in religion, and his uncompromising insistence on the necessity of personal realization of Nirvāṇa, moreover ensured that they should be distinguished, if at all, according to their intrinsic merits rather than their socio-ecclesiastical status.

> Even though a man be richly attired, if he develops tranquillity, is quiet, subdued and restrained, leading a holy life and abstaining from injury to all living beings – he is a *brāhmaṇa*, he is a *samaṇa*, he is a *bhikkhu*.[131]

That the homeless wandering monk, totally free from all worldly concerns, had a far better chance of reaching the Goal, was admitted, even emphasized; but that a householder, if sufficiently resolved, might sometimes reach it too, and that in the last resort it was transcendental attainment that mattered, not the wearing of yellow robes, more than one such saying of the Buddha testifies. In a passage tucked away in the *Aṅguttara-Nikāya* he indeed speaks of the righteous of all four *vargas* as illuminating the Sangha:

> Brethren, these four persons, who are full of wisdom and insight, are well-disciplined, learned [in the Dharma] and have reached complete righteousness, shed lustre upon the Sangha. Which are the four? Brethren, the bhikkhu, the bhikkhuṇī, the upāsaka the upāsikā, who are full of wisdom and insight, well-disciplined, and learned, and have reached complete righteousness, shed lustre upon the Sangha. Brethren, these four beings do indeed shed lustre upon the Sangha.[132]

Here the *vargas* are clearly placed on a footing of complete spiritual equality.

With the growth of the coenobium, and the consequent tendency of religious life towards claustration in the *āvāsas*, a change took place. Dharma developed into Abhidharma, and Vinaya, originally signifying the practical side of a universal spiritual ideal, into Abhivinaya, in the sense of a body of rules and regulations for ordained monks only. Spiritual life was identified with monastic life. Though the Pāli scriptures, even after having passed through the hands of generations of monk redactors, preserve the names of twenty-one lay disciples who had attained Release, it was now generally agreed that a layman was incapable of the higher transcendental attainments. Arhantship, in the narrower, more individualistic Hīnayāna sense which the term now assumed, was regarded not as the common goal of the entire Buddhist community, irrespective of socio-ecclesiastical status, but as the prerogative of monks and nuns. The laity could aspire only to the inferior goal of rebirth, after death, in a happy heavenly abode. To the two different goals there appertained two different paths. The monk traversed the stages of *śīla, samādhi*, and *prajñā*, culminating in *vimukti*; the layman or laywoman cultivated *dāna, śīla*, and (*śamathā-*) *bhāvanā*. In practice, the latter were expected simply to give alms to the monks and to observe the Five or, on *poṣadha* days at least, the Eight, Precepts; *bhāvanā*, in the sense of 'cultivation' (the literal meaning of the term) of the mundane *dhyānas*, though it could not be forbidden, was hardly encouraged. As the Buddha apparently had taught them, the two paths overlapped, the first and second stages of the one coincided with the second and third stages of the other, thus in effect forming between them a single path of five stages from *dāna* to *vimukti* which could be traversed, according to their capacity, by any member of the Buddhist community. During the period of which we are speaking, however, the first path was interpreted so exclusively in terms of the current type of monastic spiritual culture, and the second so exclusively in terms of ordinary lay ethics, that inevitably they assumed the appearance of independent 'careers'. The laity not being personally concerned with the higher spiritual life, it was held unnecessary for them to know much about the Buddha's teaching. Restrictions were therefore imposed. It became an offence for a monk to make one who was not ordained recite the *suttas* line by line (Pāli *Pāṭimokkha, pācittiya no.4*). Śāriputra was represented as consoling Anāthapiṇḍada on his death-bed with a religious talk and telling him, when he had shed tears of emotion, that such teachings were not communicated to the white-robed householders, but only to those who had gone forth.[133]

This virtual exclusion of the laity from spiritual life, resulting in the identification of the Sangha with the Monastic Order, did not pass unchallenged. The Buddha had, incontestably, exhorted his first sixty disciples to wander about 'for the good of the many, for the happiness of the many (*bahujana hitāya, bahujana sukhāya*)' (see p.17). Śāriputra's alleged remark was, as a generalization, even untrue, being contradicted by the Buddha's own practice as recorded in, for example, the *Aṭṭhaka-vagga* and the *Pārāyana-vagga* – the oldest portions of the *Sutta-Nipāta* – wherein various brahmins ask him, and he answers, questions on the profoundest of themes. In any case, far from being wholly dependent on the monks for their knowledge of the Dharma, the laity possessed certain unsystematized traditions of their own regarding the Buddha's life and teachings, handed down not from master to disciple but from father to son. They were therefore unwilling to accept the position of second-class Buddhists, or to participate in the spiritual life of the community merely to the extent of acquiring *puṇya* (Pāli *puññā*) or merit by patronizing and supporting the monks. Even though it might be for them a remoter possibility, to be consummated only after innumerable lives, they persisted in regarding Supreme Enlightenment as their proper goal, not rebirth as a deva or even the attainment of Arhantship in the current monastic sense. In this aspiration they enjoyed the sympathy of a section of the monks themselves, many of whom felt that an exclusively monastic interpretation of Buddhism, in terms of Abhidharma and Abhivinaya, besides failing to do full justice to the depth and universality of the Master's teachings, suffered from the further defect of ignoring the splendid lessons of his personal example.

Between 100 and 200 years after the parinirvāṇa these tensions in the Buddhist community resulted in a schism. Despite its crucial importance, the traditions regarding this event are late, unreliable, and far from unanimous, there being no concurrence of testimony as to the initiators of the break, its immediate cause, its venue, and the age in which it took place. Fortunately the identity of the parties involved, and the general nature of the grounds of difference between them, as disclosed partly by their subsequent development as independent schools, is perfectly clear, and this is all that concerns us now. The Sthaviravāda, or 'School of the Elders' (i.e. of the senior monks), who are represented as Arhants, was the extreme monastic party, according to whom Buddhism was primarily, if not exclusively, a religion for monks, and who not only insisted that they alone had the right of determining what was Buddhism and what was not but sought to impose their own one-sided version of the Master's teaching on the entire Buddhist community. On the other side stood the Mahāsāṁghikas, 'Those of the Great Order' or 'The Great Assemblists'. They were the liberal party. Unlike their opponents, they did not represent only the more conservative elderly coenobites but, as their name suggests, all the four *vargas*. They maintained that the Dharma having been preached for the benefit of everyman and everywoman, irrespective of socio-ecclesiastical status, the right of determining the true nature of the religion inhered in the whole Buddhist community, not in any one section of it exclusively, and that in compiling a standard version of the Master's teaching all surviving traditions should be taken into account, including those current among the laity. They also felt that there should be a common spiritual ideal, not a higher one for monks and nuns and a lower one for lay people. As the Mahāsāṁghikas were, by all accounts, the larger party, they probably represented contemporary Buddhist thought more faithfully than the Sthaviravādins, who consisted, not even of all monks, but only of some of the senior members belonging to a particular group of *āvāsas*.

Once begun, the process of division could not be checked. Out of the Sthaviravāda arose, in the course of the next century or two, a succession of schools afterwards known collectively to their opponents as the Hīnayāna or 'Little Way'. Similarly among the Mahāsāṁghikas there sprang up various schools which gave rise to, and partly merged with, a movement terming itself the Mahāyāna or 'Great Way' which, taking its stand on the more liberal and catholic aspects of the tradition, aimed at not less than a complete restatement of the Buddha's message in terms more in keeping with its original spirit. Whether conservative or liberal, however, none of the schools could afford to ignore the fact that the Monastic Order was economically dependent on the laity, whether in the form of the general public, a few wealthy burgesses and merchants, or the king. A complete separation, even in the religious sphere, between the two monastic and the two lay *vargas* was, therefore, as unthinkable as a complete identification. A place for the aspirations of the laity had to be found. Eventually, owing to both the necessities of their common economic situation and the interactions which took place between them, the Hīnayāna and the Mahāyāna worked out solutions to the problem which, certainly in India and to a large extent in the rest of Asia too, in practice coincided to a greater extent than the difference between their respective attitudes might have led one to expect.

The Mahāyāna solution was the more radical. Impelled by the universalism and optimism that had given it birth, it evolved for all followers of the Buddha a common spiritual ideal which, integrating devotion and understanding, derived inspiration as much from the living personal example of the Buddha as from the records of his teaching. This was the bodhisattva ideal (see Chapter 2). At the same time it worked out a common path, the Path of the Six (or Ten) Pāramitās (see p.155), which was in fact a revised and enlarged edition of the old series of stages from *dāna* to *prajñā*. By restoring this ideal and this path to their proper place at the very centre of the Buddha's teaching whence, as from a heart, flowed the lifeblood of the religion, as well as by stressing the fact that all, whether monks or laymen, were bodhisattvas, and thus potential Buddhas, the Mahāyāna was able to lessen the tensions between the *vargas*, which were now united through the pursuit of a common spiritual objective by means of the same, or similar, spiritual methods. This meant that for the Mahāyāna the mahā-sangha coincided with the bodhisattva-sangha in the widest sense of the latter term. The lay Buddhist ideal was no longer embodied in a figure such as Anāthapiṇḍada, patron and supporter of the Order in the Buddha's day, but in Vimalakīrti, the wealthy householder of Vaiśālī, the profundity of whose spiritual understanding was such that he could give a lesson in wisdom even to the bodhisattva Mañjuśrī.

As time went on, a common Vinaya for all bodhisattvas, whether monks or laymen, was also evolved. Though much less systematized than its Hīnayāna counterpart – as from the very nature of the Mahāyāna had to be the case – it included both an ordination ceremony and a code of discipline. The first of these, known as the *bodhisattva-saṁvara*, could be conferred by any spiritually qualified bodhisattva on any person in whom the Will to Enlightenment had arisen (see p.152). Though longer than the *upasampadā-saṁvara* it was concerned, as the following short extract reveals, less with the punctilious observance of ceremonial minutiae than with the promotion of a certain type of spiritual attitude:

> I (person's name), who have thus caused the thought of enlightenment to arise, accept the infinite world of living beings as my mother, father, sister, brother, son, daughter, and any other blood-relations, and having accepted them as far as is in my power, strength, and knowledge, I cause the roots of goodness to grow in them. From now on, whatever gift I shall give or moral rule I shall keep, or act of patience I shall perform, acting vigorously, or whatever meditation I shall attain, or acting with wisdom shall learn skill in means, all that shall be for the profit and welfare of living beings.
>
> And having undertaken to win supreme, perfect enlightenment, and having done homage to those Bodhisattvas of great mercy who

> have entered the Great Stage, I go forth after them. Having gone forth, a Bodhisattva am I, a Bodhisattva. From now on may my teacher support me.[134]

If no teacher was available, self-ordination was, as an exceptional measure, permitted. The code of discipline, known as the *bodhisattva-śīla*, seems to have been derived partly from its Hīnayāna counterpart, the *prātimokṣa*, and partly from passages in the Mahāyāna sūtras, dealing with the life and duties of the bodhisattva, of the type which Śāntideva collected and arranged in his *Śikṣā-samuccaya* or 'Compendium of Instruction'. The possibility that the *bodhisattva-śīla* is based on an early, precoenobitical form of the Hīnayāna *prātimokṣa* current among the Mahāsāṁghikas and their offshoots should not be overlooked. According to the *Brahmajāla-bodhisattva-śīla Sūtra*, or 'Grand Net of the Bodhisattva's Precepts', a work of great influence and authority in China and Japan, one who has received the bodhisattva ordination should observe ten major and forty-eight minor rules of conduct. The first four major rules are identical with the four *pārājikas*. The additional six are:

(1) trading in intoxicating drinks or inducing others to do the same;

(2) divulging the offences committed, or the way in which they were committed, by a householder, bhikṣu-bodhisattva, monk, or nun;

(3) vaunting one's own qualities and disparaging others;

(4) giving nothing to the destitute, and even ignoring them;

(5) not forgiving a person who has injured the bodhisattva but asked for pardon; and

(6) speaking ill of the Triratna.

The minor rules are even more Mahayanic in emphasis, and cover a wide range of topics, ranging from abstention from garlic to the development of the bodhicitta; they are applicable, some to monks and nuns, some to householders, and some to all four *vargas*.[135] As extant in Tibet the *bodhisattva-śīla* consists of a rather different set of sixty-four rules, eighteen major and forty-six minor, the major rules being available in two recensions. All these versions of the *bodhisattva-śīla* breathe the same spirit of unbounded altruism.

The evolution of the Mahāyāna Vinaya, as it may be called, did not result in the supersession of its Hīnayāna counterpart. After receiving the bodhisattva ordination a follower of the Mahāyāna remained faithful to, and continued to observe, either the Five or Eight Precepts, in the case of a householder-bodhisattva, or the Monastic Code, in that of a bhikṣu- or bhikṣuṇī-bodhisattva; *but they observed them in the spirit of the Mahāyāna*. Such, at least, was the Sino-Indian and Central Asian tradition. In China the bodhisattva ordination, though also conferred on lay people, invariably followed within a few days of monastic ordination, with which it comprised as it were an extended Hīnayāna-cum-Mahāyāna ceremony. Developments in Japan were less fortunate. The *upasampadā* lineage having become practically extinct, so that, except in the Ritsu Shū, or Vinaya School, there were really no bhikṣus and bhikṣuṇīs in the country, the bodhisattva ordination in effect took its place. As in most schools of Japanese Buddhism the latter now came to be conferred only on those engaged in pastoral activities, it became to this extent a dividing rather than a uniting factor in the Buddhist community.

The measures taken by the offshoots of the Sthaviravādins to accommodate the spiritual aspirations of the laity were less thoroughgoing. They were in fact a compromise. Unwilling to recognize a common spiritual ideal for all *vargas*, and unable either to ignore the growing popularity, or resist the influence, of the bodhisattva ideal, these schools eventually conceded that the laity as such might aim not merely at heavenly rebirth but at being a bodhisattva and becoming, after three whole aeons of striving, a Supreme Buddha. A list of ten *pāramitās*, less systematic than their Mahāyāna original, was drawn up in time to be included in some of the later, more obviously apocryphal, books of their respective canons. In the case of the Pāli Tipiṭaka, the only one of these collections to survive complete, the fact that the bodhisattva ideal finds admission only to such books has unfortunately helped confirm an impression that the ideal is a late and spurious one, whereas, on the contrary, it is as ancient as Buddhism itself, and late only in respect of its recognition by the Hīnayāna schools and its belated partial incorporation in their canonical literature. Arhantship remained however for these schools the monastic ideal. Thus a curious situation developed in which the more spiritually-minded Hīnayāna laymen could model themselves upon an ideal which, in theory, was recognized as superior to that followed by the monks and nuns. Doctrinal expression to this plurality of religious ideals was given in the formula of the three *yānas* or spiritual careers, a distinction the Mahāyāna rejected as merely provisional on the grounds that ultimately there was but one *yāna* for all sentient beings, that of the bodhisattva. As the Hīnayāna tradition, both doctrinal and disciplinary, had already been worked out in purely monastic terms and systematically oriented towards the attainment of Arhantship, its attempt to 'contain' – rather than really to incorporate – the bodhisattva ideal by recognizing it as suitable for lay people failed to result in any deep or lasting modification of its basic attitude. The *Jātaka* stories were treated as matter for edification rather than for exemplification and the style of bodhisattva was appropriated, not to pious lay folk, but more often to rulers who, being obviously unfitted for Arhantship in the present life, might be regarded as aiming at Buddhahood in the distant future.

The Theravādin countries of South-east Asia, unable to formulate a common spiritual ideal without violating the basic assumptions of the Hīnayāna, have tended to rely on a social rather than on a purely religious solution to the problem. Recourse to such an expedient was facilitated by the fact that, practically the entire population of these countries being Buddhist, national and religious loyalties have tended if not to coincide then at least strongly to reinforce each other. With the exception of Sri Lanka, which might have inherited Indian prejudices in the matter, they all introduced a system of temporary monastic ordination which, though hardly in keeping with the spirit of the Vinaya, nevertheless contributed to the solidarity of the community to an extent that more than compensated for any shortcomings. On the completion of the more secular side of his education (which might in any case have been received under monastic auspices), and before assuming the responsibility of marrying and bringing up a family, a young man would, and often still does, enter the Sangha and devote a few months to the acquisition of spiritual knowledge. An upāsaka moreover enjoyed the privilege of repeating this invaluable experience at any time during his life, as often as he wished, and for however long or short a period. Wherever the ancient traditions are honoured a male Buddhist who has not been a monk for at least three days is even now regarded as scarcely human, and certainly not fully educated. The bhikṣuṇī-ordination having died out in the Theravādin countries the system does not extend to women. Its popularity even among the male section of the community has, however, sufficed to ensure a general understanding of and sympathy with the monastic vocation, and an appreciation of its special requirements, which are of immense value in creating among the laity a feeling of participation in the spiritual life of the religion. The system has also been largely responsible for the wide diffusion of elementary religious knowledge in those parts of the Theravādin world where it obtains.

Just as it was impossible for the Hīnayāna, even at its most rigid, entirely to ignore the higher aspirations of the laity, so the Mahāyāna, even in its most liberal form, could not overlook the fact that it was easier for a monk to be a bodhisattva than a layman and that there existed, in consequence, a real difference between the Monastic Order and the community of lay devotees. According to the Mahāyāna, this difference was socio-ecclesiastical rather than spiritual; or, if spiritual, one of degree only, not of kind. For the classical Hīnayāna the danger consisted in making too absolute a distinction between bhikṣus and upāsakas and interpreting Buddhism too exclusively in terms of monasticism; for the Mahāyāna it lay rather in confounding the spiritual with the socio-ecclesiastical order of things in such a way that the Sangha was submerged in the laity. Albeit from opposite extremes each of these two great traditions in practice tended, when dealing with the laity, to converge upon a common mean position. This in combination with the facts previously mentioned was responsible for the creation of a common pattern of Sangha–laity relations throughout practically the entire Buddhist world. Though the Sangha in Mahāyāna lands may be characterized more by compassionate participation in the affairs of secular life, and the Sangha in Theravādin lands more by cool aloofness from them, such a difference of emphasis by no means obscures the fact that whether in Sri Lanka or Tibet, Burma or Vietnam, Buddhist laymen and laywomen everywhere look up to the members of the Sangha as to their elder brothers in religion, reverencing them as (1) and (2) their teachers, both spiritual and secular, as (3) objects of devotion, as (4) sources of merit, as (5) a means of magical protection and blessing, and as (6) their trusted advisers in worldly affairs.

(1) Since they devote not a part but the whole of their time to the study and practice of the Dharma the standard of religious knowledge and spiritual experience is naturally higher among monks than laymen. Consequently, though a bhikṣu sometimes has a spiritually advanced upāsaka for his guru, especially in the Mahāyāna countries, the lay community as a whole stands in a relation of discipleship to

the Sangha, the members of which function primarily as *spiritual teachers* and are honoured as such.

Instruction in the Dharma is imparted in various ways. One of the most ancient and popular is the religious discourse, which the preacher delivers sitting cross-legged on a special raised seat, and which may consist of an exposition of the Scriptures, of edifying stories and moral exhortations, of hints on the practice of meditation, or of an original presentation of the Doctrine. Whatever its theme, such a discourse is distinguished from an ordinary lecture by an ethical and spiritual emphasis powerful enough to inspire the congregation with a distaste for worldly things and an ardent desire for the realization of Nirvāṇa. Religious discourses are generally delivered in that integral part of any large monastery, the preaching hall. Sometimes they are delivered in the homes of the laity. On such occasions they often follow a ceremonial food-offering (*bhojana-dāna*) to one or more monks, a practice symbolic of the system of mutual dependence wherein upāsakas support bhikṣus with the gift of material things (*amisa-dāna*) and bhikṣus, in return, sustain upāsakas with that greatest of all gifts, the gift of the Dharma (*dhamma-dāna*).

The monks are not only preachers but writers. For the benefit of the laity they translate the Scriptures into the vernacular, compose religious songs, stories, and dramas, compile tracts and manuals, and engage in a variety of other literary undertakings. Nor is the importance of visual aids to religious education unknown. Through sculptured images of the Buddhas and bodhisattvas and mural paintings such as those of Ajaṇta, where incidents from the Scriptures are vividly depicted, generations of monk-artists have sought to impress the facts of the Master's life and the truths of his teaching upon the minds even of the illiterate. Religious instruction is also imparted through special classes and courses, the 'meditation week' being particularly popular in some areas. Being endowed with a greater mobility and freedom of action than the laity, the monks are moreover able not only to consolidate the Dharma at home but to propagate it abroad. Apart from the intermittent patronage of kings, the story of the spread of Buddhism throughout Asia is largely that of the missionary enterprise of individual members of the Sangha.

(2) As the most literate section of the community, the monks tended to function not only as spiritual but as secular teachers. Once the Scriptures had been committed to writing, an event that occurred

about four centuries after the parinirvāṇa, literacy became almost a Buddhist virtue. Many Mahāyāna sūtras contain colophons detailing the merit to be derived from copying them.

> Peeling your own skin for paper [says Locana Buddha in the *Brahmajāla-bodhisattva-śīla Sūtra*] with blood for your inkstick and using spinal fluid for the water to mix it, using your own bones for a pen, you should copy out the precepts of the Buddha.[136]

With exhortations such as these ringing in its ears, it is hardly astonishing that wherever the Sangha penetrated literacy was encouraged and education became more widespread. The monasteries, both large and small, were simultaneously centres of spiritual life, of cultural activity, and of learning. If the standard of popular education is even today higher in the Buddhist than in the non-Buddhist regions of Asia it is due mainly to the fact that, in the former, the village temple has been for centuries the village school. Individual monks often ranked as poets and artists with the most celebrated. Siri Rāhula, the best classical Sinhalese poet, was Sangharāja of Ceylon, while Milarepa enjoys the double distinction of being both the greatest poet and the greatest yogin of Tibet. The earliest and at least the second best epic and dramatic poet to have written in Sanskrit was Aśvaghoṣa, a Buddhist monk. In China and Japan, among hundreds hardly less illustrious, there was Wu Tao-tzu, the poet-painter, whose dragon flew away as soon as he had painted in its eyes, and Kōbō Daishi, the founder of the Shingon Shū, a man of many-sided religious and artistic genius who is traditionally credited with the invention of the Japanese system of syllabic writing. Apart from educational and cultural activities, the monks also engaged in social work. Some, inspired by the bodhisattva ideal, and desirous of alleviating suffering, studied medicine and gave free treatment to the sick. Others built roads and bridges, introduced useful arts and crafts, and popularized improved methods of agriculture.

(3) Inasmuch as the monks not only preach the Dharma but practise it more intensively than anybody else, they become *objects of devotion* to the laity. This is natural. The impulse to admire, to revere and worship, is deep-rooted in the human psyche, and requires for its full satisfaction as concrete an embodiment of one's ideals as possible. The Buddhas, in their golden aureoles, tend to appear remote, perhaps a little unreal, to the average man and woman. Entangled in doctrinal

formulas, and submerged beneath layers of scholastic commentary, the Dharma seems abstruse. The members of the Ārya Sangha, and even the bodhisattvas, recede into the sunset glow of the legendary past. Only the bhikṣus, the members of the Monastic Order, fall within range of the layman's experience. From them he hears the Dharma. In their lives he sees more intelligence, more kindness, more self-control – in short a fuller realization of the Buddhist ideal – than in his own. Thus seeing, his faith in the Three Jewels is confirmed and strengthened. Throughout the Buddhist world, therefore, the laity treats the Sangha with a respect and devotion that at times astonishes the outsider. In a thoroughly orthodox community the most junior bhikṣu takes precedence over kings. No one sits on a higher level than a bhikṣu, or sits while he stands. Particularly on formal occasions, the members of the Sangha are commonly saluted with a threefold prostration. In several Buddhist lands special honorific speech-forms are used in addressing monks or referring to them.

(4) *Dāna* or giving, the first *pāramitā*, was a virtue to be practised, in one form or another, by the whole Buddhist community. From ancient times the belief prevailed that the amount of merit accruing to the donor was, in part, determined by the worthiness of the recipient. On account of the holiness of its members, the Sangha was the *puṇya-kṣetra* (Pāli *puññā-khetta*) or field of merit *par excellence*; for, as seed planted in fertile soil yielded more abundantly than that planted in barren, any offering made to the Sangha was productive of greater *puṇya* than one bestowed elsewhere. With a sufficient quantity of *puṇya* to his credit one could pass, at death, to rebirth in a happy heavenly abode. The latter, as we saw above (p.195), was according to the Hīnayāna the proper goal of the lay devotee. In Theravādin countries, therefore, the religious life of the devout laity consists largely of making offerings to the monks in the hope of getting to heaven. This is no more spiritual than a shrewd investment in stocks and shares. Carried to extremes, it can even prove dangerous. A layman preoccupied with the accumulation of a private stock of merit may, unintentionally, do harm to the Sangha by thrusting upon the bhikṣus articles for which they have no need, or which are forbidden by the Vinaya, or which are so luxurious as to be obviously unsuitable for anyone intent on the higher life. Undue emphasis on the doctrine of *puṇya*, and on the Sangha as the most worthy recipient of gifts, also leads to a channelling of public generosity so exclusive that other

deserving objects of charity, such as the sick, the poor, and the aged, are neglected. Burmese 'nuns' who are not technically bhikṣuṇīs, being considered barren soil in respect of the harvest of merit to be obtained from them, are often left to fend for themselves. In Mahāyāna countries, where the altruistic emphasis is more pronounced and where bhikṣus are not so exclusively the object of devotion, such abuses are rare. Even in Theravādin countries they are not without their corresponding compensations. Throughout almost the entire Buddhist world, in fact, the practice of regarding the Sangha as *puṇya-kṣetra*, to whatever degree, has for centuries past ensured for it the steady, continuous, and most lavishly generous support of the faithful.

(5) By virtue of their austerities, particularly the practice of *dhyāna*, the monks were able to exercise control over not only their own mental states but the objective correlates of those states in the external world. They were thus *a means of magical protection and blessing*. The laity, though devout, was generally interested more in material gains than in spiritual attainments; they wanted long life, health, riches, progeny, success in all their undertakings, and a host of other mundane things. Sometimes what they wanted could not be obtained, or obtained only with great difficulty, by the ordinary methods. The Sangha was therefore called upon to invoke the hidden powers on their behalf.

It is wrong to view this aspect of Buddhism as a regrettable lapse from the purity of a strictly rational, 'scientific' original teaching. As far back as literary evidence goes, even to what are apparently the oldest portions of the Scriptures, belief in the existence of occult forces which the monk, through a high degree of concentration, can manipulate for the benefit of humanity, is present; the life of the Buddha himself, as it has come down to us, cannot be wholly dissociated from such elements. Neither is the magical aspect of Buddhism the prerogative of any particular school. Though the Vajrayāna may be richer in specifically magical expressions, which are for this school symbolic of higher, even transcendental, forces and values, magical practices are equally characteristic of the Mahāyāna and the Hīnayāna, and constitute an important aspect of Buddhist life in every age and clime.

The occult forces are invoked through repetition of the Sacred Word. The more intrinsically sacred the Word, as well as the holier and more numerous the reciters, the more powerful will be the effect produced. Consequently it is the Tripiṭaka, or a selection of texts from it, which, as the Word of the Buddha, the most sacred of all utterances, is commonly employed. This sometimes results in curious situations. The grosser the object desired, the stronger the desire for it is likely to be, and the more powerful, therefore, the forces that must be conjured up for its acquisition. In Thailand the *upasampadā-kammavācā* is recited as a love charm. The diary of the Japanese monk Jojin describes how, when on pilgrimage to Wu-ta'i-shan in 1073CE, he was commanded by the Chinese emperor to make rain; which he did by setting up a lotus altar and reciting the *Saddhārma-puṇḍarīka*.[137] No portion of the Scriptures excels in sublimity the discourses on the 'Perfection of Wisdom', yet in one of the most famous of them the Lord says, addressing Śakra:

> If a follower of perfect wisdom were to go into battle, to the very front of it, he could not possibly lose his life in it. It is impossible that he should lose his life from the attack of somebody else. If someone strikes at him – with sword, or stick, or clod of earth, or anything else – his body cannot be hit.[138]

Here an exalted teaching is clearly made to function as a lucky charm or talisman. Sometimes the magical potency of a sūtra is condensed into a *dhāraṇī*, a 'meaningless' combination of syllables the repetition of which produces the same results as the recitation of the sūtra.

However strange such a view may seem today, the ceremonial recitation of the sacred texts by the monks, for magical purposes, has ever been regarded in all Buddhist countries as an important public service, for performing which the Sangha was entitled to the gratitude of the laity. Indeed the mere presence of a body of austere and saintly monks exerted, it was believed, a beneficial influence on the entire national economy, and acted as an insurance against such calamities as fire, flood, epidemics, earthquakes, and invasion. Monks were therefore regarded as a national asset.

(6) On the principle that the spectator sees more of the game than the players, the monks, with their more detached attitude towards life, often had a clearer and more balanced understanding even of worldly affairs than the laity. They were therefore greatly in demand as *advisers*. In a traditional Buddhist community, no matter is too trivial or too important to be brought to them for their consideration, from the settlement of a dispute to the choice of a new site for the

village. Especially when sought in connection with those matters with which it is improper for a monk to concern himself, such as marriage, the advice given may be couched not in categorical but in hypothetical terms, the monk doing no more than indicate the probable consequences of certain lines of action. Whatever the advice given, it would tend to promote the best interests of the community, both material and spiritual. In times of sickness and bereavement, and at the hour of death, the monk administers spiritual consolation. According to some traditions, his care for the laity extends even beyond this life, continuing in the form of instructions which can be heard and acted upon, in the 'intermediate state' (*antarabhava*), by a stream of consciousness newly dissociated from the physical body. At a time of national emergency the government may call upon the Sangha, or upon prominent individual monks, not only for magical protection and blessing but for counsel. Monks are also sometimes employed as ambassadors to negotiate terms of peace. Though invested thereby with the power of doing a great deal of good, the Sangha is simultaneously exposed to the corrupting influence of politics. Examples of politically ambitious ecclesiastics are, of course, not lacking in Buddhist history, but on the whole the political record of the Sangha is not only far cleaner but incomparably more tolerant and pacific than that of its counterparts in other religions.

19

POPULAR BUDDHISM

BETWEEN THE PURELY spiritual exercises pertaining to the Path, and the predominantly mundane activities of lay society, there intervenes an aspect of the religion which may be termed Popular Buddhism. Like Diotima's Eros, who was neither divine nor human but daimonic, it is neither wholly sacred nor wholly profane in character, but of a mixed or intermediate nature. As such it constitutes an important link between the intenser but more confined religious life of the monasteries and temples, with their monks and nuns, and their small bands of more seriously-minded lay devotees, and the more widely diffused but lukewarm and fitful piety of the vast mass of more or less nominal adherents of the Teaching. Both in the past and now, being a Buddhist always consisted, for the average person, in participation in this popular aspect of the religion rather than the systematic cultivation of the Eightfold Path or the Six Perfections. This is no more than may be expected. Few strive for Enlightenment; the majority are concerned with other things. What is required, under such circumstances, is not recriminations and regrets, but provision for at least a peripheral contact with, or a partial and occasional participation in, the life of the religion, on the part of those who for the time being demand nothing more. This is the function of Popular Buddhism. Ideally it is an *upāya*, a skilful means, perpetuating the flame of popular awareness of spiritual values, however dimly, and keeping open the channels of communication between the spiritual and secular worlds.

In practice this aspect of Buddhism is an extremely rich and composite one, consisting of an immense number of elements that do not easily lend themselves to generalization. Apart from the recitation of the Three Refuges and Five Precepts, without which one is not even nominally a Buddhist, it comprises elements evolved out of the Teaching itself by a natural process of development and adaptation, elements assimilated from non-Buddhist cultures, and, at the lowest level, foreign elements that may, in extreme cases, even be incompatible with Buddhism. Popular devotional observances, as an expression of faith in, and adoration of, either the Enlightened and compassionate master or his teaching, generally belong to the first category. Likewise observances connected with the Sangha. The celebration of the New Year, and other seasonal festivities, belong to the second, having been carried over from pre-Buddhist times and given a Buddhistic colouring. The Tibetan New Year, for example, is now connected with the advent of Maitreya. Sometimes it is not definitely known whether a particular element was developed from within the religion or assimilated from without. Such is the case with regard to one of the main focal points of Popular Buddhism, the Buddha image. Astrology and divination, though widespread in all Buddhist lands, both Theravāda and Mahāyāna, belong to the third category, that of the foreign elements. So too does the caste system which, though prevalent among the Buddhists of Sri Lanka, is incompatible with the Buddha's teaching even as handed down in that country.

Among the varied elements making up Popular Buddhism there exists, also, a relative distribution of emphasis, which varies from one age and one part of the Buddhist world to another, and even, perhaps, from school to school. Ideally, if Popular Buddhism is really to function as an *upāya*, not only should it be counterbalanced, in the community as a whole, by a sufficiency of activities pertaining directly to the Path, but within this aspect of Buddhism itself the first and second categories should take precedence over the third. With regard to any form of Popular Buddhism, from the adoration of relics to the wearing of amulets, what falls to be considered, in the present context, is not so much its intrinsic value in comparison with the activities connected with the Path, so much as the degree of prominence assigned to it within the whole system of popular observance. The worship of the bodhi tree, beneath which the Bodhisattva gained Supreme Enlightenment, is an integral part of traditional practice; but a Buddhism, even a Popular Buddhism, that consisted exclusively in the veneration of such trees, would not be deserving of the name. The 'corruptions' in Buddhism of which some observers complain are generally found to consist, whenever the complaints are well founded, either in an imbalance between the Dharma proper and Popular Buddhism or in a wrong distribution of emphasis among the latter's various constituent elements. As a historical phenomenon Buddhism has carried tolerance of what did not belong to it and sometimes of what was bad in itself – to adapt Sir Charles Eliot's language in respect of Indian religions generally – to an extreme that constituted almost a betrayal of its own principles. It has therefore perpetually stood in danger of forfeiting its distinctive character. Eliot points out that

> The weakness comes from the absence of any command against superstitious rites and beliefs. When the cardinal principles of Buddhism are held strongly these accessories do not matter, but the time comes when the creeper that was once an ornament grows into the walls of the shrine and splits the masonry.[139]

The present account deals with some of the more truly Buddhistic components of Popular Buddhism, and presupposes them to occupy no more than their rightful place in the total tradition.

Lay Buddhists have always tended to be more emotionally than intellectually inclined. They are Faith-Followers rather than Doctrine-Followers. In fact, the development of the devotional element in the Teaching was originally due to their influence rather than to the efforts of the monks, the more conservative minority of whom indeed admitted it with reluctance as the result of popular pressure. Being more the creation of the laity than of the Sangha, whose function is generally limited to supplying doctrinal connections, Popular Buddhism is therefore strongly emotional, consisting largely of fervent expressions of faith in and devotion to the Three Jewels, or, more correctly, to their various symbols and representatives.

Among symbols of the Buddha, one of the most ancient and best known is the *caitya* (Pāli *cetiya*) or *stūpa* (Pāli *thūpa*), a tumulus or artificial mound consisting, originally, of a cube surmounted by a hemisphere on which rested an honorific umbrella. One kind of stūpa, the *dhātugarbha* (Sinhalese *dagoba*) or reliquary, enshrines a portion of the bone-relics of the Buddha, worship of which tended to be assimilated to the cult of the stūpa. Besides being connected with his *rūpakāya*, the stūpa as an assemblage of architectural elements symbolic of the Doctrine is also an embodiment of the Lord's *dharmakāya*. As might have been expected, the *Mahāvastu Āvadāna* of the Lokottaravāda, an offshoot of the Mahāsāṁghika, supports the worship of stūpas much more enthusiastically than does the Theravāda Tipiṭaka. Speaking of the events immediately following the parinirvāṇa, the latter merely says

> At the four cross-roads a thūpa should be erected to the Tathāgata: and whoever shall there place garlands or perfumes or paint, or make salutation there or become in its presence calm in heart, that shall long be to them for a profit and a joy.[140]

The former is more explicit. It represents the Buddha himself as declaring

> He who, having turned his thoughts to enlightenment for the sake of all living things, reverentially salutes the tope of the Saviour of the world, becomes everywhere in all his lives as he fares on the way to enlightenment, mindful, thoughtful, virtuous and assured.[141]

The text then eulogizes stūpa worship at length in the most extravagant terms, attributing to it all possible merits. Despite the initial lack of enthusiasm, in certain quarters, for this expression of popular devotion to the Buddha, it was firmly established by the time of Aśoka, whom later traditions indeed represent as being himself a great builder of stūpas. Today, as in the past, the veneration of stūpas of various shapes, sizes, and materials is as striking a feature of Asian Buddhism as the whitewashed, gaily tiled, gilded, or moss-grown structures themselves are of the landscapes of Buddhist countries.

A slightly less ancient symbol of the Buddha, but a no less popular one, is the image. So much is image worship a part of Buddhist devotion, and so highly characteristic of popular practice, that its comparatively late introduction into the religion is sometimes overlooked. It has, in fact, no canonical sanction. The commentarial literature does, however, incorporate late traditions about the carving of a wooden likeness of the Master during his lifetime. Though its time and place of origin were long a matter of scholarly dispute, it now seems probable that the Buddha image was first introduced among the Sarvāstivādins of Mathura during the first century CE. Despite its late appearance, so admirably did it meet the requirements of the masses that as an object of devotion its popularity soon rivalled even that of the stūpa. Artistically it is the most beautiful expression of the spirit of Buddhism. Images of bodhisattvas, Arhants, guardian deities, and saintly teachers are also widely venerated. Theravādin worship usually consists of offering only flowers, lights, and incense, and chanting verses in praise of the Three Jewels and passages from the Scriptures. In the Mahāyāna, and even more so in the Vajrayāna, the ritual is not only more complex and artistic but symbolical of psychological processes and spiritual experiences.

Other popular ancient objects of devotion are the bodhi tree and the Buddha's footprint. According to tradition, the bodhisattva attained Supreme Enlightenment while meditating at the foot of an *asvattha* or *pīpal* (*ficus religiosa*). What appear to be the oldest canonical accounts of this event make no mention of this circumstance, but by the time of Aśoka the cult of the bodhi tree, as it came to be known, was evidently well established, for one of the gates of the Great Stupa at Sanchi depicts that monarch himself in the act of adoration before it. According to the *Mahāvaṁsa*, which devotes two whole chapters to the incident,[142] Aśoka's daughter Sanghamittā brought with her to Sri Lanka a cutting from the original tree which the king and people of that country received with tremendous jubilation. The worship of the bodhi tree seems to represent an incorporation into Buddhism of primitive tree-worship and its associated solar-cosmic symbolism. Due to climatic reasons the cult is confined to India and the Theravādin countries of South-east Asia, though it is said that in China the *pīpal* is commonly identified with a sacred tree connected with Taoism. Bodhi trees are worshipped by decorating their branches with flower-garlands and coloured flags, by lighting rows of lamps, and by sprinkling their roots with milk and perfumed water. The worship of the *śrīpāda* (Pāli *siripāda*) or sacred footprint may owe something to the Indian custom, referred to in the Tipiṭaka, of touching, stroking, and even kissing the feet of a religious teacher as a mark of the profoundest devotion. Such footprints are of two kinds, those believed to have been left by the Buddha himself in the course of his legendary visits to different parts of the Buddhist world, and facsimiles in gold, silver, and other substances. According to Sinhalese tradition, the Buddha impressed his footprint on the bank of the Narmada River and on Mount Elumalai near Tirūpati, both in South India, on 'Adam's Peak' in Sri Lanka, and in Yonaka-pura, which is probably

Gāndhāra.[143] Another, over which stands an imposing pinnacled shrine, is found in the Sarapuri province of Thailand. The footprint at Gayā, in Bihar, having been appropriated by Hinduism after the virtual disappearance of Buddhism from India, is now popularly venerated as that of the god Viṣṇu.

Associated as they are with the chief events of his life, the four great centres of pilgrimage – Lumbinī, Bodh Gayā, Sārnāth, and Kusinārā – are also in a way symbolical of the Master. One might even claim that involving as it does the worship of stūpas and images, and of the bodhi tree, as well as a certain amount of hardship, pilgrimage is the most comprehensive of all popular devotional practices. A passage in the *Mahāparinibbāna Sutta* attests the antiquity of the custom. Addressing Ānanda, the Buddha declares that there are four places upon which the believer should look with emotion: the Tathāgata's birthplace, the place of his Supreme Enlightenment, the place where he set in motion the Wheel of the Dharma, and the place of his parinirvāṇa. He continues

> And whosoever, Ānanda, shall make an end with peaceful heart, while wandering in pilgrimage to (such) shrines, upon the breaking up of the body all such shall be reborn beyond death in the blissful heaven-world.[144]

These words have over the centuries inspired millions of monks, nuns, and lay people to brave all dangers and take the long road that from a remote corner of the Buddhist world led, through desert and jungle, and over mountains and seas, to the peaceful shrines of the 'Middle Country'. It was regarded as particularly meritorious to go all the way on foot and to beg one's food. Even now, when the journey is more often made by rail or air, Tibetan devotees can (or could until recently) be seen prostrating themselves the whole distance from Lhasa to Bodh Gayā. As the practice increased in popularity, the pilgrim's itinerary came to include not only numerous additional places connected with events in the Buddha's life, but also others associated with his lives as a bodhisattva and with previous accounts of many of these places, not all of which fall within the present political boundaries of India. Eventually, as Buddhism overspread Asia, and became consolidated in one country after another, historic local shrines also developed into centres of pilgrimage. In China this was the case with the sacred mountains of Wu-t'ai-shan, Omei-shan, and P'u-t'o-shan, which were the seats of special manifestations of the spiritual power of the bodhisattvas Mañjuśrī, Samantabhadra, and Avalokiteśvara respectively. In *The Wheel of Life* John Blofeld describes a modern pilgrimage to the gilded and lacquered shrines of Wu-t'ai-shan.

Though popular devotion tends to centre upon the Buddha, the two other Jewels are not neglected. If we except the stūpa, which to the masses is commemorative of the Buddha rather than symbolic of spiritual truths, the Dharma is embodied principally in the written or printed volumes of the Scriptures. In contrast to the traditionally theistic West, where the true worship that can be offered to God alone is sharply distinguished from all other acts of homage, the Buddhist East tends to regard religious worship – including ritual worship – reverence, and respect as the various manifestations, in differing degrees, of a single devotional attitude. Veneration for the Scriptures, which sprang up immediately the Dharma was committed to writing, could therefore express itself in Buddhism with the greatest freedom. Apart from the fact that the Theravādins refuse to recognize the Mahāyāna sūtras, respect is of course shown for the whole body of the Scriptures, extending by association even to commentaries and exegetical works. Popular devotion has, though, tended to crystallize round individual texts. Mahāyāna Buddhists have a special regard for the *Prajñāpāramitā* and *Saddhārma-puṇḍarīka Sūtras*. The *Perfection of Wisdom* 'in 8,000 Lines' describes how the bodhisattva Dharmodgata created for the former

> a pointed tower, made of the seven precious substances, adorned with red sandalwood, and encircled by an ornament of pearls. Gems were placed in the four corners of the pointed tower, and performed the functions of lamps. Four incense jars made of silver were suspended on its four sides, and pure black aloe wood was burning in them, as a token of worship for the perfection of wisdom. And in the middle of that pointed tower a couch made of the seven precious things was put up, and on it a box made of four large gems. Into that the perfection of wisdom was placed, written with melted vaidurya on golden tablets. And that pointed tower was adorned with brightly coloured garlands which hung down in strips.[145]

The sūtra further relates how the bodhisattva Sadaprarudita and the merchant's daughter, with her 500 maidens, who had come to hear Dharmodgata preach,

> all paid worship to the perfection of wisdom – with the flowers which they had brought along, and with garlands, wreaths, raiment, jewels, incense, flags and golden and silvery flowers.[146]

This brilliantly colourful scene, representing a highly idealized version of what must have been a common feature of Indian Buddhism, was partly responsible for the more gorgeous and extravagant aspects of Far Eastern bibliolatry. In Japan the *Saddhārma-puṇḍarīka* is the object of special, indeed exclusive, devotion for the adherents of the Nichiren sect, in the sanctuaries of whose temples it occupies a position of honour. Theravādin Buddhists often exhibit a corresponding veneration for the Abhidharma Piṭaka and the *Mahāsatipaṭṭhāna Sutta*. Narrating the meritorious deeds of Kassapa V of Lanka, the *Cūḷavaṁsa* says:

> He had the Abhidhamma-piṭaka written on tablets of gold, the book Dhammasaṅgaṇī, adorned with all kinds of jewels, and having built a splendid temple in the midst of the town he placed the book in it and caused festival processions to be held for it.[147]

Even when it stopped short of actual worship, popular devotion to the Dharma as symbolized by the Scriptures was responsible not only for the production of an immense number of beautifully written, lavishly illustrated, and magnificently ornamented copies of the canonical texts, but also for their preservation over a long period, in some cases down to the present day.

Though the Sangha is symbolized – sometimes represented – broadly speaking by the Monastic Order, this is naturally not quite so much the case for the Mahāyāna as for the Theravāda. In Tibet, for example, it is the *tulkus* or *nirmāṇakāyas*, rather than monks as such, who are the great objects of popular devotion; but as these are, more often than not, themselves members of the Monastic Order, the difference does not – in William James's phrase – really make a difference. Throughout the Buddhist world, in fact, except in Japan and Nepal, sangha and bhikṣu-sangha are for the bulk of the faithful practically synonymous terms. Devotion to the Sangha expresses itself principally by external acts of reverence and by the giving of material support. In Sri Lanka, Burma, and Thailand, where climatic conditions do not greatly differ from those in India, saffron-robed figures still flit at dawn with their begging-bowls from house to house, standing in silence for a few minutes at each door to receive alms which the laity, with joyous faces, offer them not as beggars but as honoured guests. Besides food, the laity also supplies the members of the Sangha with clothing, shelter, medical treatment, and other requisites. The scale on which this is done naturally varies from one part of the Buddhist world to another; sometimes, as in Tibet until recently and in Thailand, the responsibility is shared by the government. Though devotion to the Sangha is a regular feature of Buddhist life, it reveals itself with particular exuberance at the time of the *kaṭhina* ceremony (see p.190). In some countries the lavish, indeed spectacular, generosity of the lay people on this occasion has succeeded in transforming a purely monastic function not only into a great popular festival but also, for the monks, into the veritable highlight of the ecclesiastical year.

Festivals and celebrations, which often incorporate practically all the expressions of devotion to the Three Jewels just described, are perhaps the most direct, spontaneous, and colourful manifestations of popular religious sentiment. The most ancient and most important are, of course, those commemorating events in the Buddha's life, particularly his birth, his attainment of Supreme Enlightenment, and his parinirvāṇa. Unfortunately there is no unanimity regarding the date of these events. According to the *Mahāvaṁsa*, the kings of Ceylon sponsored elaborate celebrations on the full-moon day of the Indian lunar month Vaiśākha (Pāli: Vesakha, Sinhalese: Wesak) corresponding to the months April–May of the Roman calendar, as far back as the reign of Duṭṭhagāmini in the first century CE.[148] These celebrations were apparently in honour of the Buddha's attainment of Enlightenment, which according to the first chapter of the same work had occurred on that day. Modern Sinhalese tradition assigns his birth and parinirvāṇa also to the same full-moon day, so that Vaiśākha is now celebrated throughout the Theravādin world as a threefold festival. Japanese Buddhists celebrate the three events separately, on 8 April, 8 December, and 15 February respectively. In Tibet the Shaga Dawa (= *Śākya-pūrṇimā*) day, commemorating the Enlightenment only, falls in the fifth month of the Tibetan calendar corresponding normally to the full-moon day of the Indian month Jeystha (Pāli

Jeṭṭha), the month after Vaiśākha. Despite differences of national culture, there are, in the words of a Sinhalese Buddhist, 'two features which are very characteristic of Vesak, namely Colour and Serene Joy.'[149]

Both are certainly conspicuous in the same writer's description of Vaiśākha in Sri Lanka, which may be taken as typical of the way in which the day is celebrated by Buddhists everywhere. Houses are swept and garnished, streets decorated with lanterns and festooned with six-hued Buddhist flags and coloured streamers. At the entrances of the temples and other public buildings, and across the roadways, stand huge bamboo arches covered with greenstuff. While older devotees prefer spotless white, young people love to go clad in the gayest colours. Having worshipped at the local temple or monastery, where offerings are made and devotional stanzas chanted, many take the Eight Precepts, involving abstention from food after midday, and spend the remainder of the day meditating and listening to religious discourses. At every street corner stand free refreshment stalls, the contents of which are practically forced upon passers-by. Roads are thronged with people, some on foot and others riding in every type of vehicle from a bullock cart to a car, while at intervals elephants, dancers, drummers, and long lines of yellow-robed monks sweep past in procession bearing, amidst a glitter of gold and jewels, and with royal pomp, a sacred image or relic from one shrine to another. When night falls both town and countryside are transformed into a fairyland of lights. The temples, redolent of flowers and incense, are packed with devotees, and such is the spiritual fervour generated by the events of the day that worship continues until long past midnight.[150]

In Japan the Buddha's birthday is the most popular of the three great festivals connected with his life.

> In temples [writes Beatrice Lane Suzuki] a miniature canopy, 12 to 16 inches high, is erected over the statue of the Buddha in the form of a child, the shrine with its flower decoration representing the grove of Lumbinī where the Buddha was born.[151]

On account of its floral decorations this anniversary is popularly known as the Flower Festival. The image of the infant Bodhisattva is also ceremonially bathed in tea, to represent the bath which, according to tradition, he was given immediately after birth by the four *lokapālas* or 'world protectors'. Several other anniversaries of events in the life of the Buddha are celebrated in different parts of the Buddhist world. They include the anniversaries of the First Sermon, sometimes known as Dharmachakra Day, and his descent from the Trayastriṁśa Heaven where, some years after his Enlightenment, he had spent the rains residence preaching (according to the Hīnayāna) the Abhidharma or (according to the Mahāyāna tradition) the 'Perfection of Wisdom' to his deceased mother, who had been reborn as a goddess there.

Besides those which are, in principle, common to the entire Buddhist world, each Buddhist country has national festivals commemorating events and personalities connected with its own religious history. Thus Sri Lanka celebrates the arrival of the Arhant Mahinda, who according to tradition was responsible for the introduction of Buddhism to the island, while Japanese Buddhists observe the death anniversary of Shōtoku Taishi, who on 1 February, 594CE, promulgated an imperial ordinance supporting and urging the worship of the Three Jewels. The foundation days of monasteries and temples, as well as the anniversaries of the consecration of an image or stūpa, are also celebrated with more or less pomp by the devotees of the area over which their influence extends. Among Mahāyāna Buddhists, individual Buddhas and bodhisattvas are honoured on particular days and special services are held on the death anniversaries of founders of schools and sects, initiators of new spiritual movements, and other prominent religious personages. In Japan, where for historical reasons sectarianism is much stronger than is usually the case in Buddhism, the death anniversaries of Dōgen, Kōbō Daishi, Shinran Shonin, Nichiren, and other founders of sects are said to be celebrated, by their respective adherents, in an even more gorgeously elaborate manner than the Buddha's birthday. New Year's Days and national days, though non-Buddhist in origin, as well as the birthdays of kings, presidents, and party chairmen, are often observed as semi-religious festivals and made occasions for a display of traditional Buddhist piety and pageantry. With the exception of Sri Lanka, the Theravādin countries of South-east Asia celebrate the New Year's Day principally as a water-throwing festival which, though not devoid of religious significance, in Burma at least sometimes results in ugly scenes of vulgarity and violence.

In addition to these more public manifestations Popular Buddhism also possesses a domestic aspect which, since it touches them more nearly, in the eyes of the lay followers is of no less importance. This aspects relates, not to the powerful upward surge of emotion towards the transcendental represented by the various devotional observances connected with the Three Jewels, but rather in the desire for a descent of the transcendental into ordinary human affairs in such a way as to bless and sanctify them on their own level. This desire finds typical expression in the practice of maintaining a household shrine and performing various religious ceremonies at the time of birth, marriage, and death. A miniature shrine, consisting of a representation of the Buddha and accessories, is found in most Buddhist homes, and may range from a separate richly-appointed chapel, complete with image or images, to a scroll-painting hung in an alcove or a framed lithograph on a shelf. In Theravādin countries the Buddha is sometimes accompanied by the Arhant Sivali who, according to tradition, was distinguished among the disciples of the Master by the fact that his begging-bowl was never empty. Mahāyāna household shrines often contain images or pictures of the more approachable bodhisattvas, such as Avalokiteśvara and Tārā, from whom, on account of their compassionate nature, help in worldly affairs might be expected. Representations of teachers and initiators of traditions such as Tsongkhapa and Padmasambhava fulfil a similar function. In the Far East, instead of an icon, there may be a column of ideograms, in beautiful calligraphy, or a flower or landscape painting instinct with wordless meaning. From the spiritual point of view the household shrine, with its symbol of Enlightenment, stands for the presence of the Unconditioned in the midst of the conditioned, Nirvāṇa in saṁsāra, as well as for the presence of the Enlightened mind behind the dust and dirt of mundane consciousness. Ultimately it stands for the unconditioned non-duality of these pairs of opposites. Yet despite the fact that lamps may be lit, incense burned, and flowers and other offerings presented, if not daily, at least on special occasions, the Buddha image or other symbol of Enlightenment is popularly conceived not even as an object of actual worship – much less still metaphysically – but rather as a talismanic source of blessing and magical protection. All the same, obscured by secondary considerations though its real signification may be, the practice of maintaining a household shrine is of value to the laity as providing a constant unobtrusive reminder of the existence of a higher world of spiritual values to the realization of which they ought, as followers of the Buddha, to direct themselves.

Buddhism being concerned primarily, if not exclusively, with the Path to Enlightenment, no provision was originally made in it for the performance of domestic ceremonies. In all communities, however, from the most primitive to the most highly developed, the great turning-points of human life, especially birth, puberty, marriage, and death, are marked by observances which, by linking them with the vaster social and cosmic order around, simultaneously invest them with a deeper significance and invoke upon them the blessing and protection of higher powers. The domestic ceremonies now current in Buddhist countries consist, broadly speaking, of a substratum of local, more or less secular, pre-Buddhist practices upon which have been superimposed religious observances of Buddhist origin. While the local element naturally varies enormously from one part of the Buddhist world to another, the religious part follows a fairly constant pattern, of which inviting monks to the house for the recitation of sacred texts is the commonest feature. The Thai tonsure ceremony, as described by B. Ananda Maitreya, is a good example of this type of observance:

> On the first day, Buddhist monks are invited to the home and seated on a raised platform. The child then enters dressed in his best clothes and accompanied by appropriate music and, after saluting the monks, places his head upon a cushion while the leading monk ties a cotton cord around the topknot. Then all the people repeat the Triple Refuge and the Five Precepts. After that religious ceremony, all the guests are entertained for the rest of the day. On the second day the Bhikkhus return and chant Parittas, the sayings of the Buddha which have been selected because they create in the hearers a suitable psychic condition. On the third day, again, the monks chant passages from the canon, and the topknot is cut off by the guest of highest rank.... The long hairs severed from the head are saved until the child makes his first pilgrimage to the shrine of the Buddha's footprint at Prabat, and then they are offered to the footprint to be used as a brush for sweeping the holy shrine; the short hairs are put in a tiny boat made from banana leaves and cast into the nearest stream to float to the sea.[152]

It is significant that the actual cutting off of the topknot is done, not by a monk, but by the guest of highest rank, that is to say by a layman. The initiation ceremonies which, in many communities, take place at the time of puberty, are represented, in some Theravādin countries at least, by the practice of temporary ordination (see p.201). The marriage ceremony is almost entirely a secular affair. Not only is it performed by an elderly upāsaka, never by a bhikṣu, but normally monks are not even present on the occasion. Instead, they are invited to bless the newly married couple shortly afterwards, or, alternatively, the latter go themselves to the nearest monastery or temple and there, after worshipping the Buddha, receive the blessings of the Sangha.

On the other hand monks take a prominent part in the performance of the death ceremony, which throughout the Buddhist world is not only the most elaborate of the domestic ceremonies but the one most closely associated with Buddhism. So elaborate are these rites, indeed, and so greatly do they vary from one country to another, that generalization is out of the question. Travellers have in any case often described them, though descriptions as well informed and sympathetic as Evans-Wentz's account of the Sikkimese death ceremony are rare.[153] Only a very few of the most salient features can be touched upon. As rebirth takes place in accordance mainly with the nature of the last thought, great importance is attached to making 'a good death'. Buddhists are expected to pass away peacefully, either reciting the name of the Buddha or remembering their past good deeds. Spiritually advanced persons die in the *dhyāna* state, as the Buddha himself is reported to have done. Both the Nyingmapas of Tibet and the Japanese Jōdō Shin Shū have, in fact, sought to give effect to an ancient tradition of liberation at time of death, the former by addressing to the dying or 'dead' person instructions which will enable him to recognize the various visions he then experiences as the creations of his own mind.[154] Noisy deathbed scenes, with women beating their breasts, tearing their hair, and wailing, are regarded with disapproval, since by disturbing the mind of the dying person they jeopardize his chances of a happy rebirth. The actual funeral, in the sense of the ceremonies connected with the immediate disposal of the dead body, is usually short and simple, compared with the post-mortem observances. Cremation is general, though burial, and dismemberment and exposure to birds of prey and wild beasts are also practised. The most elaborate funerals are those of famous monks or other outstandingly holy persons. In Burma, China, and Tibet the embalmed and gilded body is the centre of ceremonies and festivities that may last for a year or two, even before it is finally cremated or, as sometimes happens, either enclosed in a stūpa or enshrined image-wise in a temple for the veneration of the faithful. In Theravādin countries the post-mortem observances consist mainly in the performance of meritorious acts, such as the making of a ceremonial food-offering to the Sangha in the name of the deceased person and transferring to him the merit accruing therefrom. Throughout the Far East, where they have tended to amalgamate with the deeply-rooted indigenous ancestor-worship, the corresponding Mahāyāna observances though identical in principle are much more elaborate in form. Chinese monks are in fact traditionally concerned mainly with the performance of such rites. In Japan, according to Beatrice Lane Suzuki, the O-Bon

> is perhaps the most striking, most important and most observed [of all the religious observances of that country]. It is a ... three day reunion of the living with the spirits of the dead.... Graveyards are visited, incense burned, flowers offered, and lanterns lighted.... Throughout the ceremony temple priests are busy holding services and reciting sūtras.[155]

Apart from devotional and ceremonial expressions, Popular Buddhism pervades the domestic and social life of the entire Buddhist community in the form of hospitality and good manners. Both are, in fact, esteemed as religious virtues, one being classified under *dāna* or giving, the first perfection, the other under *śīla* or morality, the second. Despite the disturbing effects of modern civilization, the impact of which has now been felt almost universally, they continue to impart a grace and charm to life wherever the Three Jewels are revered.

NOTES AND REFERENCES

1 P.V. Bapat (ed.), *2500 Years of Buddhism*, Publications Division, Ministry of Information and Broadcasting, Government of India, New Delhi 1956, p.144.
2 T.W. Rhys Davids, *Buddhist India*, Motilal Banarsidass, Delhi 1971, ch.xi.
3 See Francis Story, *The Case for Rebirth*, Buddhist Publication Society, Kandy 1959.
4 For a detailed account see Sangharakshita, *A Survey of Buddhism*, Windhorse, Birmingham 1999 (forthcoming), chapter 4.
5 Ananda Coomaraswamy, *Buddha and the Gospel of Buddhism*, Asia Publishing House, Bombay 1956, p.6 (after *Nidānakathā*).
6 I.B. Horner (trans.), *Mahāvagga* I.II.ii. *The Book of the Discipline* (*Vinaya-Piṭaka*), vol.iv (Mahāvagga), Pali Text Society, London 1982, p.28.
7 *Cūḷavagga* X.6.i.
8 *Digha-Nikāya* ii.81.
9 T.W. and C.A.F. Rhys Davids (trans.), *Dīgha-Nikāya* ii.119. *Dialogues of the Buddha*, part ii, Pali Text Society, London 1951, p.127.
10 E. Conze (trans.), *The Perfection of Wisdom in 8,000 Lines and Its Verse Summary (Aṣṭasāhasrikā Prajñāpāramitā)*, Four Seasons Foundation, Bolinas 1973, p.172.
11 *Mahāvagga* i.7.ii.
12 J.J. Jones (trans.), *The Mahāvastu*, Luzac, London 1952, vol.ii, pp.154–5.
13 *Buddhacārita* v.47–62.
14 J.G. Jennings (ed. and trans.), *The Vedantic Buddhism of the Buddha*, Motilal Banarsidass, Delhi, 1947.
15 *Aṅguttara-Nikāya* i.145.
16 E.J. Thomas, *The Life of the Buddha as Legend and History*, Routledge and Kegan Paul, London 1949, p.51.

17 *Udāna* II.I.i.
18 See *A Survey of Buddhism*, op.cit., p.282 *et seq.*
19 See *A Survey of Buddhism*, op.cit., p.398 *et seq.*
20 E.M. Hare (trans.), *Sutta-Nipāta* 1076 (*Woven Cadences*), Oxford University Press, London 1945, p.155.
21 *Saṁyutta-Nikāya* iii.118.
22 *Majjhima-Nikāya* i.488.
23 E. Conze (trans.), *Vajracchedikā Prajñāpāramitā* 26a&b, in *Buddhist Wisdom Books*, Unwin Hyman, London 1988, p.63. Also in *Selected Sayings from the Perfection of Wisdom*, Buddhist Society, London 1955, p.111, and *Vajracchedikā Prajñāpāramitā*, Serie Orientale Roma, Rome 1957, p.89.
24 *Selected Sayings from the Perfection of Wisdom*, op.cit., p.113.
25 D.T. Suzuki, *Outlines of Mahāyāna Buddhism*, New York 1963, p.222 *et seq.*
26 Aśvaghoṣa, *Discourse on The Awakening of Faith in the Mahāyāna*, D.T. Suzuki (trans.), cyclostyled edition, London Dharma Group, p.24.
27 *Udāna* vi.4.
28 E. Conze, *Buddhism: Its Essence and Development*, Bruno Cassirer, Oxford 1951, p.28.
29 Lin Yutang (trans.), *Tao-Teh-King* xxv.
30 *Udāna* v.5.
31 *Majjhima-Nikāya* i.34. For a detailed discussion see *A Survey of Buddhism*, op.cit., p.233.
32 Bangkok, 'Buddhist Era 2500'.
33 For scriptural and other references see T.R.V. Murti, *The Central Philosophy of Buddhism*, George Allen and Unwin, London 1955, p.36, n.2.
34 *Saṁyutta-Nikāya* ii.178ff.
35 For detailed account see Junjirō Takakusu, *Essentials of Buddhist Philosophy*, Motilal Banarsidass, Bombay 1956.
36 *Majjhima-Nikāya* 134 & 135.
37 The world of the *asuras* and that of the *pretas* are sometimes transposed.
38 *Essentials of Buddhist Philosophy*, op.cit., p.30.
39 Ben Shahn, *A Matter of Life and Death*, Ark Press, Marazion, Cornwall 1959, pp.17–18.
40 *The Sūtra of Wei Lang*, London 1947, p.43.
41 E. Conze, *Vajracchedikā Prajñāpāramitā*, op. cit., p.92; *Buddhist Wisdom Books*, op.cit., p.68.
42 I.B. Horner (trans.), *Udāna* iii.2; E. Conze (ed.), *Buddhist Texts Through the Ages*, Harper and Row, New York 1964, p.35.
43 F.L. Woodward (trans.), *Digha-Nikāya* iii.34–5, in *Some Sayings of the Buddha*, Buddhist Society, London 1973, p.139.

44 D.L. Snellgrove, *The Hevajra Tantra*, Oxford University Press, London 1959, vol.1, p.134.
45 *Buddhist Texts Through the Ages*, op.cit., pp.246–8.
46 Herbert V. Guenther, *Philosophy and Psychology in the Abhidharma*, Shambhala, Berkeley 1976, p.152.
47 Jean-Paul Sartre, *Existentialism and Humanism*, Methuen, London 1948, p.28.
48 See e.g. *Sutta-Nipāta* vv.801, 1060, & 1068.
49 *Saṁyutta-Nikāya* xii.23.xxviii.
50 *Dhyana For Beginners*, ch.i, in *A Buddhist Bible*, Dwight Goddard (ed.), Beacon, Boston 1970, pp.441–4.
51 *Philosophy and Psychology in the Abhidharma*, op. cit., p.51.
52 Maung Tin, M.A. (trans.), *The Expositor (Aṭṭhasālinī)*, Pali Text Society, London 1920, vol.i, p.154.
53 Ibid., p.153.
54 Ibid., pp.155–6.
55 e.g. *Majjhima-Nikāya* 36.
56 Lama Anagarika Govinda, *The Psychological Attitude of Early Buddhist Philosophy*, Rider, London 1961, p.63.
57 *Aṅguttara-Nikāya* x.2.
58 I.B. Horner (trans.), *Majjhima-Nikāya* i.246, *The Middle Length Sayings* vol.i, Pali Text Society, London 1954, p.301.
59 *The Philosophy of our People*, Presidential Address at the Indian Philosophical Congress, 1925. *Indo-Asian Culture*, New Delhi, vol.ix, no.3, January 1961, p.233.
60 Bhikkhu Ñānamoli (trans.), *The Path of Purification* (*Visuddhimagga*) xxi.7, Colombo 1956, p.761.
61 *Lam Gyi Gtso Bo Rnam Gsum Gyi* ('The Three Chief Paths [to Enlightenment]'), verse 6.
62 *Philosophy and Psychology in the Abhidharma*, op.cit., p.207.
63 *Saṁyutta-Nikāya* iv.251, in E. Conze (trans.), *Buddhist Texts Through the Ages*, op.cit., p.94.
64 *Udāna* viii.1–4, in *Buddhist Texts Through the Ages*, op. cit., pp.94–5.
65 Kenneth W. Morgan, (ed.) *The Path of the Buddha*, Ronald Press, New York 1956, p.178.
66 F. Max Müller (ed.), *Sacred Books of the East*, London 1894, vol.xlix, part.ii, p.181.
67 Beatrice Lane Suzuki, *Mahāyāna Buddhism*, George Allen and Unwin, London 1959, p.117.

68 Christmas Humphreys (ed.), *The Wisdom of Buddhism*, Michael Joseph, London 1960, p.147.
69 *Smṛti, dharma-pravicaya, vīrya, prīti, praśrabdhi, samādhi, upekṣā*; in Pāli *sati, dhamma-vicaya, viriya, pīti, passadhi, samādhi, upekkhā.*
70 *Digha-Nikāya* ii.119.
71 *The Central Philosophy of Buddhism*, op. cit., p.280.
72 *Digha-Nikāya* i.223.
73 *Aṅguttara-Nikāya* i.10.
74 *Sumangala-Vilāsinī* (Indian Historical Quarterly, II,i), p.33.
75 Lama Anagarika Govinda, *Foundations of Tibetan Mysticism*, Rider, London 1969, p.106.
76 See *Buddhist Wisdom Books*, op.cit., p.103.
77 E. Conze (trans.), *The Large Sūtra on Perfect Wisdom (part 1)*, University of California, Berkeley 1975, p.1.
78 Nyanatiloka, *Buddhist Dictionary*, Kandy 1988, p.72.
79 N. Dutt, *Early Monastic Buddhism*, Calcutta Oriental Book Agency, Calcutta 1960, pp.268–9.
80 *Abhidharmakośa* vi.56.
81 See e.g. Shwe Zan Aung and Mrs Rhys Davids (trans.), *Kathāvatthu* i.2. *Points of Controversy*, Pali Text Society, London 1915, pp.64–70.
82 *Philosophy and Psychology in the Abhidharma*, op.cit., p.211.
83 Bimala Charan Law (trans.), *Designation of Human Types (Puggala-Paññatti)*, Pali Text Society, London 1922, p.104.
84 *Philosophy and Psychology in the Abhidharma*, op. cit., p.232, n.2.
85 Ibid., p.198, n.4.
86 E. Conze (trans.), *The Large Sūtra on Perfect Wisdom*, pp.37–8.
87 E. Conze (trans.), *Aṣṭasāhasrikā Prajñāpāramitā*, op. cit., pp.238–9.
88 Ministry of Information and Broadcasting, Govt. of India, *The Way of the Buddha*, New Delhi 1956, p.198.
89 *Aṣṭasāhasrikā Prajñāpāramitā*, op.cit., pp.223–4; *Buddhist Texts Through the Ages*, op.cit., pp.128–9.
90 *Buddhist Texts Through the Ages*, op. cit., pp.131–2.
91 *Buddhist Wisdom Books*, op. cit., p.25.
92 D.T. Suzuki, *Essays in Zen Buddhism, Third Series*, Rider, London 1970, p.172.
93 Ibid., p.178–9.
94 Ibid., p.180.
95 Ibid., p.170.
96 H.V. Guenther (trans.), *The Jewel Ornament of Liberation*, Rider, London 1959, p.34.

97 Ibid., p.35.
98 Ibid., p.114.
99 D.T. Suzuki, *Manual of Zen Buddhism*, Rider, London 1956, p.14.
Alternative translation: *Essays in Zen Buddhism, Third Series*, op. cit., p.169.
100 Bunyin Nanjio (trans.), *Mahāyāna Buddhist Texts*, Sacred Books of the East, vol.xlix, Oxford and London 1894, part ii, p.73.
101 *Essays in Zen Buddhism, Third Series*, op. cit., p.181.
102 Ibid., pp.186–7.
103 *Aṣṭasāhasrikā Prajñāpāramitā*, op.cit., p.206.
104 E. Conze (trans.), *Abhisamāyalaṇkara* iv.8, Serie Orientale Roma, Rome 1954, pp.66–70.
105 *Aṣṭasāhasrikā Prajñāpāramitā*, op.cit., p.200.
106 Ibid., p.202.
107 Ibid., pp.227–9.
108 D. Snellgrove, *Buddhist Himalaya*, Bruno Cassirer, Oxford 1957, p.57.
109 Benoytosh Bhattacharya, *The Indian Buddhist Iconography*, K.L. Mukhaopadhyay, Calcutta 1958, pp.100–23.
110 Ibid., pp.124–44.
111 *Digha-Nikāya* iii.76.
112 *Essays in Zen Buddhism, Third Series*, op. cit., p.83.
113 Sir Charles Eliot, *Hinduism and Buddhism: An Historical Sketch*, Routledge and Kegan Paul, London 1921, vol.ii, p.24.
114 *The Path of the Buddha*, op.cit., pp.256–8.
115 S. Dutt, *Early Buddhist Monachism*, Asia Publishing House, Bombay 1960, p.55.
116 G.F. Allen, *The Buddha's Philosophy*, London 1959, p.72.
117 *Early Buddhist Monachism*, op. cit., pp.66–7.
118 *Sutta-Nipāta* i.3.
119 Ibid., iv.13,900.
120 *Early Buddhist Monachism*, op. cit., p.90.
121 Ibid., p.69.
122 Nalinaksha Dutt and Krishna Datta Bajpai, *Development of Buddhism in Uttar Pradesh*, Govt. of Uttar Pradesh, Lucknow 1956, p.277.
123 Anukul Chandra Banerjee, *Sarvāstivāda Literature*, D. Banerjee, Calcutta 1957, p.118.
124 For details see W. Pachow, *A Comparative Study of the Prātimokṣa*, Santiniketan 1955.
125 *Development of Buddhism in Uttar Pradesh*, op. cit., p.277.
126 *Early Buddhist Monachism*, op. cit., p.123.
127 *Sarvāstivāda Literature*, op. cit., pp.187–8.

128 *Udāna* v.5.
129 Bhikkhu Ñānamoli (trans.), *The Path of Purification (Visuddhimagga)*, Colombo 1956, p.96.
130 Ibid., p.122.
131 *Dhammapāda* 142.
132 *Aṅguttara-Nikāya* ii.15.
133 *Majjhima-Nikāya* iii.261.
134 E.J. Thomas, *The Perfection of Wisdom*, John Murray, London 1952, p.58.
135 Philip Karl Eidmann, 'A Synopsis of the Sūtra of Brahma's Net of the Bodhisattva's Precepts', *Maha Bodhi Journal*, vol.66, 1958, p.392.
136 Ibid., p.398.
137 *Buddhist Texts Through the Ages*, op.cit., p.302.
138 *Aṣṭasāhasrikā Prajñāpāramitā*, op.cit., p.104.
139 *Hinduism and Buddhism: An Historical Sketch*, op.cit., vol.i, p.xciv.
140 S. Dutt, *Buddhism and Four After Centuries*, p.169.
141 J.J. Jones (trans.), *The Mahāvastu*, op.cit., vol.ii, p.329.
142 *Mahāvaṁsa* xviii and xix.
143 *The Path of the Buddha*, op.cit., p.131.
144 *Dīgha-Nikāya* ii.141.
145 *Aṣṭasāhasrikā Prajñāpāramitā*, op.cit., p.288.
146 Ibid., p.289.
147 Wilhelm Geiger (trans.), *Cūlavaṁsa*, part i, Pali Text Society, London 1929, p.167.
148 Wilhelm Geiger (trans.), *The Mahāvaṁsa*, Pali Text Society, London 1912, p.223.
149 D.T. Devendra, *The Greatest Buddhist Festival (Vesak)*, Kandy 1961, p.x.
150 Ibid., p.4 *et seq.*
151 *Mahāyāna Buddhism*, op. cit., p.83.
152 *The Path of the Buddha*, op.cit., p.137.
153 W.Y. Evans-Wentz, *The Tibetan Book of the Dead*, Oxford University Press, London 1957, pp.18–28.
154 See ibid., p.91 *et seq.*
155 *Mahāyāna Buddhism*, op. cit., pp.82–3.

INDEX

Where both Sanskrit and Pāli forms are in use, priority has been given to the Sanskrit, with the Pāli in brackets. Entries under Buddha, Dharma, and Sangha deal primarily with material found *outside* the sections dedicated to those subjects.

The Windhorse symbolizes the energy of the enlightened mind carrying the Three Jewels – the Buddha, the Dharma, and the Sangha – to all sentient beings.

Buddhism is one of the fastest-growing spiritual traditions in the Western world. Throughout its 2,500-year history, it has always succeeded in adapting its mode of expression to suit whatever culture it has encountered.

Windhorse Publications aims to continue this tradition as Buddhism comes to the West. Today's Westerners are heirs to the entire Buddhist tradition, free to draw instruction and inspiration from all the many schools and branches. Windhorse publishes works by authors who not only understand the Buddhist tradition but are also familiar with Western culture and the Western mind.

For orders and catalogues contact

WINDHORSE PUBLICATIONS
11 PARK ROAD
BIRMINGHAM
B13 8AB
UK

WINDHORSE PUBLICATIONS
P O BOX 574
NEWTOWN
NSW 2042
AUSTRALIA

Windhorse Publications is an arm of the Friends of the Western Buddhist Order, which has more than sixty centres on five continents. Through these centres, members of the Western Buddhist Order offer regular programmes of events for the general public and for more experienced students. These include meditation classes, public talks, study on Buddhist themes and texts, and 'bodywork' classes such as t'ai chi, yoga, and massage. The FWBO also runs several retreat centres and the Karuna Trust, a fund-raising charity that supports social welfare projects in the slums and villages of India.

Many FWBO centres have residential spiritual communities and ethical businesses associated with them. Arts activities are encouraged too, as is the development of strong bonds of friendship between people who share the same ideals. In this way the FWBO is developing a unique approach to Buddhism, not simply as a set of techniques, less still as an exotic cultural interest, but as a creatively directed way of life for people living in the modern world.

If you would like more information about the FWBO please write to

LONDON BUDDHIST CENTRE
51 ROMAN ROAD
LONDON
E2 0HU
UK

ARYALOKA
HEARTWOOD CIRCLE
NEWMARKET
NH 03857
USA

ALSO FROM WINDHORSE

KAMALASHILA

MEDITATION: THE BUDDHIST WAY OF TRANQUILLITY AND INSIGHT

A comprehensive guide to the methods and theory of Buddhist meditation, written in an informal, accessible style. It provides a complete introduction to the basic techniques, as well as detailed advice for more experienced meditators seeking to deepen their practice.

The author is a long-standing member of the Western Buddhist Order, and has been teaching meditation since 1975. In 1979 he helped to establish a semi-monastic community in North Wales, which has now grown into a public retreat centre. For more than a decade he and his colleagues developed approaches to meditation that are firmly grounded in Buddhist tradition but readily accessible to people with a modern Western background. Their experience – as meditators, as students of the traditional texts, and as teachers – is distilled in this book.

304 pages, with charts and illustrations
ISBN 1 899579 05 2
£12.99/$25.95

SANGHARAKSHITA

A SURVEY OF BUDDHISM:
ITS DOCTRINES AND METHODS THROUGH THE AGES

Now in its seventh edition, *A Survey of Buddhism* continues to provide an indispensable study of the entire field of Buddhist thought and practice. Covering all the major doctrines and traditions, both in relation to Buddhism as a whole and to the spiritual life of the individual Buddhist, Sangharakshita places their development in historical context. This is an objective but sympathetic appraisal of Buddhism's many forms that clearly demonstrates the underlying unity of all its schools.

'It would be difficult to find a single book in which the history and development of Buddhist thought has been described as vividly and clearly as in this survey.... For all those who wish to "know the heart, the essence of Buddhism as an integrated whole", there can be no better guide than this book.' *Lama Anagarika Govinda*

'I recommend Sangharakshita's book as the best survey of Buddhism.' *Dr Edward Conze*

544 pages
ISBN 0 904766 65 9
£12.99/$24.95

ANDREW SKILTON

A CONCISE HISTORY OF BUDDHISM

How and when did the many schools and sub-sects of Buddhism emerge? How do the ardent devotion of the Pure Land schools, the magical ritual of the Tantra, or the paradoxical negations of the Perfection of Wisdom literature, relate to the direct, down-to-earth teachings of Gautama the 'historical' Buddha? Did Buddhism modify the cultures to which it was introduced, or did they modify Buddhism?

Here is a narrative that describes and correlates the diverse manifestations of Buddhism – in its homeland of India, and in its spread across Asia, from Mongolia to Sri Lanka, from Japan to the Middle East. Drawing on the latest historical and literary research, Andrew Skilton explains the basic concepts of Buddhism from all periods of its development, and places them in a historical framework.

272 pages, with maps and extensive bibliography
ISBN 0 904766 92 6
£9.99/$19.95

SANGHARAKSHITA

WHAT IS THE DHARMA?
THE ESSENTIAL TEACHINGS OF THE BUDDHA

Guided by a lifetime's experience of Buddhist practice, Sangharakshita tackles the question 'What is the Dharma?' from many different angles. The result is a basic starter kit of teachings and practices, which emphasizes the fundamentally practical nature of Buddhism.

In turn refreshing, unsettling, and inspiring, this book lays before us the essential Dharma, timeless and universal: the Truth that addresses the deepest questions of our hearts and minds and the Path that shows us how we can renew our lives.

272 pages, illustrated
ISBN 1 899579 01 X
£9.99/$19.95

SUBHUTI

SANGHARAKSHITA: A NEW VOICE IN THE BUDDHIST TRADITION

Sangharakshita was one of the first Westerners to make the journey to the East and to don the monk's yellow robe. In India he gained unique experience in the main traditions of Buddhist teaching and practice. His involvement with the 'mass conversion' of ex-Untouchable Hindus to Buddhism exposed him to a revolutionary new experiment in social transformation. More recently he founded one of the most successful Buddhist movements in the modern world – pioneering a 'living Buddhism' that seems ideally suited to our times.

Highly respected as an outspoken writer and commentator, he has never been afraid to communicate his insights and views, even if they challenge venerated elements of Buddhist tradition.

But what are those insights and views? How have they arisen and developed? Here one of Sangharakshita's leading disciples offers an account of his evolution as a thinker and teacher.

336 pages
ISBN 0 904766 68 3
£9.99/$19.95

P.D. RYAN

BUDDHISM AND THE NATURAL WORLD:
TOWARDS A MEANINGFUL MYTH

P.D. Ryan takes a fresh look at our relationship with the living world and offers a radical analysis of our consumerist attitudes. Applying the Buddha's fundamental message of non-violence to these crucial issues, he draws out a middle way between destructiveness and sentimentality: a way which recognizes the truth of the interdependence of all life and places universal compassion at the very centre of our relationship with the world.

In *Buddhism and the Natural World* Ryan emphasizes the importance of living in accord with this truth – and reminds us of the Buddha's insistence that to do so calls for nothing less than a revolution in consciousness.

144 pages
ISBN 1 899579 00 1
£6.99/$13.95

SANGHARAKSHITA

KNOW YOUR MIND:
THE PSYCHOLOGICAL DIMENSION OF ETHICS IN BUDDHISM

Know Your Mind is an accessible introduction to traditional Buddhist psychology, offering a clear description of the nature of mind and how it functions.

Sangharakshita guides us expertly through the Abhidharma classification of positive and negative mental states and shows us how we can work with them. In exploring the part we play in creating our own suffering and happiness, he elucidates the relationship of the mind to karma and rebirth, and stresses the ethical, other-regarding nature of Buddhist psychology.

304 pages
ISBN 0 904766 79 9
£11.99/$23.95

RICHARD P. HAYES

LAND OF NO BUDDHA: REFLECTIONS OF A SCEPTICAL BUDDHIST

Witty, honest, and thought-provoking, Richard Hayes casts a critical eye over modern society and the teachings of Buddhism as they flow into the West. Written with the perspective that comes from more than twenty years of study and practice, *Land of No Buddha* examines the pitfalls awaiting those who search for the truth. A sceptical Buddhist, Hayes nevertheless proposes the radical path of the Buddha – becoming free from self-indulgent passions and delusions – to those seeking genuine wisdom, not just slogans to stick on the bumpers of their cars.

288 pages
ISBN 1 899579 12 5
£9.99/$19.95